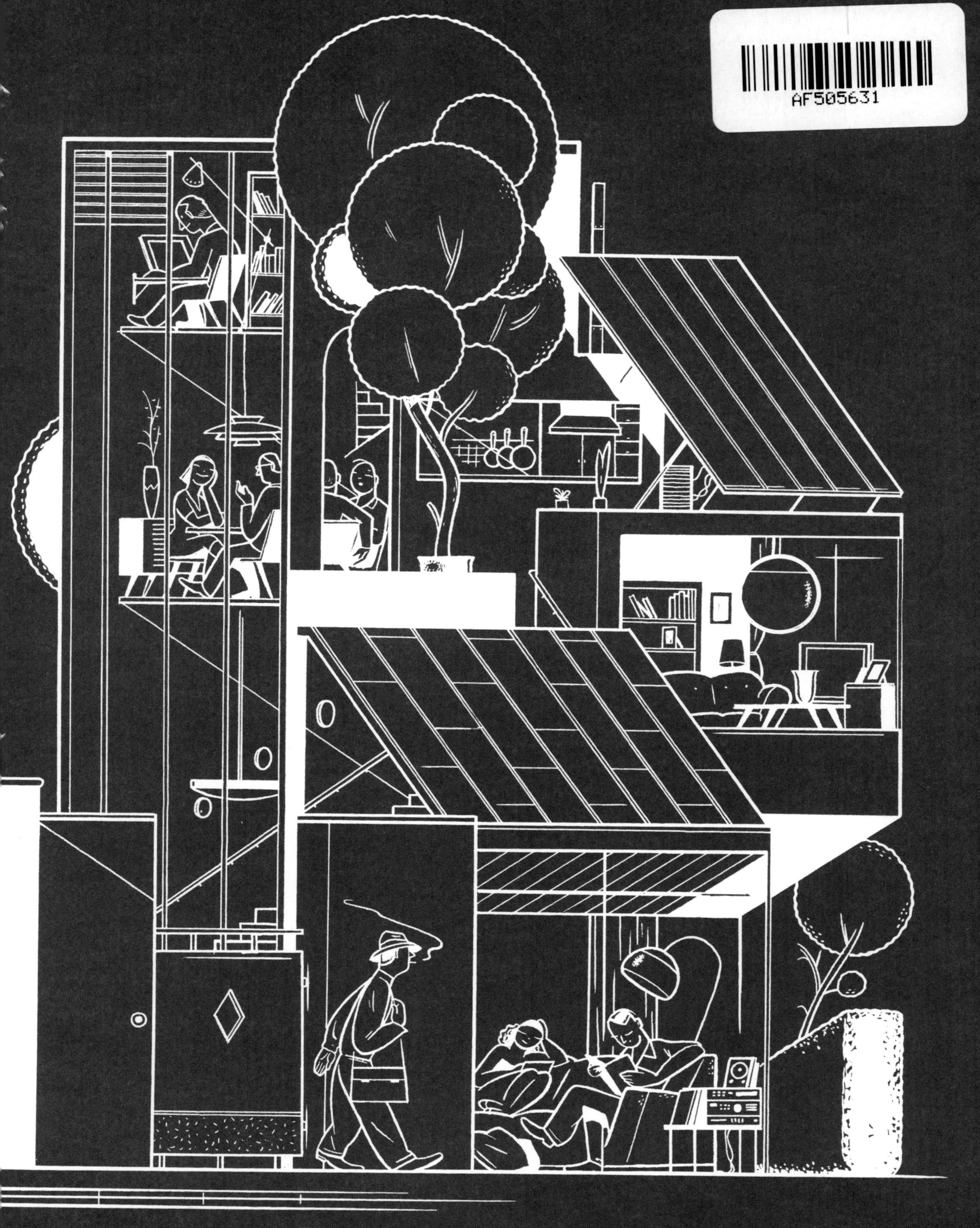

Custom-made graphics
with a retro, atomic-style, clear line

JAN VAN DER VEKEN

fabrica grafica

gestalten

James Cartwright

THE FUTURE STARTED YESTERDAY

THE ILLUSTRATION & ARTWORK OF JAN VAN DER VEKEN

The first time I had the pleasure of writing about Jan Van Der Veken's work there was little information available about him online or, it seemed, in print. I'd come across a poster of his while browsing at Nobrow's shop in London – a screen print entitled *City Lights* that depicted a man gazing wistfully at an autumnal evening, the soft glow of neighboring tower blocks illuminating a solitary tree in front of him – and was immediately drawn to his agile lines, classically-styled characters and subtle use of color. Although Nobrow described Jan

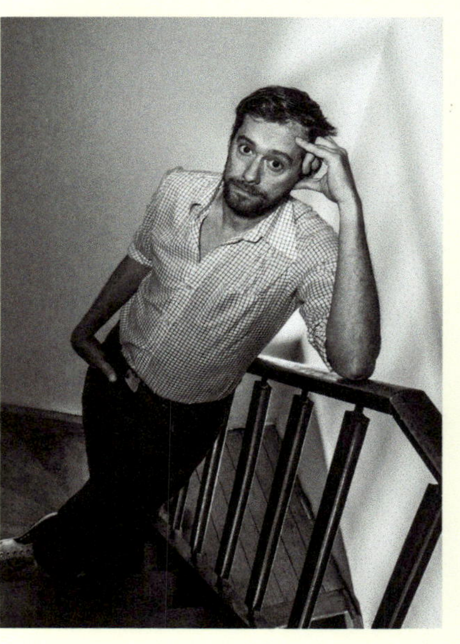

as "one of the leading Belgian illustrators of today" and *Drawn & Quarterly* had long been utilizing his trademark style to define their online presence, I was perplexed by how hard it was to find anything more about him.

But now all that's about to change as here you sit, with a monograph of Jan's work in front of you, ready to feast upon a prolific body of work and witness his rise from mildly-obscure illustrator genius to worldwide household name. Likewise, my own understanding of Jan has developed somewhat since those early days of ignorance and through a prolonged period of badgering him via email for continued updates on his progress, a couple of interviews, and innumerable hours staring at his images. I've come now to know him and his work much better; certainly enough to confirm Nobrow's brief appraisal of him and almost definitely enough to be summarising his career so far.

Like many of his contemporaries Jan's first brushes with illustration came from the greats. "Being Belgian, I grew up with comics like Tintin and Blake and Mortimer by Edgar P. Jacobs – the really traditional stuff. *The Yellow Mark* [one of Jacobs' most celebrated works] in particular was a great influence. It's like Tintin but more detailed and the atmosphere and the quality of the images are really great, the story lines, too. I was really influenced by that kind of thing and eventually started to draw in that way."

In spite of having this rich source of imagery at his disposal during his formative years it wasn't until later on that Jan truly became inspired to put pen to paper, and the impetus came from a much less respectable place. "The first thing that really got me into drawing was Iron Maiden. I bought a small cassette in a local music shop, even though I didn't know the music – I just really liked the cover art. It was *Powerslave* with the Egyptian drawing on the front by Derek Riggs, and it just made me think ‚Wow!' Then of course I listened to the music and I really liked it, but it was the cover art that made me want to buy the cassette. So I copied it with all the things I had at my disposal at the time. I just redrew it literally again and again and that was the first thing that started me off."

In his mid–teens Jan was able to channel his interest in drawing within an educational environment, taking formal lessons in place of scribbling in his free time. "I studied arts at a technical school where we had lessons in printing techniques and screen printing, learning how to make the artwork. Studying very early graphic art made my world a bit larger. Then we had lessons in aesthetics and I started to develop my own way of making work and learned a lot on my own, too,

---

Being Belgian, I grew up with comics like Tintin and Blake and Mortimer by Edgar P. Jacobs – the really traditional stuff... The first thing that really got me into drawing was Iron Maiden,... even though I didn't know the music – I just really liked the cover art.

but the main focus was always on technique. Later I went to St. Lucas in Ghent and the focus was on being an author – a creator of images rather than a reproducer – so I had both the technical qualities, the technical understanding of how to print a book, and the understanding of how to make a proper drawing.

"In that way I had an advantage because I knew both sides of image making and it's important to have those technical skills. We illustrators have to make illustrations to go into print or out onto the net, which is a technical way of doing things. You don't have your original image and that's it: you have your original image and you have to apply it to another medium. It's very important that you know how to do these things so you can reproduce your image in the best way possible. Once you know the rules you can work out how to bend them because you understand how things have to be done."

Jan's understanding of how things "have to be done" can be traced back to his early education in graphic design. Before he'd purchased his first tube of gouache he was studying grid systems and typographic theory at St. Lucas, gaining an understanding of layout and space that's prevalent throughout all of his work and differentiates him from most of his contemporaries. "At St Lucas I studied graphic design because I thought it wouldn't be so easy to make a living from illustration. I wanted to make typography together with illustrations, so I thought it would be better to study graphic design and have a proper job, and in the evenings I could focus on drawing. In the end, instead of creating graphic design that included pictures I made everything with drawings."

It was through this developing interest in image-making that Jan came to meet his mentor, Ever Meulen, or ‚Eddie', as Jan refers to him. Eddie taught an illustration class at St. Lucas and although Jan was not enrolled on the course, he would turn up weekly to show his drawings. Eddie was supportive of Jan's work from the start and encouraged him to do more with his illustration. "After four years of graphic design I learned I was quite able to make drawings and I really enjoyed it – perhaps even more than graphics, though that was my first love. I showed more and more illustration to Eddie and he was really enthusiastic about it, so in the end I thought, what the hell, I'm going to be an independent artist and we'll just see what happens."

What happened was an immensely successful first show that enabled Jan to show his work to nearly all of his heroes in a single week. In 2001 he held an exhibition in Holland that comprised a series of silk screens he'd created since leaving university. During that time he'd moved home to live with his parents and build his reputation as a commercial image-maker without having to worry about paying the rent. One of the first visitors to the show was an as-yet unestablished Chris Ware. "At the time he wasn't really known, he'd made his second or third Acme Novelty Library, but I knew who he was thanks to one of my teachers at art school. Anyway, he came to my exhibition and said he loved my work and all I had was this series of silk screens, so I gave them to him. Two days later he came back to the exhibition and to say thanks for the silk screens he gave me an original." That original still sits on Jan's wall in his studio; half an inked spread from a decade-old Acme – framed, of course and still in mint condition.

> I thought it would be better to study graphic design and have a proper job, and in the evenings I could focus on drawing. In the end, instead of creating graphic design that included pictures, I made everything with drawings... I thought, what the hell, I'm going to be an independent artist and we'll just see what happens.

"That was a crazy week actually because I was then invited for breakfast at Joost Swarte's house and everyone was there, from Chris Ware and Daniel Clowes to Matotti and Robert Crumb. So there I am, a twenty-year-old timidly eating my croissant and really wanting to present my prints to Joost Swarte. I couldn't find him though, but I'd met Robert Crumb at a market place in Holland earlier so I said to him, 'I want to give these silk screens to Joost, but I have to go, my parents have come to collect me and I don't have time to look for him,' and Robert Crumb – this long, thin, intimidating figure with thick round glasses – was autistically waving at me like, 'Yes, yes I will give them to him no problem.'

"I was a real nobody back then, not that I'm somebody now, but I hadn't published anything and I just had my originals, so being in that situation was quite intimidating – overwhelming even."

Nowadays it seems strange to think of Jan nervously eating breakfast with a group of men that increasingly feel more like his peers than his heroes. All of them make work in a similar style that emphasises clarity, precision and good design within illustration (Robert Crumb, perhaps, is the exception to that rule), and Jan now has a body of work large enough to intimidate even the illustrative juggernaut that is Chris Ware. At the time though, he still felt very much like he was finding his feet. "At first I was very clumsy in my approach, making normal drawings with curved lines, but more and more I was looking for structure. I'm very interested in architecture, and of course in architecture the walls have to be straight, so I applied that to my illustration and combined it with the organic feel of trees and plants. That provided a great contrast and I enjoyed working in that way very much."

The structure in Jan's drawing became increasingly important as time progressed and now it's innate within his work. His process is incredibly labored and involves the construction of an underlying grid before the drawing is made, followed by numerous hand-drawn layers placed one on top of the other. In this way he builds up imagery piece by piece, moving elements until

> In graphic design when you make a layout it's all very rigid. You have an underlying structure... the design appears to be logical. It fits. I want my drawings to have that same kind of quality; they fit, they should be like that, there's no other way they could be.

they seem intuitively placed. "In graphic design when you make a layout it's all very rigid. You have an underlying structure that isn't visible, the design appears to be logical. It fits. I want my drawings to have that same kind of quality; they fit, they should be like that, there's no other way they could be. When you see it you should think it's always been there."

Without looking at the work, all this talk of structure and rigidity comes across as overly serious for an illustrator, but alongside his geometric precision is an undeniable humor. Jan's images exude a playfulness that's tangible and infectious. Everything from the impossible architecture that punctuates his images to the myriad facial expressions he's capable of rendering upon his characters with a few simple lines expresses fun and excitement. Even when his subject matter is serious, Jan manages to communicate it with a sense of optimism and wit. "I like to refer to Jaques Tati as one of my main influences as he's a master in how he likes to frame things. Everything is well-timed and nothing is left to chance. He's funny but not funny haha, like a stand-up comedian – it's very introverted. I approve of that. I like that way of presenting life, with a quiet humor."

Jaques Tati is one of many influences that links Jan to the past. Although his work is distinctly contemporary and deals almost exclusively with modern life, it maintains a stylistic quality that belongs to the 1950s, through the application of color, the angular way in which Jan renders his characters, and their retro sense of fashion. Like Eddie and Joost before him, Jan's work comes under the broad definition of *atoomstijl*, or atomic-style, a name invented by Joost in the 1970s to describe a school of clear-line illustration that specifically referenced the modernism of Belgium's Expo '58. "The Expo of 1958 was a display of incredible technological advancements. Sputnik was there, the Citroen DS was presented there without wheels – like a rocket – and all the unbridled enthusiasm for the future and space travel was embraced at this one event. I like the optimism of that era. People had just started to live again after the war and their optimism was like a bare necessity. There was a certain happiness about everything back then. Things were made to look good in a naïve kind of way, but people really meant it. In the 1950s everyone had big plans and then in the 1960s and 1970s we found out that atomic energy had a downside and the naïvety, the childhood, was over and we had to be responsible."

Jan believes that there are numerous parallels between the 1950s and the present day. "In the era we live in now I think we're reaching another level with technology and there's a new optimism in design and architecture. It's all light and bright and playfulness is allowed again. In the 1990s everything was strict and you had interiors that couldn't be lived in because it would upset the balance, but now everything is possible again.

"People have embraced technology again and now that we know its limitations we're responsible in how we deal with it. In that way my optimism is relevant again, because now we have responsible optimism instead of naïve optimism. We know that technology has its limitations, but we believe we can do something good with it."

This notion of using technology responsibly is particularly key to Jan's image-making process, and although he's no stranger to spending hours in front of Photoshop, it's the time spent drawing in pencil, pen and ink that he finds most engaging. Computers and illustrators

I make images with pen and ink, by hand, because I want to preserve their authentic feel. I don't want to make [Adobe] Illustrator drawings. I don't want them to be that technical. You have to know that the drawing was made by a human being who is faulty.

have not always made easy bedfellows and there are many, Jan included, that find the idea of making purely digital work more than a little repugnant. "I make images with pen and ink, by hand, because I want to preserve their authentic feel. I don't want to make [Adobe] Illustrator drawings. I don't want them to be that technical. You have to know that the drawing was made by a human being who is faulty." And Jan's not the only one that thinks this. "A lot of people are going back to basics again and just like to draw things. That's the pendulum; things swing one way and then the other. At first when the computer arrived people were like, 'Oh my god, digital image-making is tops!' but now we've gone back to basics because computer image-making isn't all that exciting. But being able to draw is here forever, that will stay; that's a fact."

The thing that really distinguishes one illustrator from the other is the way they handle their image after they've drawn it. "You have many ways of handling your originals, how you proceed with them. For instance Chris Ware practically works the same way that I do; black and white inking and then coloring with Photoshop. Lots of young illustrators are doing it too, like Luke Pearson. It's a natural way of working nowadays. Drawing is like being a monk that used to write bibles back in the middle ages; it's the same slow process. But in order to be able to work in this modern world we have to embrace the computer."

In embracing the computer Jan and his contemporaries are able to do a job that would previously have been divided up among at least three people. In the heyday of comic books one man would draw, another would ink and a third would be responsible for the color separations. In fact, in many instances, the colors would be sent out to a different company altogether. Photoshop means that Jan can handle all of these processes at his own desk, without the input of anyone else. In the same way, his continuing experimentation with typography and design is born from a culture of polymathy and a desire to accomplish everything by his own hand. "To be able to draw your drawings and pair them with your own typography; that's the way to go I think. That way I can combine illustration, graphic design and typography in my own way and work on book covers and posters. Earlier in my career I'd go to meetings and be very timid and do as I was asked by art directors. So I ended up letting other people handle the typography. I'd make a beautiful illustration and then wouldn't enjoy what someone else had done with the type. Nowadays I'm more confident to produce type as well, so I'm going to put my foot down and tell people that I'll handle everything.

"The trouble is that people think in boxes. They think that you're an illustrator so they'll have you produce an illustration. Or you're a typographer so you can make some type. But there's no reason why you shouldn't do multiple things. It's all related you know, a font is an image as well."

One thing I've always expected of Jan that he's yet to try out is the production of his own comic. For someone so inspired by the medium it seemed only logical to assume that he'd one day want to branch out into telling his own stories in carefully constructed, ornate panels. But he really doesn't seem at all interested in the idea. "I'm very much inspired by comics but I've always wanted to focus on making one image. When you're a comics artist you have a story line and you use the illustration as a tool to tell that story. I don't have the patience for that. I've just never felt the urge to make my own comic. I haven't got something to say – I don't have a topic. I think in the single images that I create there's a lot of things going on, but it's not one big story. And I'm happy with that. But perhaps I just need someone to give me a hint, the start of a story line."

I suggest to Jan that for someone with such a megalomaniacal approach to image-making and such widespread interests he might find it quite easy to find a story to tell, and

The trouble is that people think in boxes. But there's no reason why you shouldn't do multiple things. It's all related you know, a font is an image as well.

some characters to give life to. "I'm like a small dictator in my own world, inhabited by people who have to obey my rules." he says, "How they look and how they stand is dictated by me. I think that feeling comes from an underlying discontent with reality, with how everything looks. When you go into the city you see certain buildings that are beautiful but you look on the other side of the road and there's trash. You want the city to be a perfect city but it isn't like that." In fact the perfect city and the perfect world – the kind Jan would be more than capable of creating in a comic of his own – isn't something he's interested in making a reality. Like his drawings Jan enjoys the human element of the everyday, the signs of fallibility error. "Things look perfectly nice on paper, but then it's different when they're real. Actually it's probably a good thing that cities aren't perfect. It would be awful."

So while Jan's plans for the future may not include the comic book some (and by that I mean myself) have been waiting for, we should expect to see great things from him in the future – though what they may be he's not yet sure. "I don't have a fixed direction but I have an eclectic mind and my influences are very diverse. I'm interested in many things because you have to draw what you know, you can't draw what you don't. You can take a picture with your eyes closed but to draw you have to really see things."

[01]

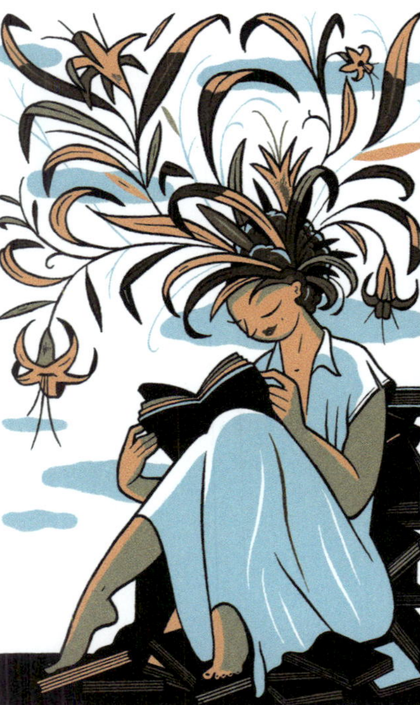

[02]

8

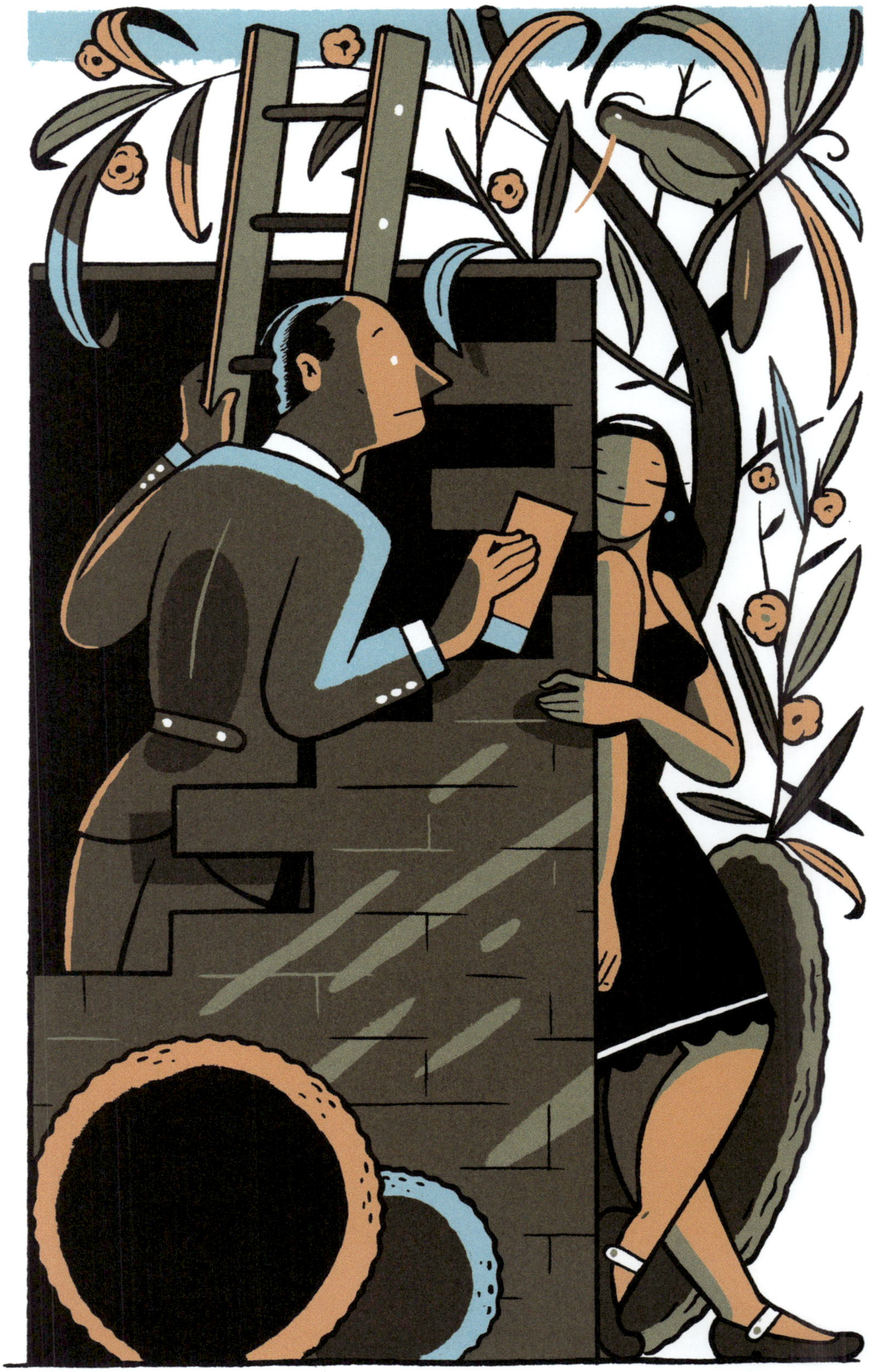

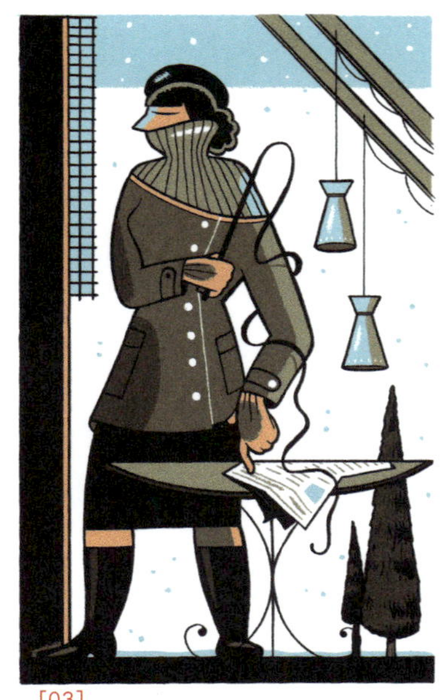

[03]

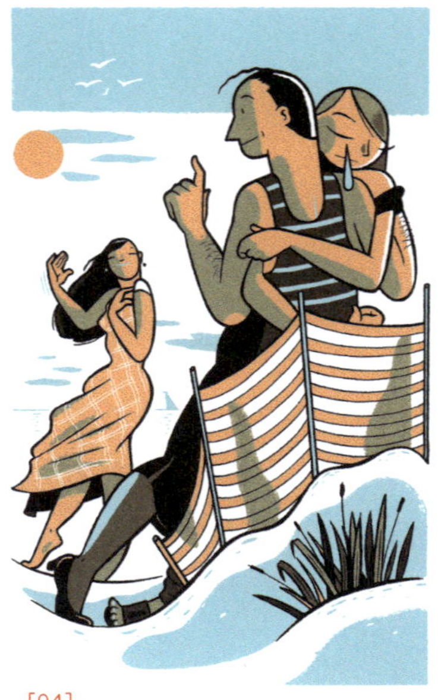

[04]

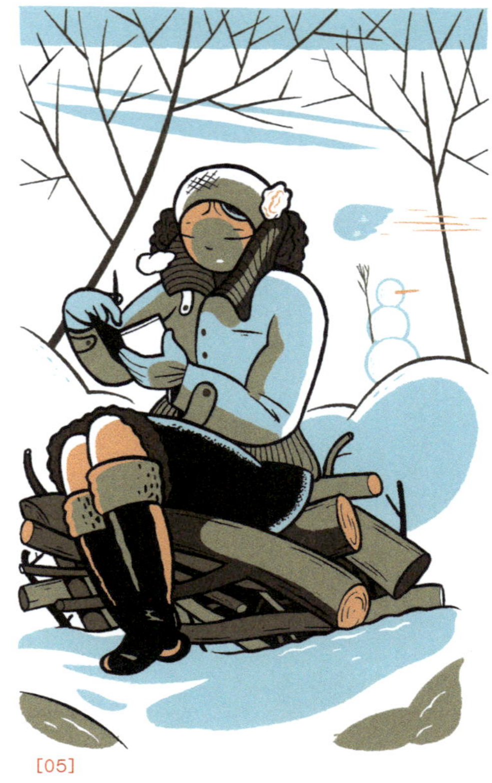

[05]

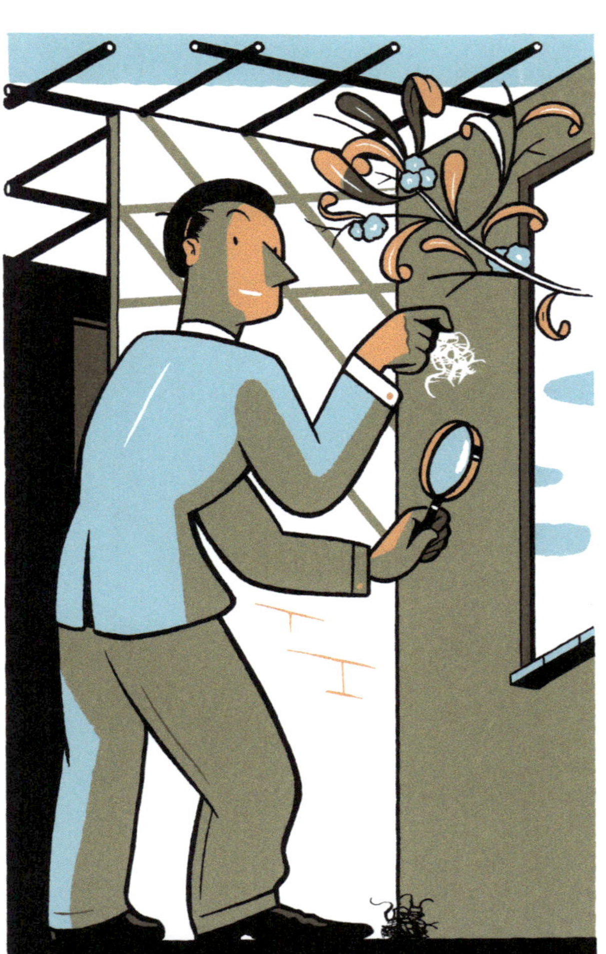

[06]

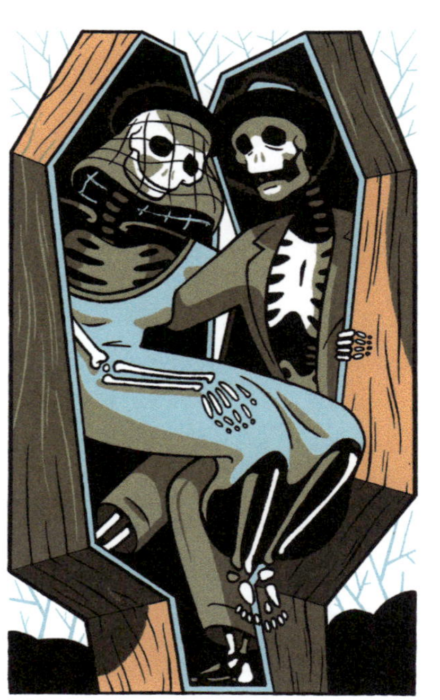

[07]

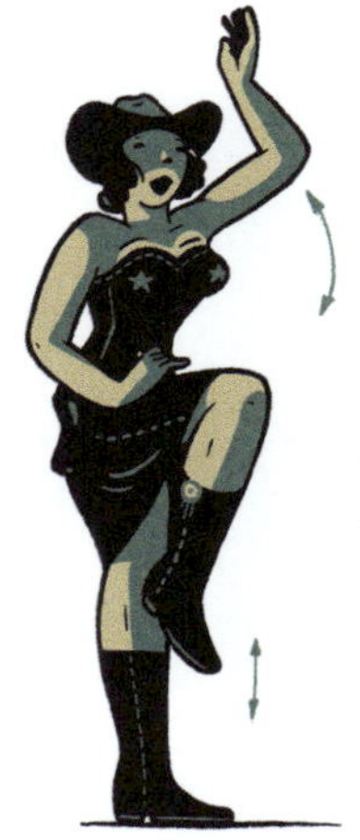

Cowboy Slap

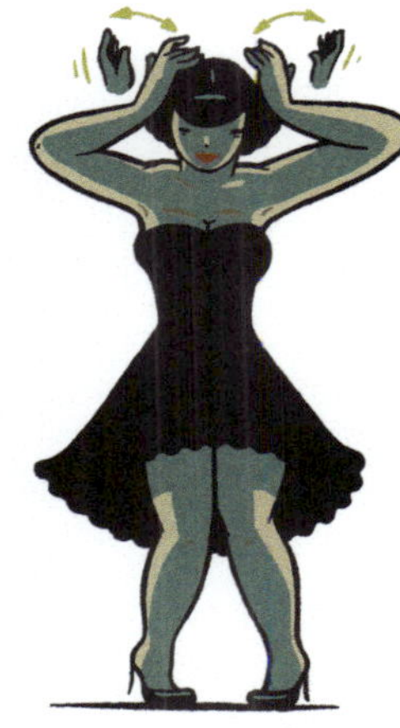

Headache

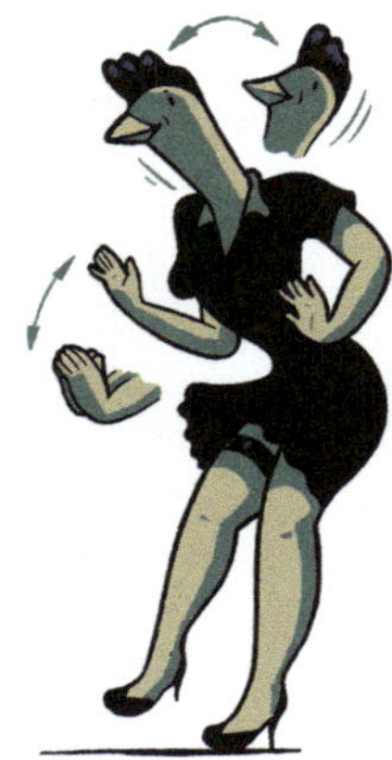

The Chicken

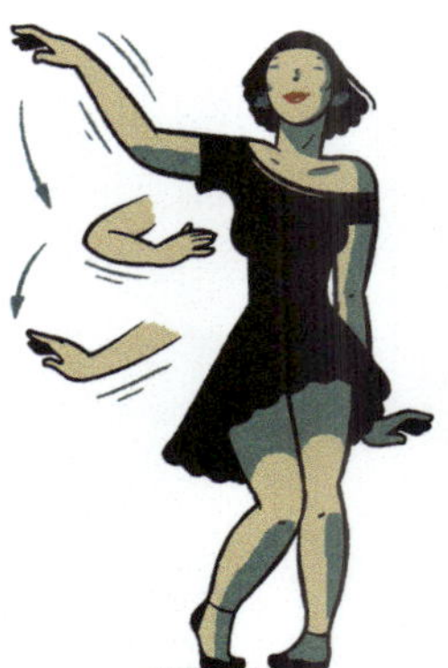

Waving Hands

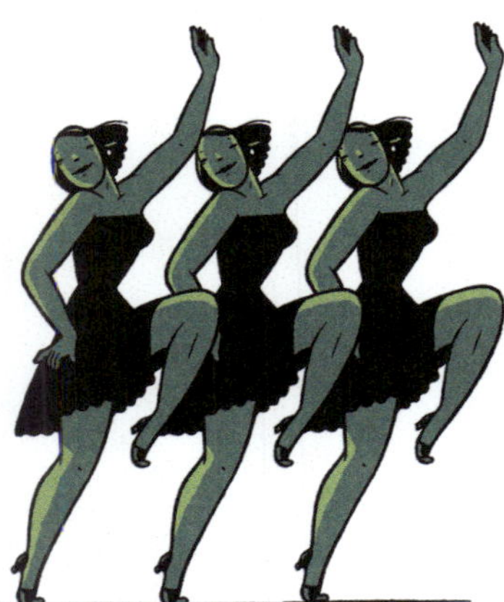

Spank the baby

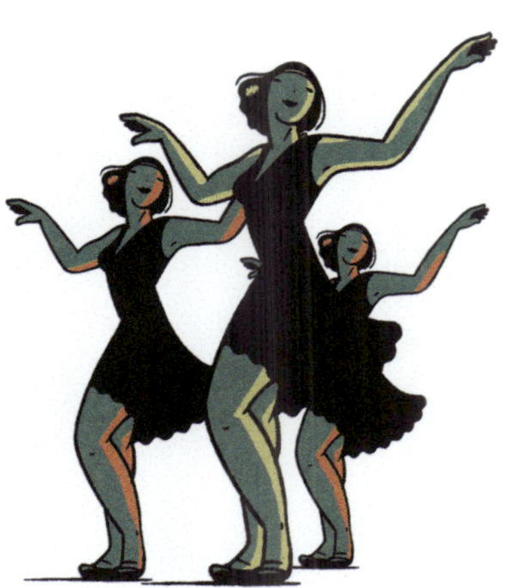

Twist

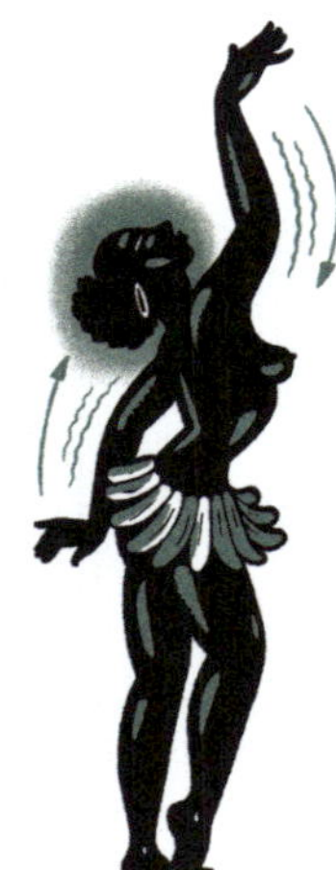

The Monkey

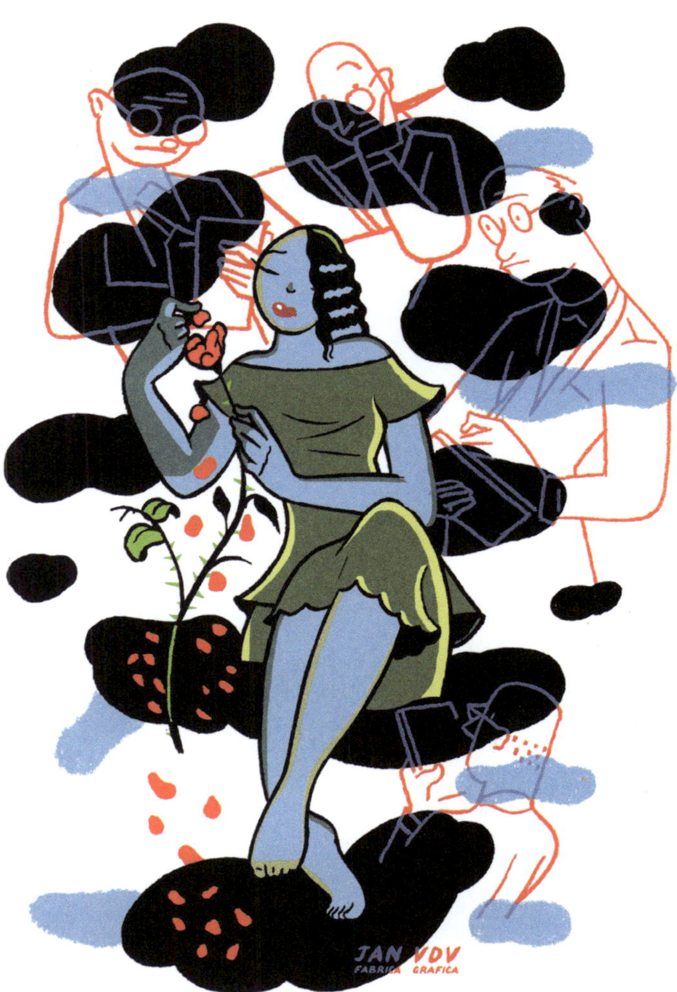

[01]

[02]

10

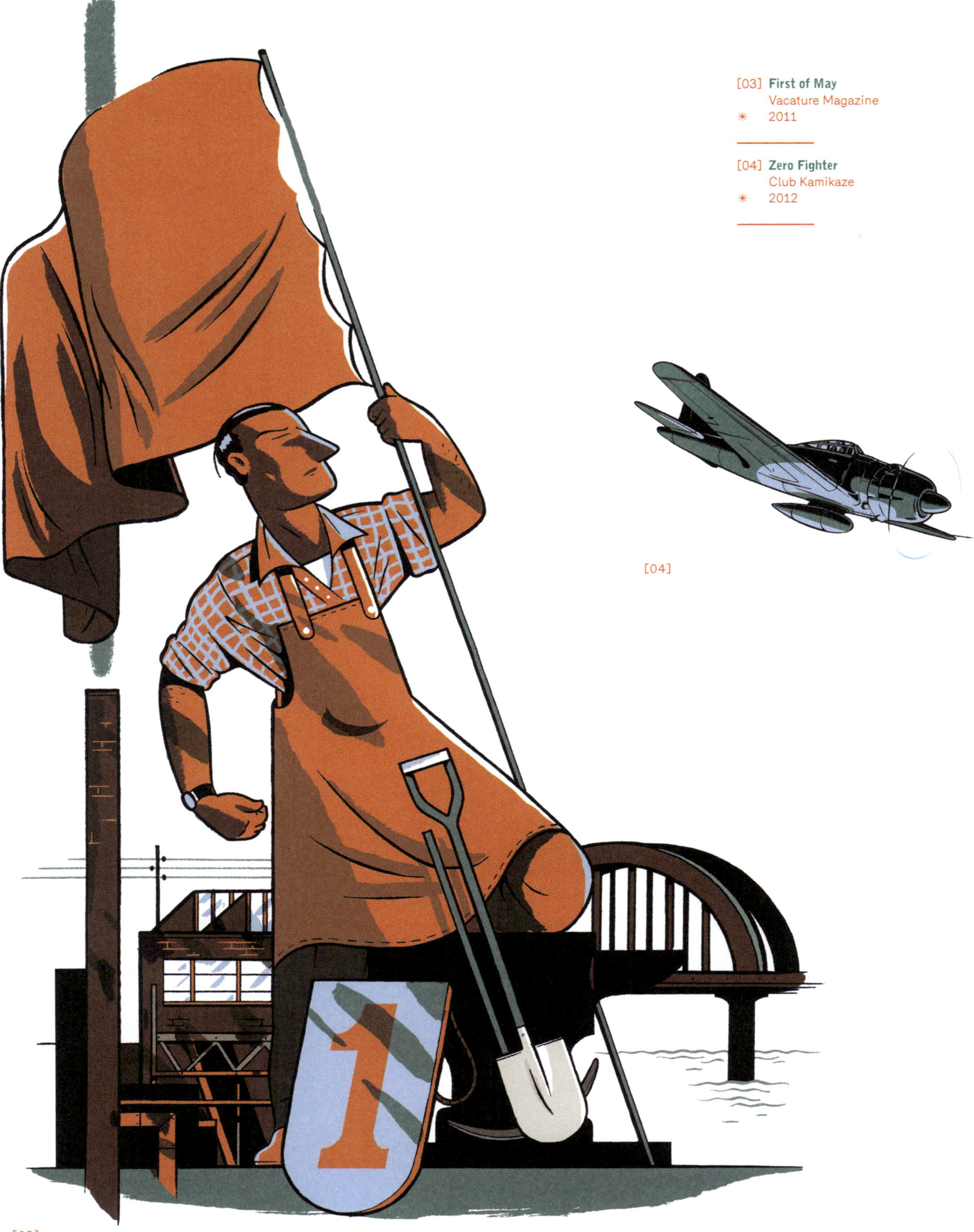

[03] **First of May**
Vacature Magazine
✳ 2011

[04] **Zero Fighter**
Club Kamikaze
✳ 2012

[04]

[03]

11

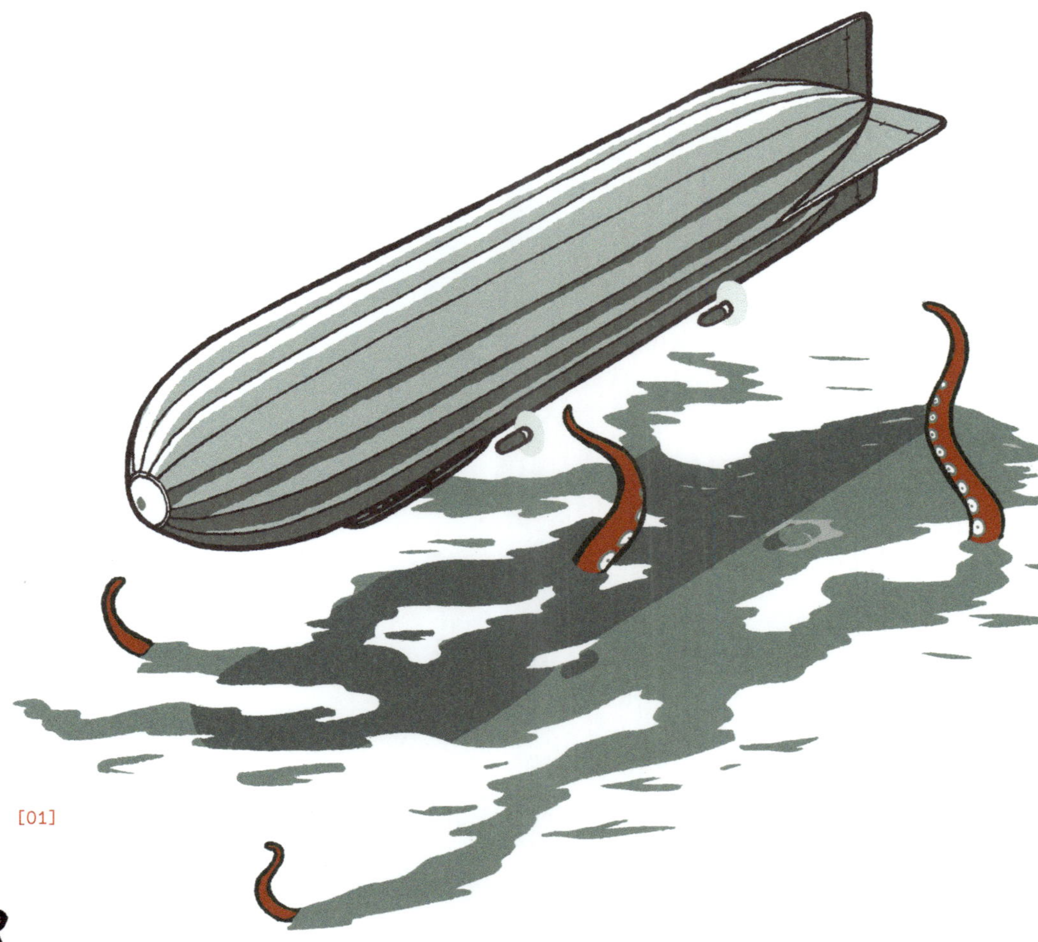

[01]

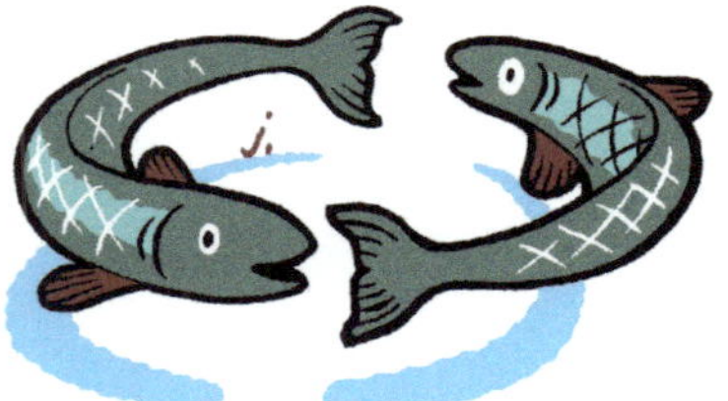

[02]

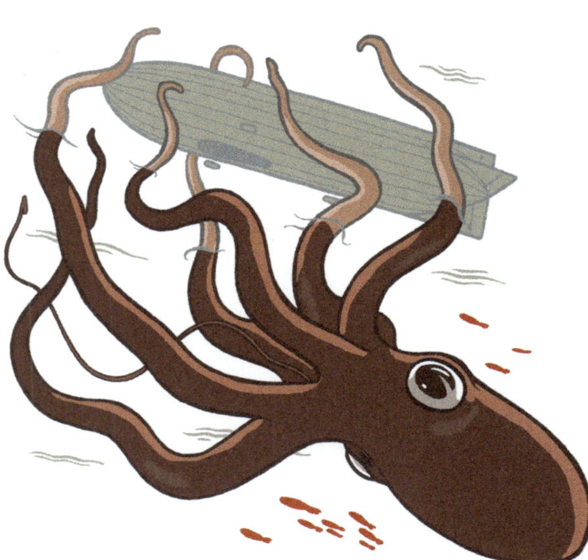

[03]

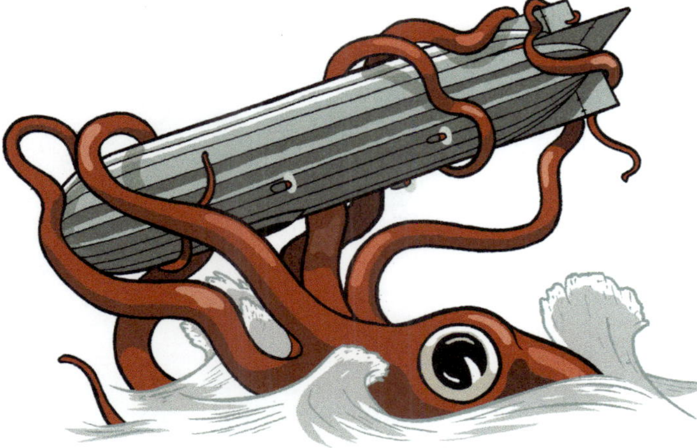

[04]

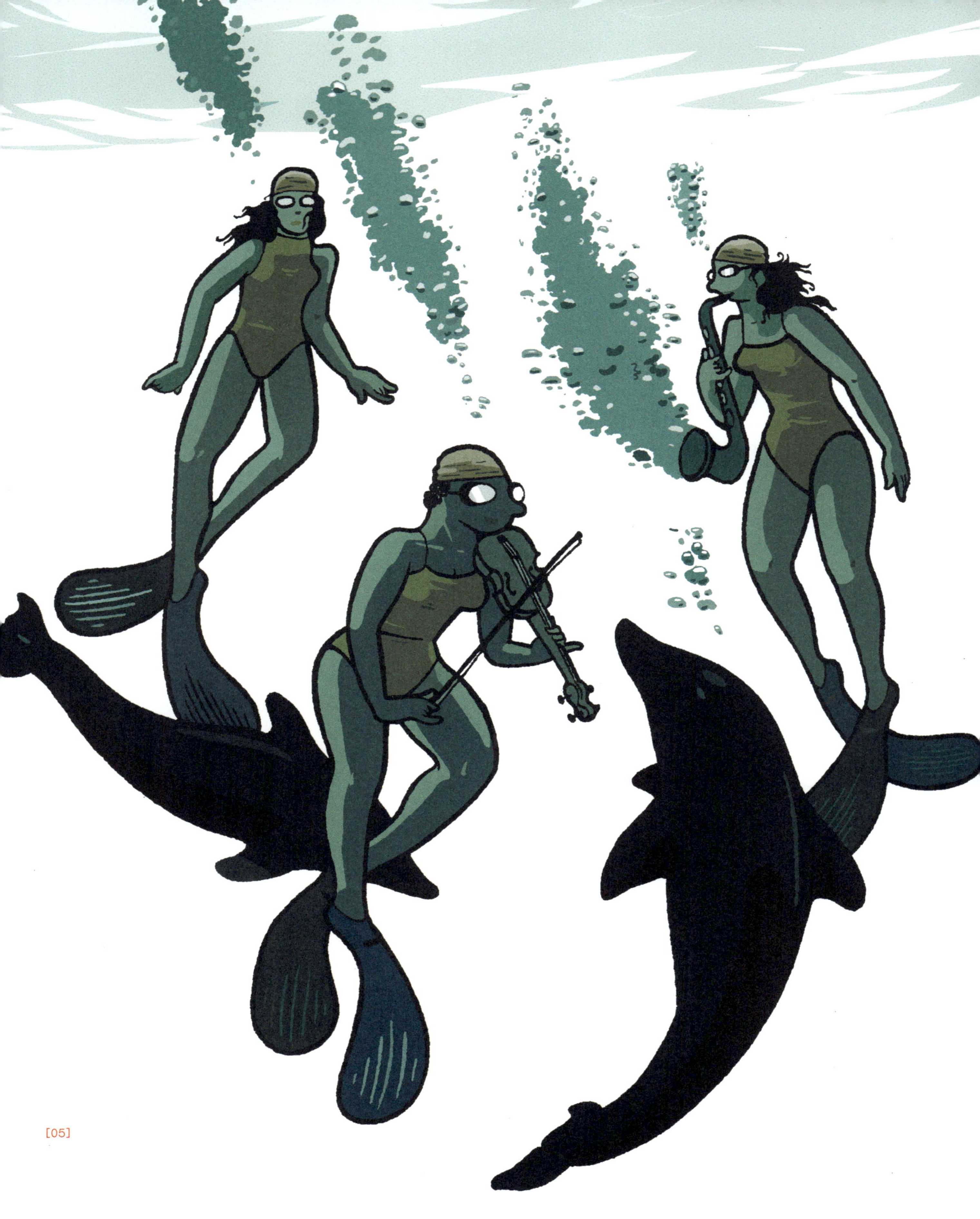

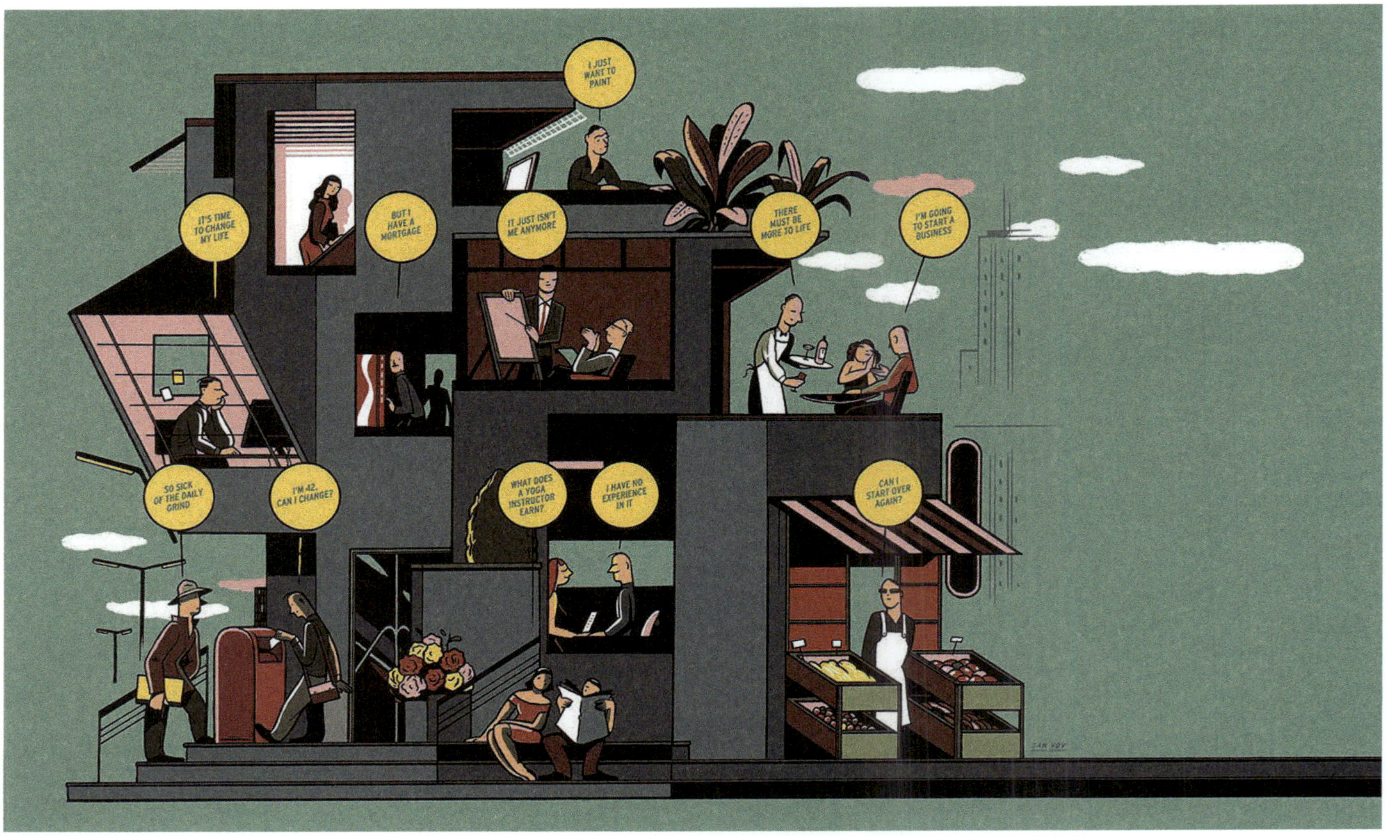

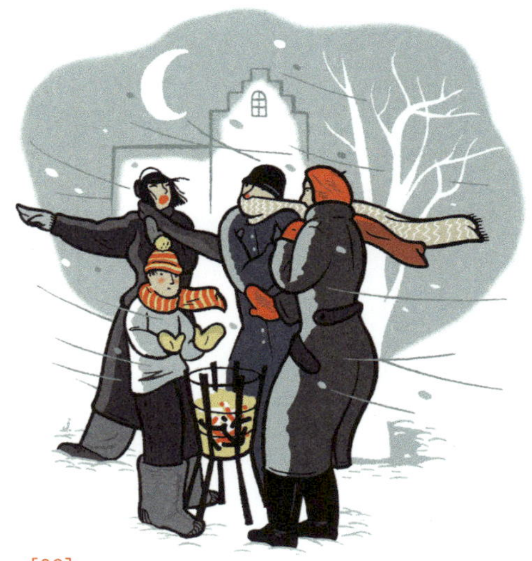

[01]

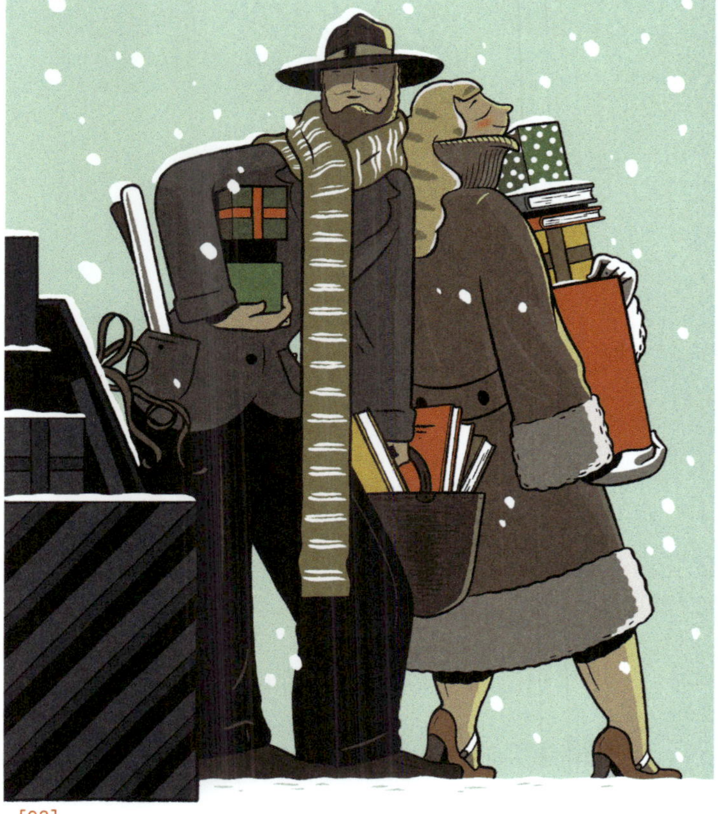

[03]

[01] **Career Moves**
Virgin Pacific
* 2011

[02] **Winter Fire**
NTG Ghent
* 2003

[03] **Christmas Shopping**
De Standaard
* 2009

[04] **December Books**
De Standaard
* 2010

14

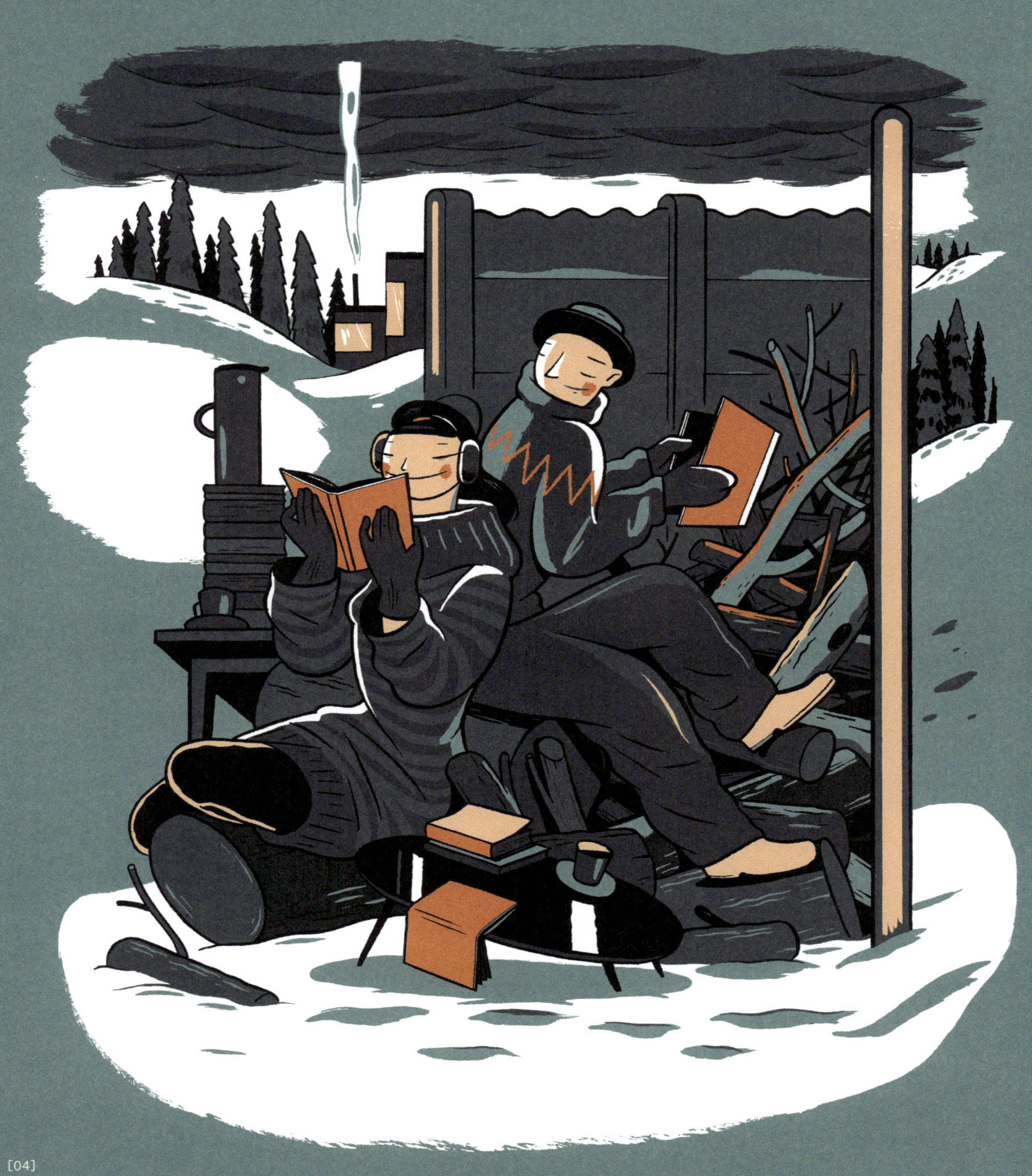

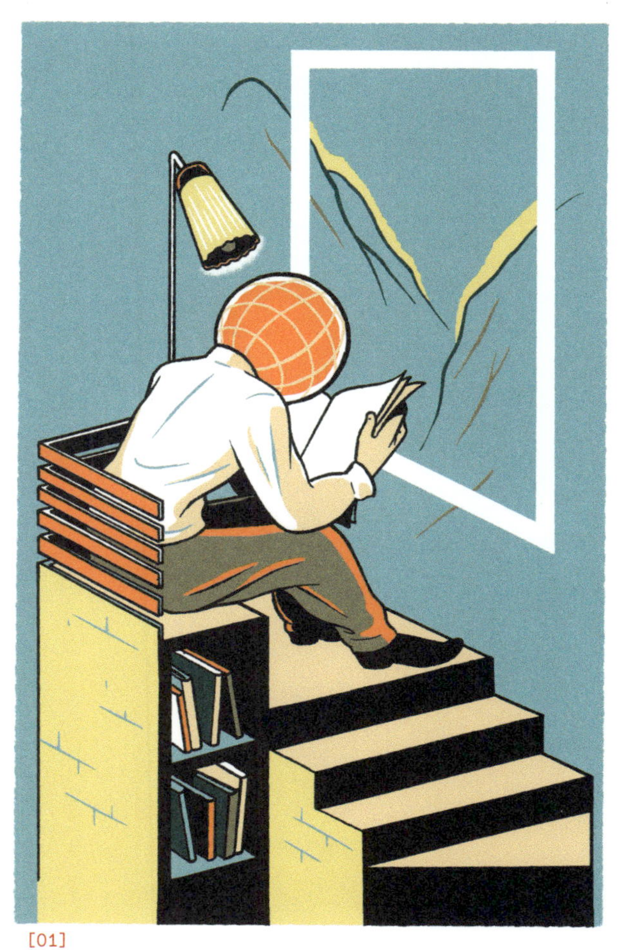

[01]

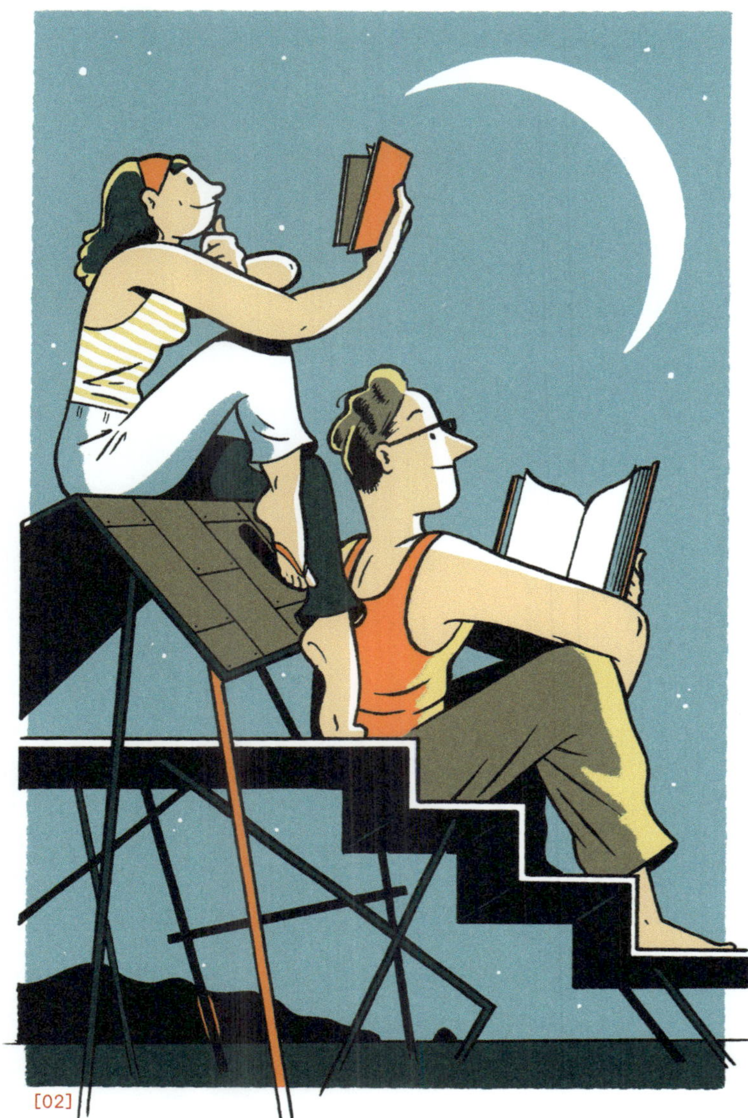

[02]

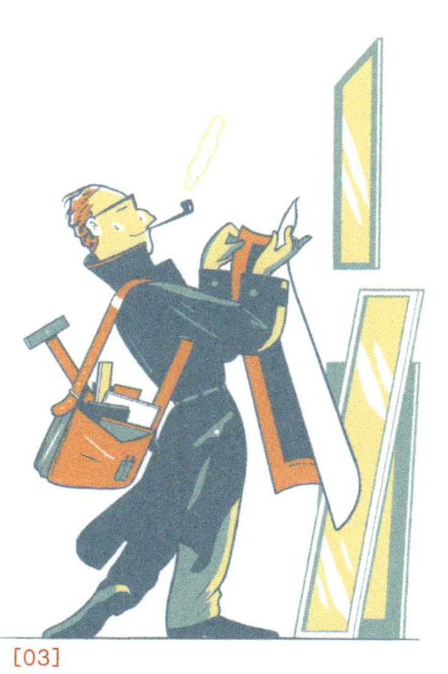

[03]

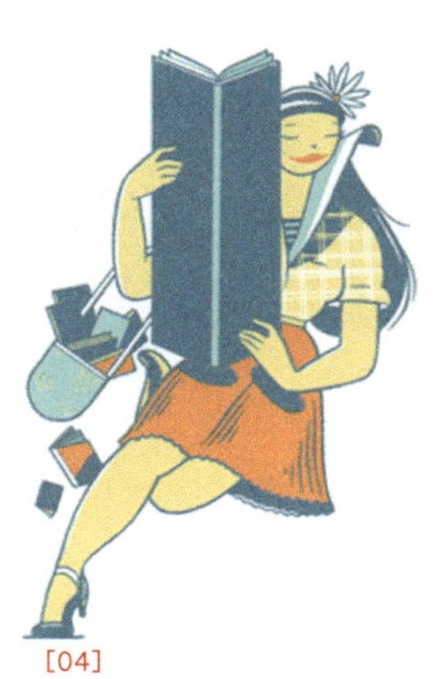

[04]

[05]

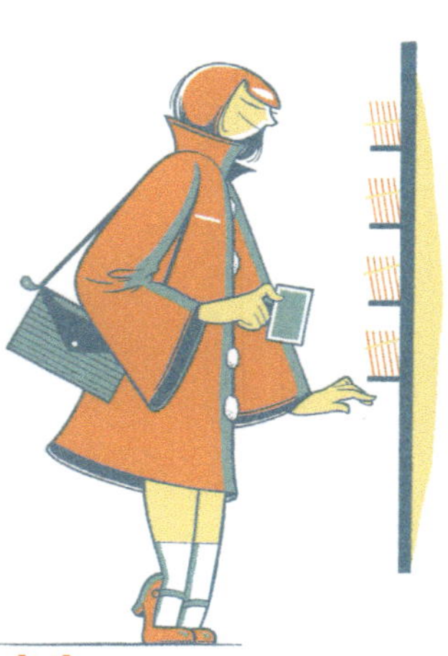

[06]

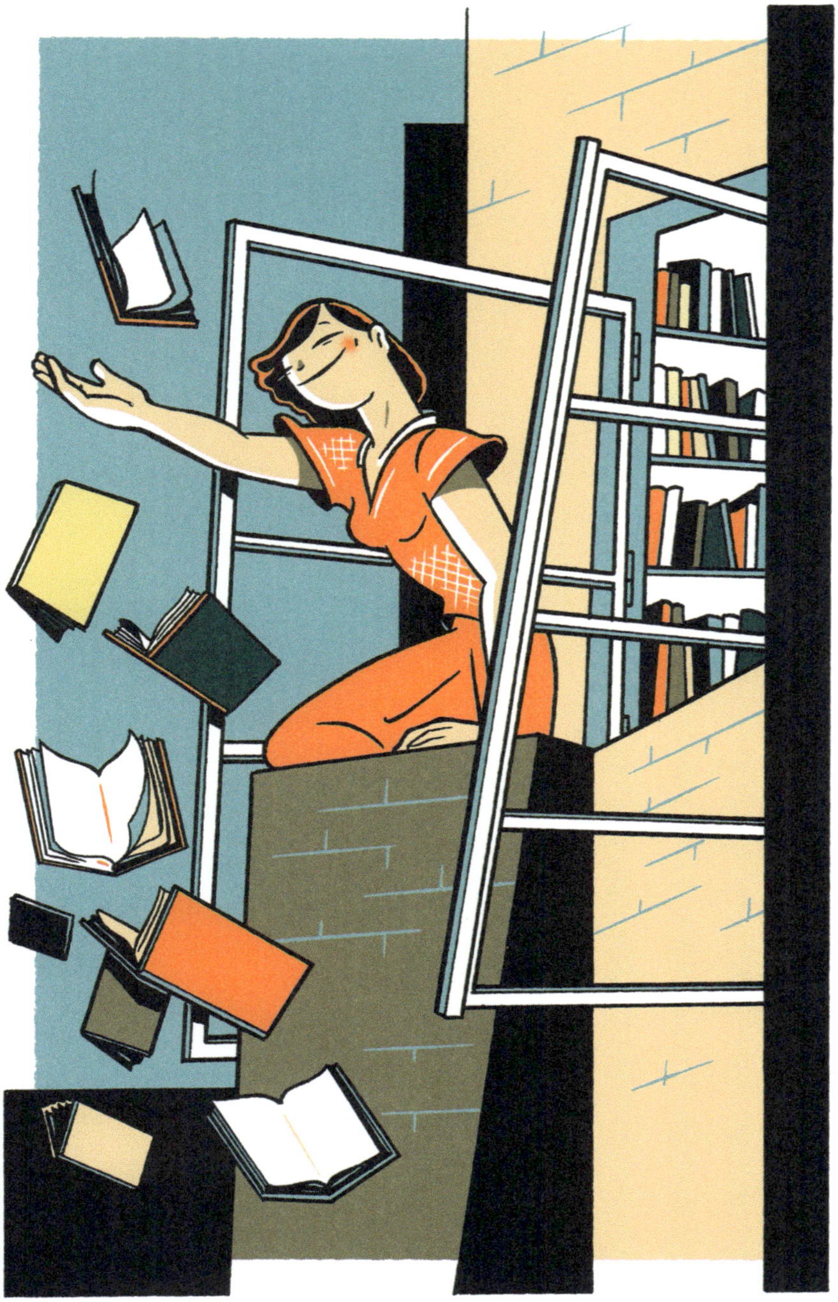

[07]

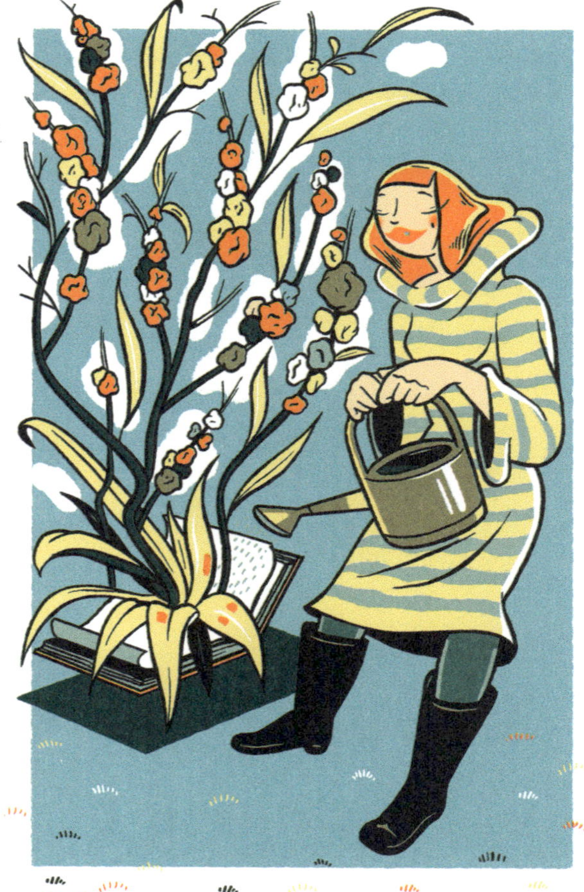

[09]

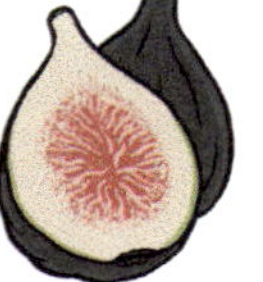
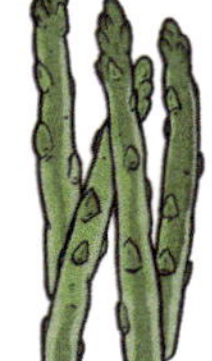
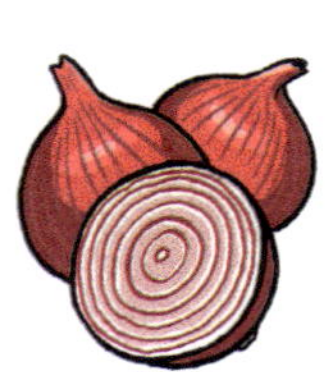
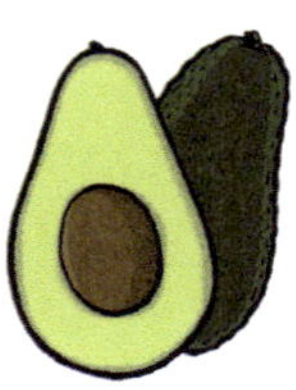
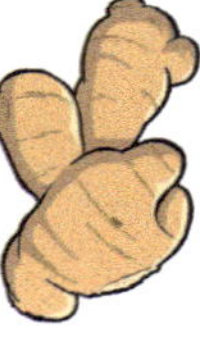

[08]

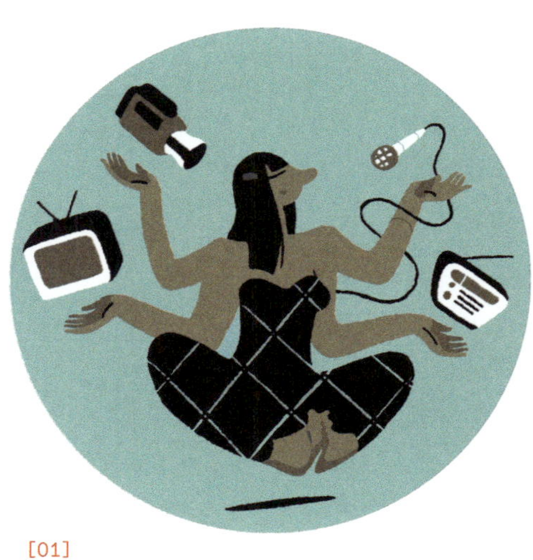

[01]

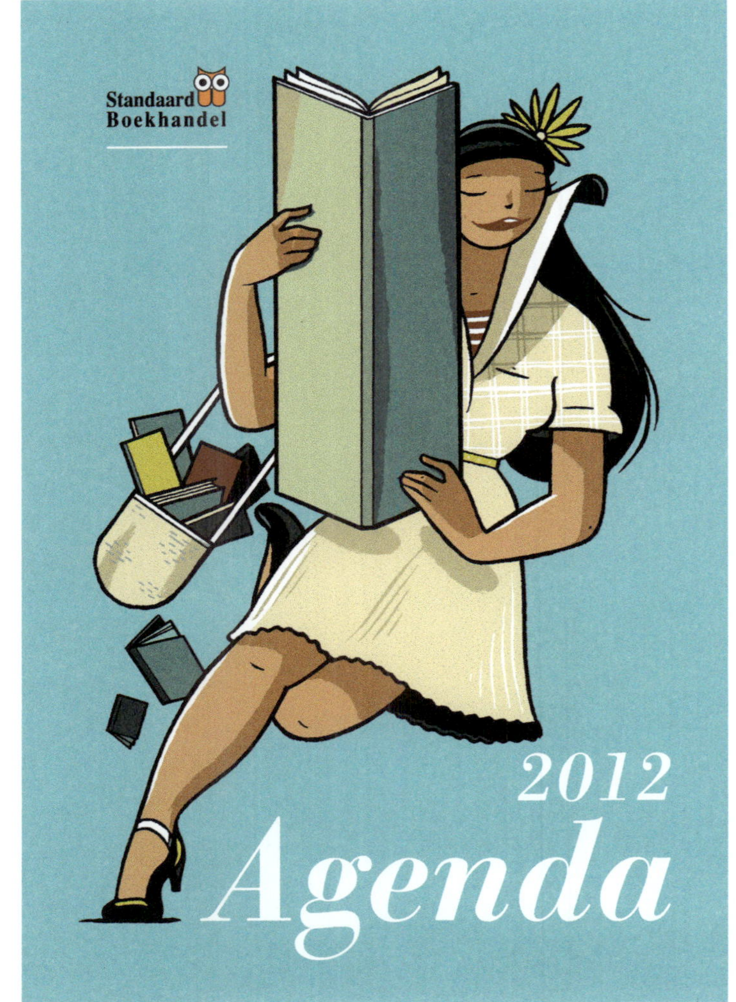

[02]

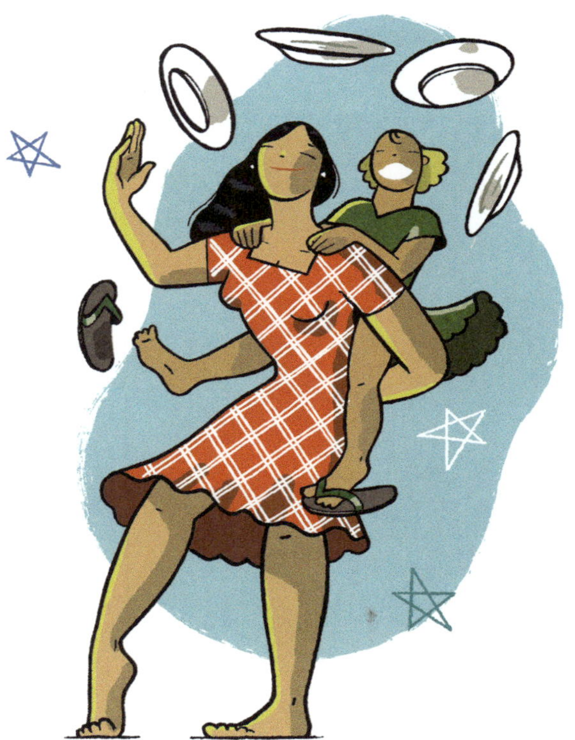

[03]

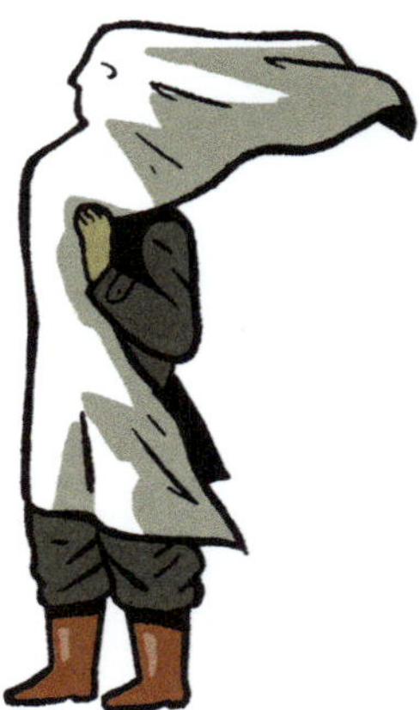

[04]

[01] **Media Girl**
Mies Meulders
✳ 2001

[02] **Refused Illustration**
Standaard Boekhandel
✳ 2009

[03] **Life is Circus**
Circus Centrum
✳ 2010

[04] **On a Windy Day**
Marketing 21
✳ 2007

[05] **Happiness**
De Standaard
✳ 2011

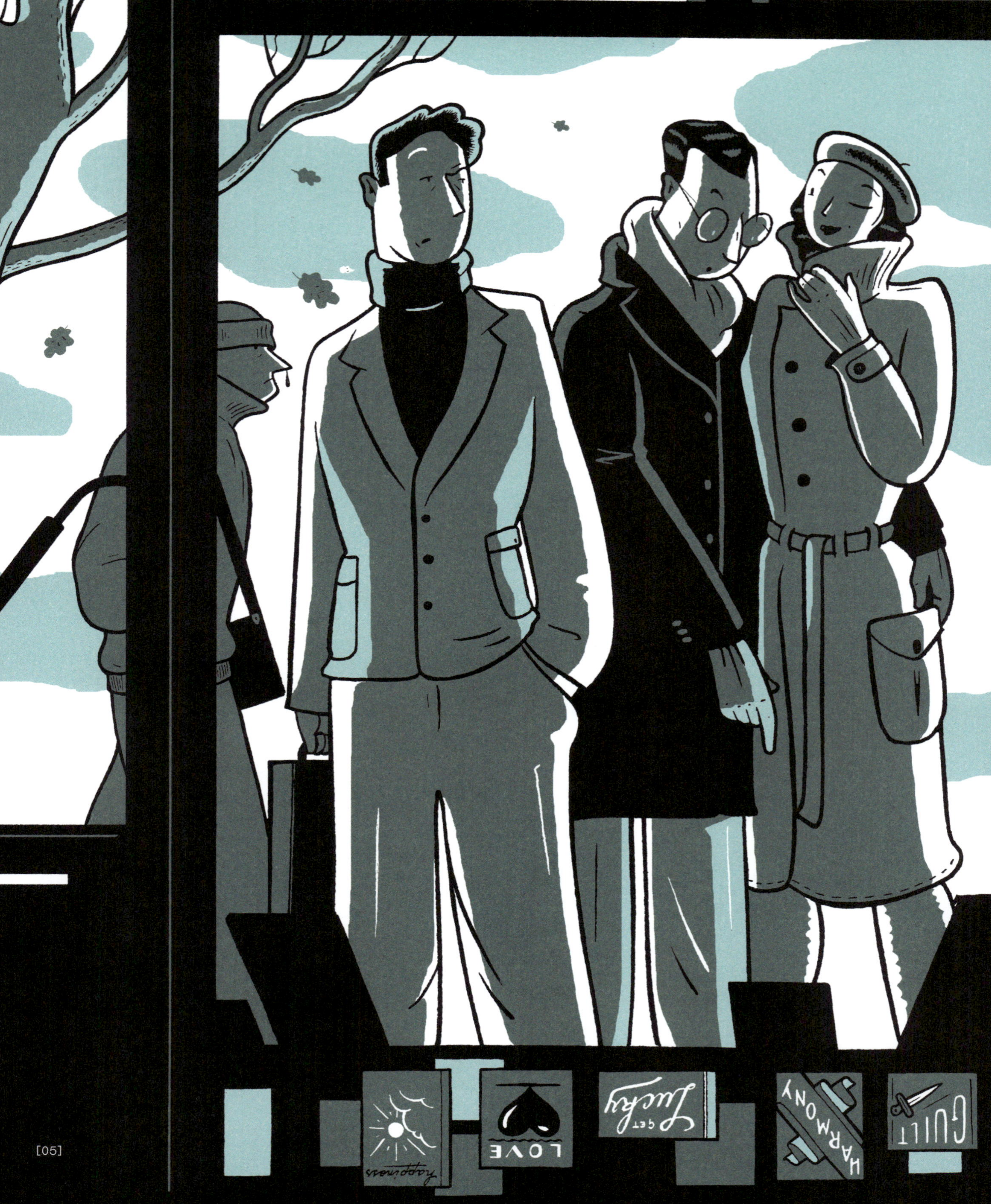

Happiness
LOVE
Get Lucky
HARMONY
GUILT

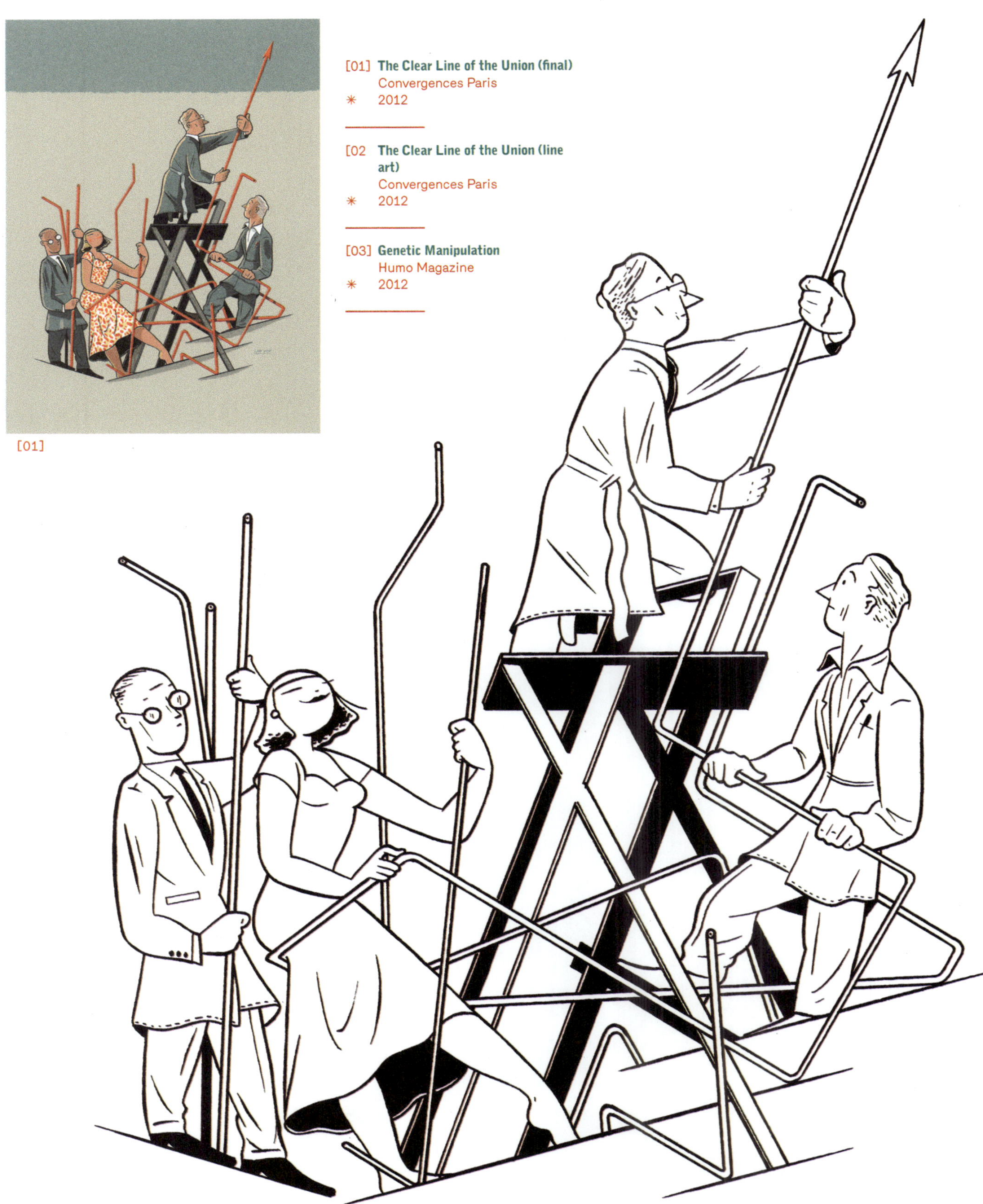

[01]

[02]

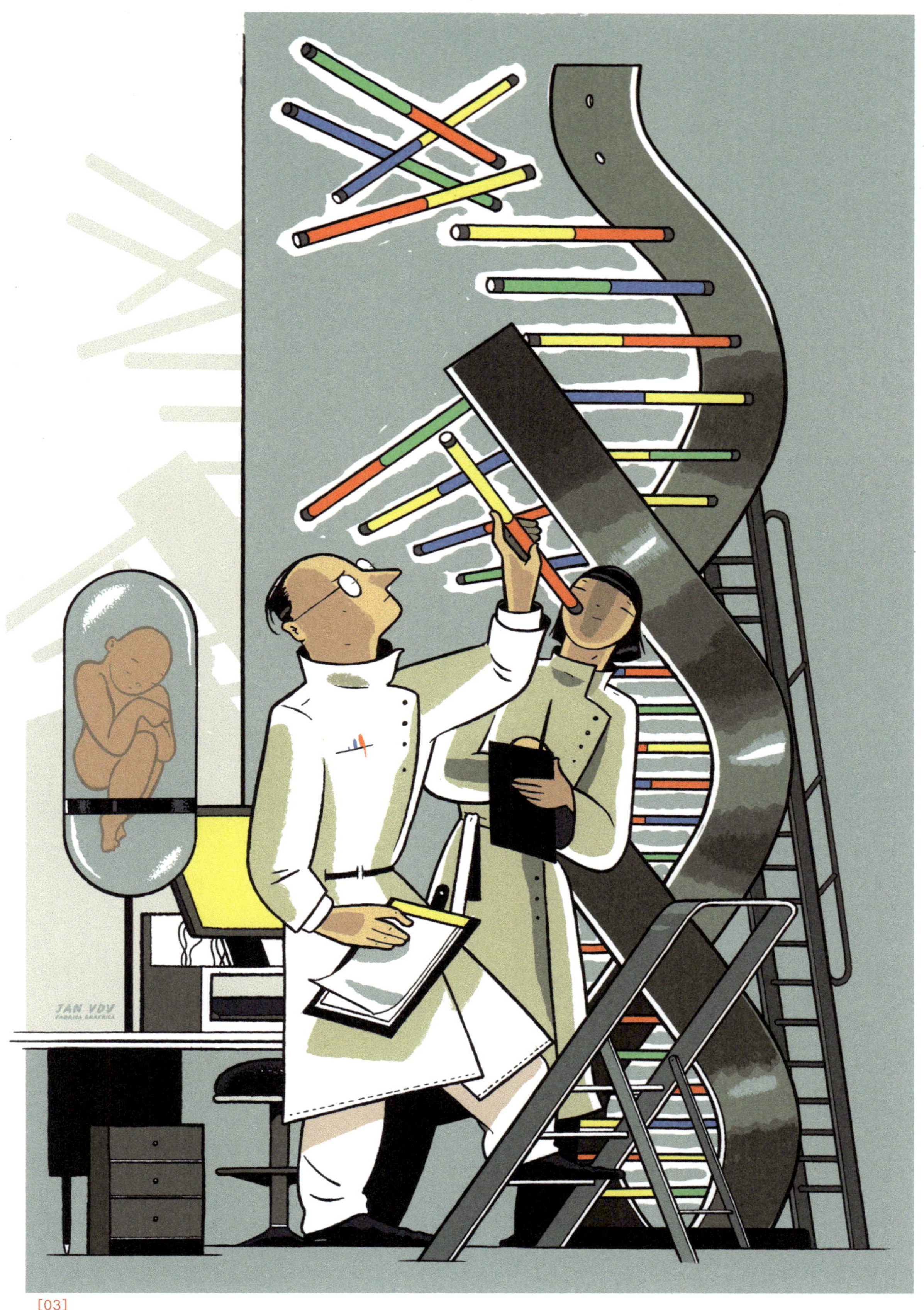
JAN VDV
FABRICA GRAFICA

[03]

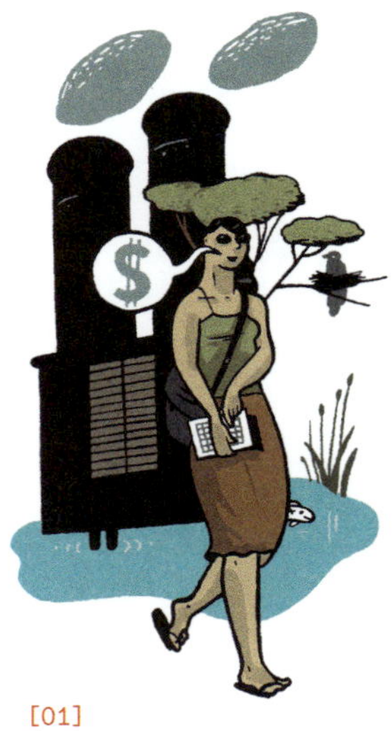

[01]

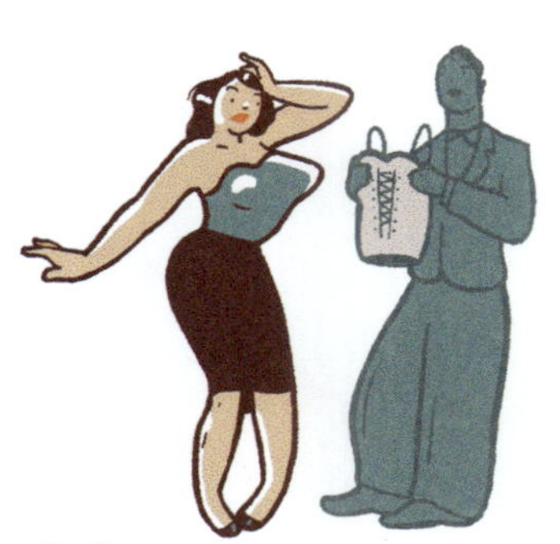

[02]

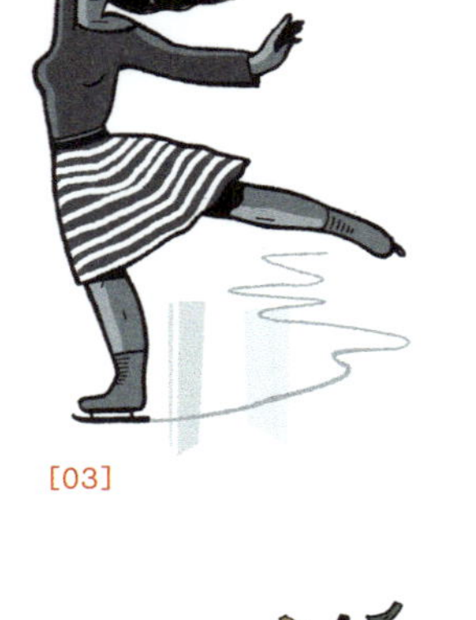

[03]

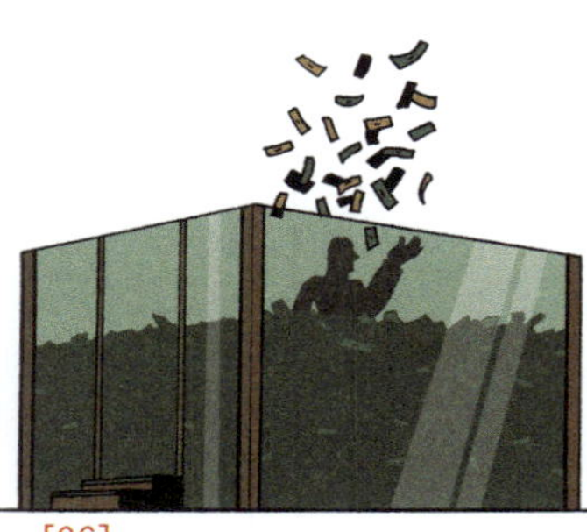

[05]

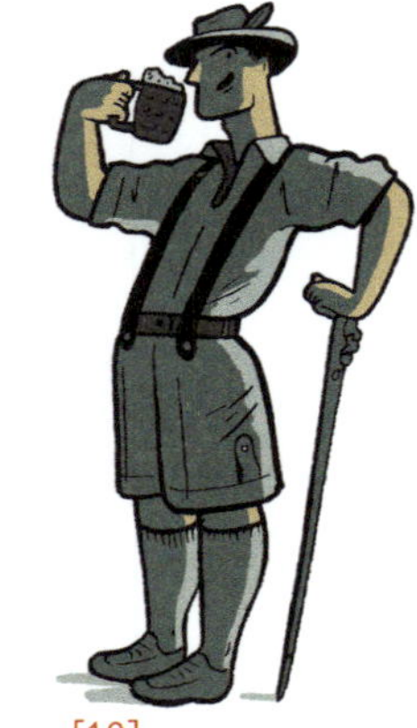

[06]

[04]

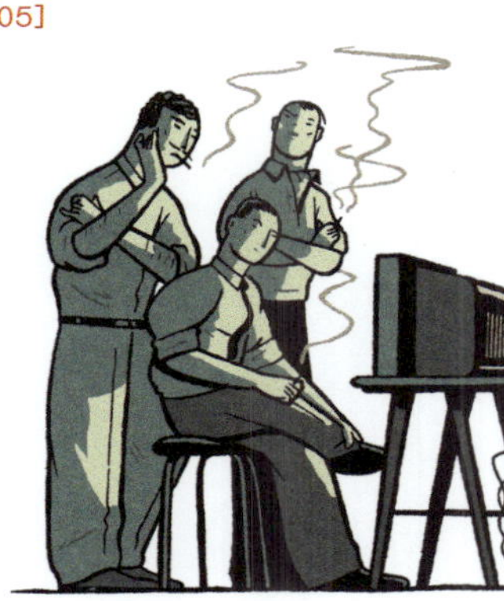

[08]

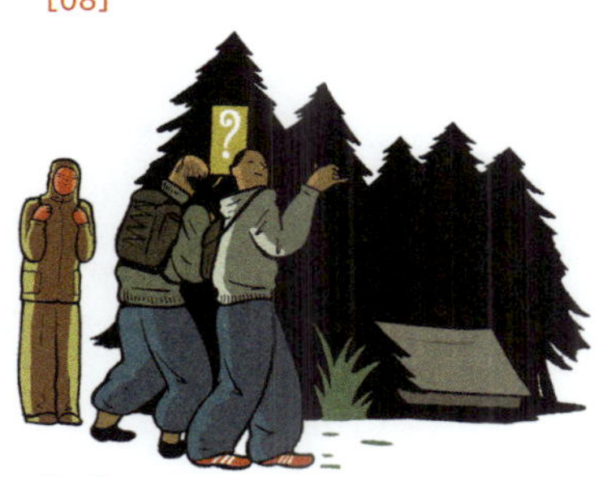

[07]

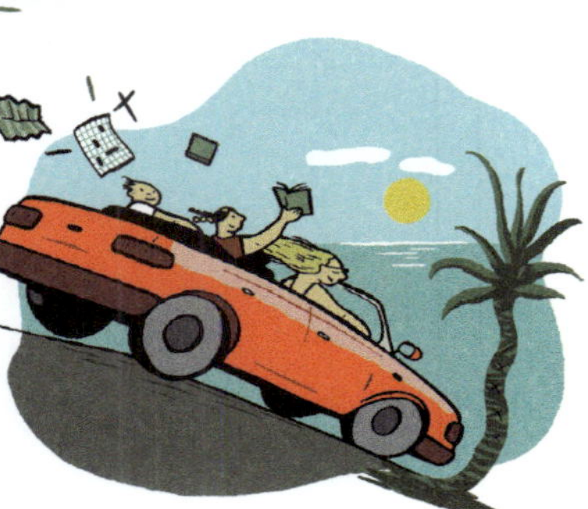

[09]

[10]

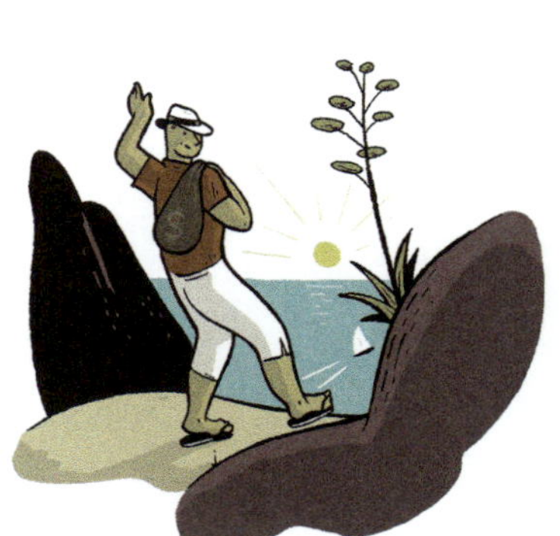

[11]

[12]

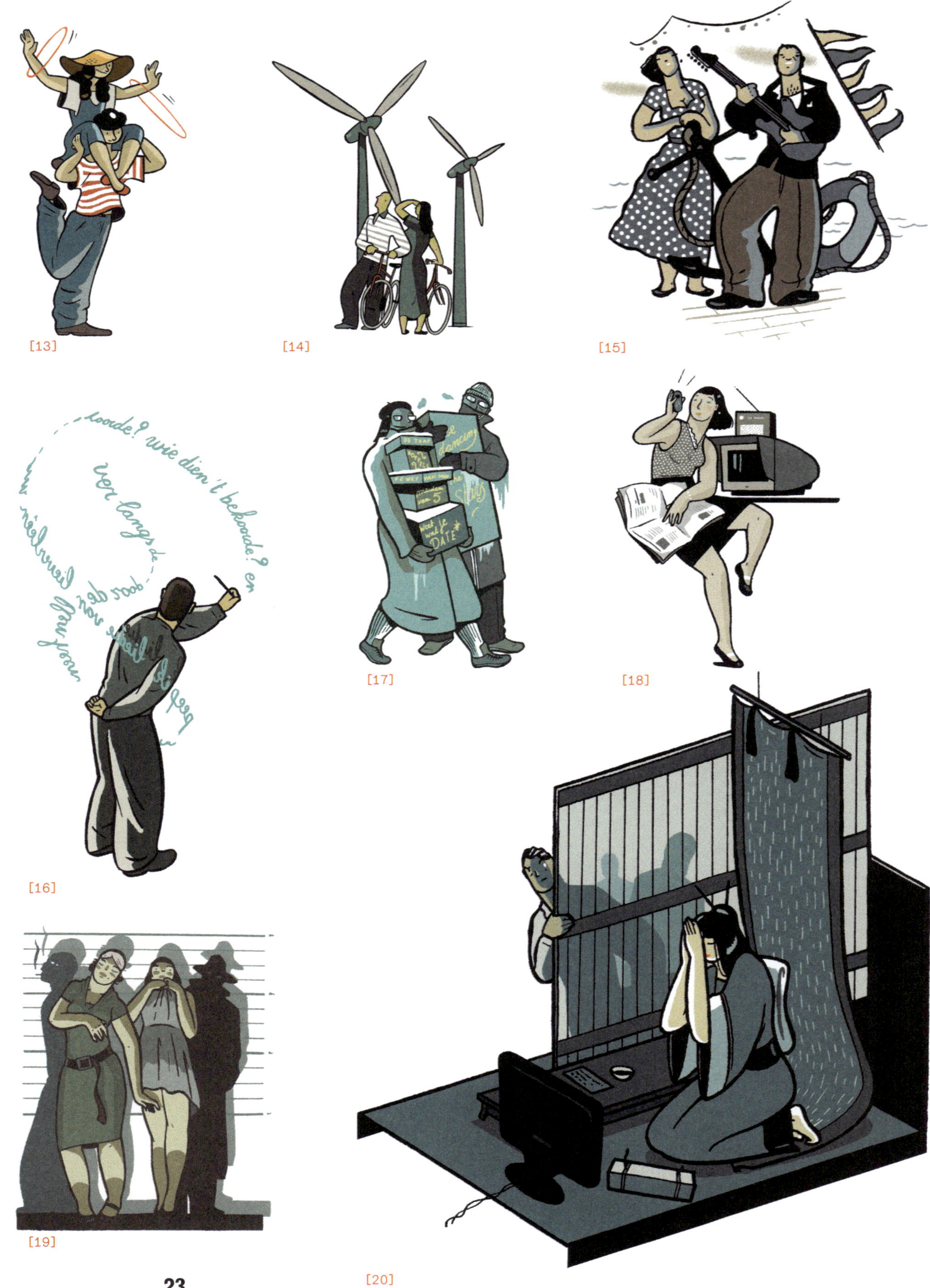
[13]
[14]
[15]
[16]
[17]
[18]
[19]
[20]

JAN VDV

[01]

1ste
UKULELE
FESTIVAL

[02]

Die Nordendwikis.

[03]

SID(t)EFFECTS
12 TOT 19 APRIL GENT !

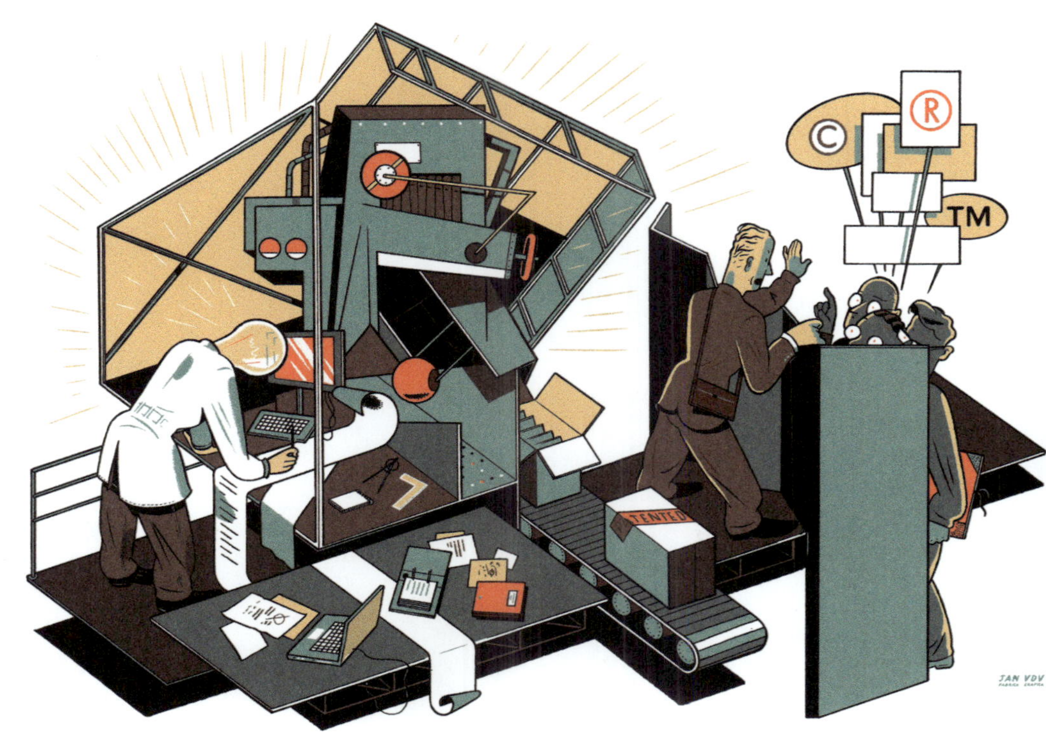

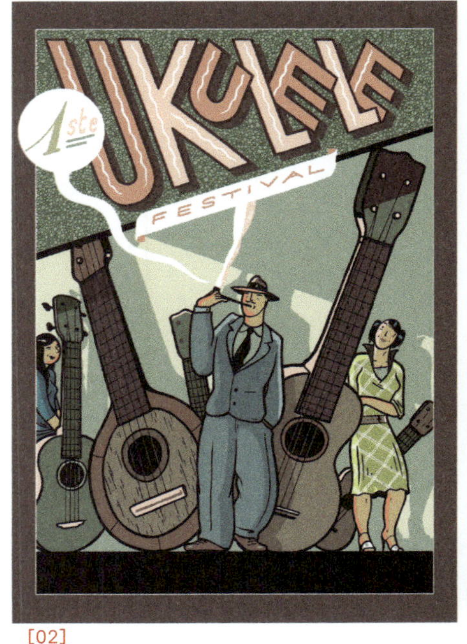

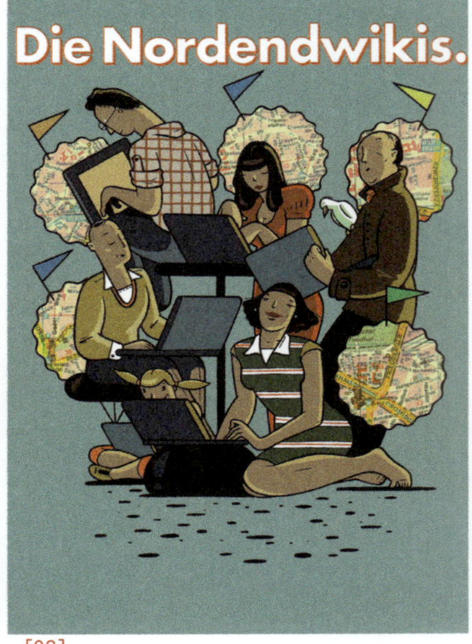

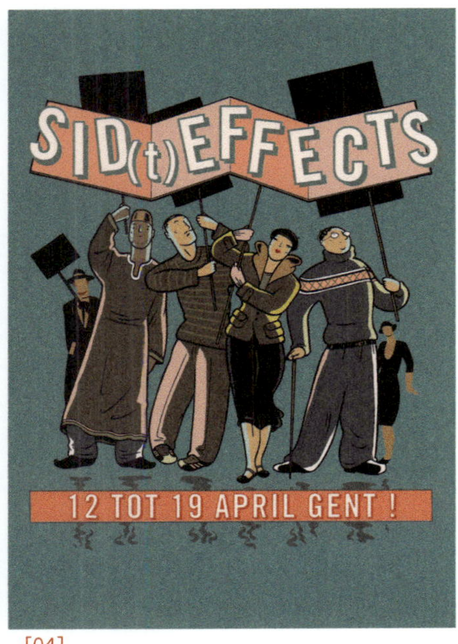

[04]

PROFICIAT
met de groeten van HOGESCHOOL GENT
JAN VDV
FABRICA GRAFICA

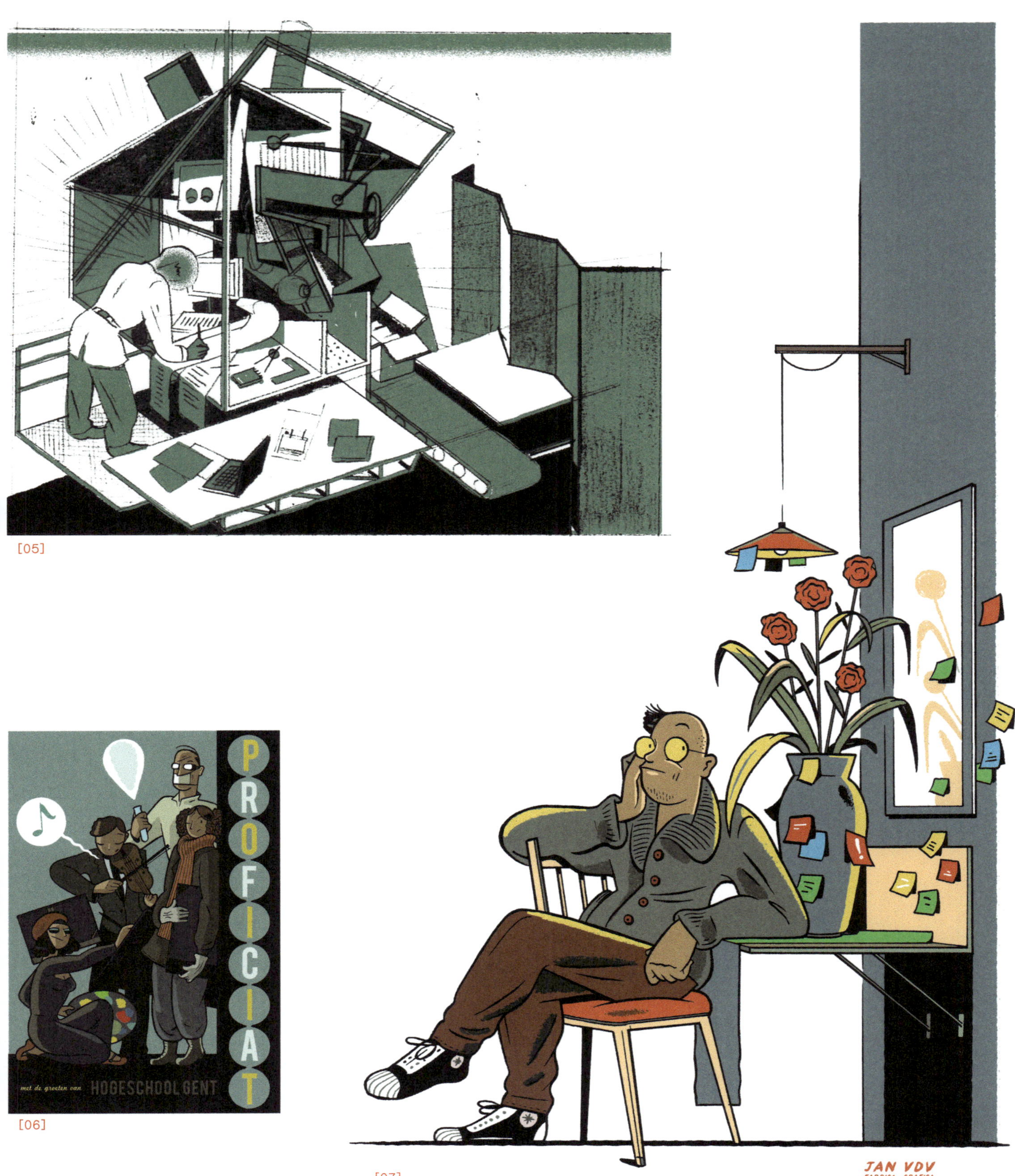

[05]

[06]

[07]

GENT 13 13
de eeuw
van de
vooruitgang !
JAN VDV
FABRICA GRAFICA

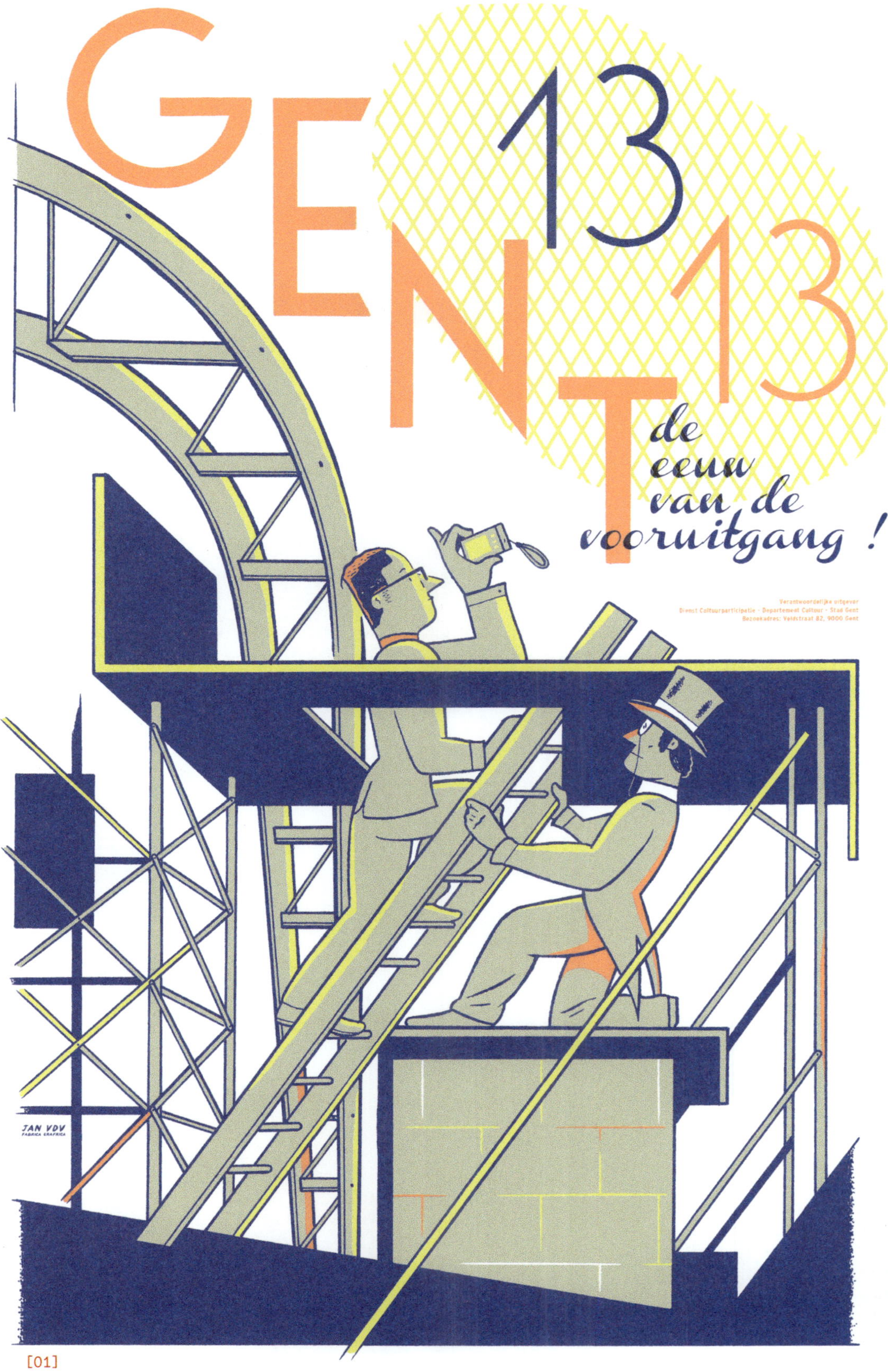

[01]

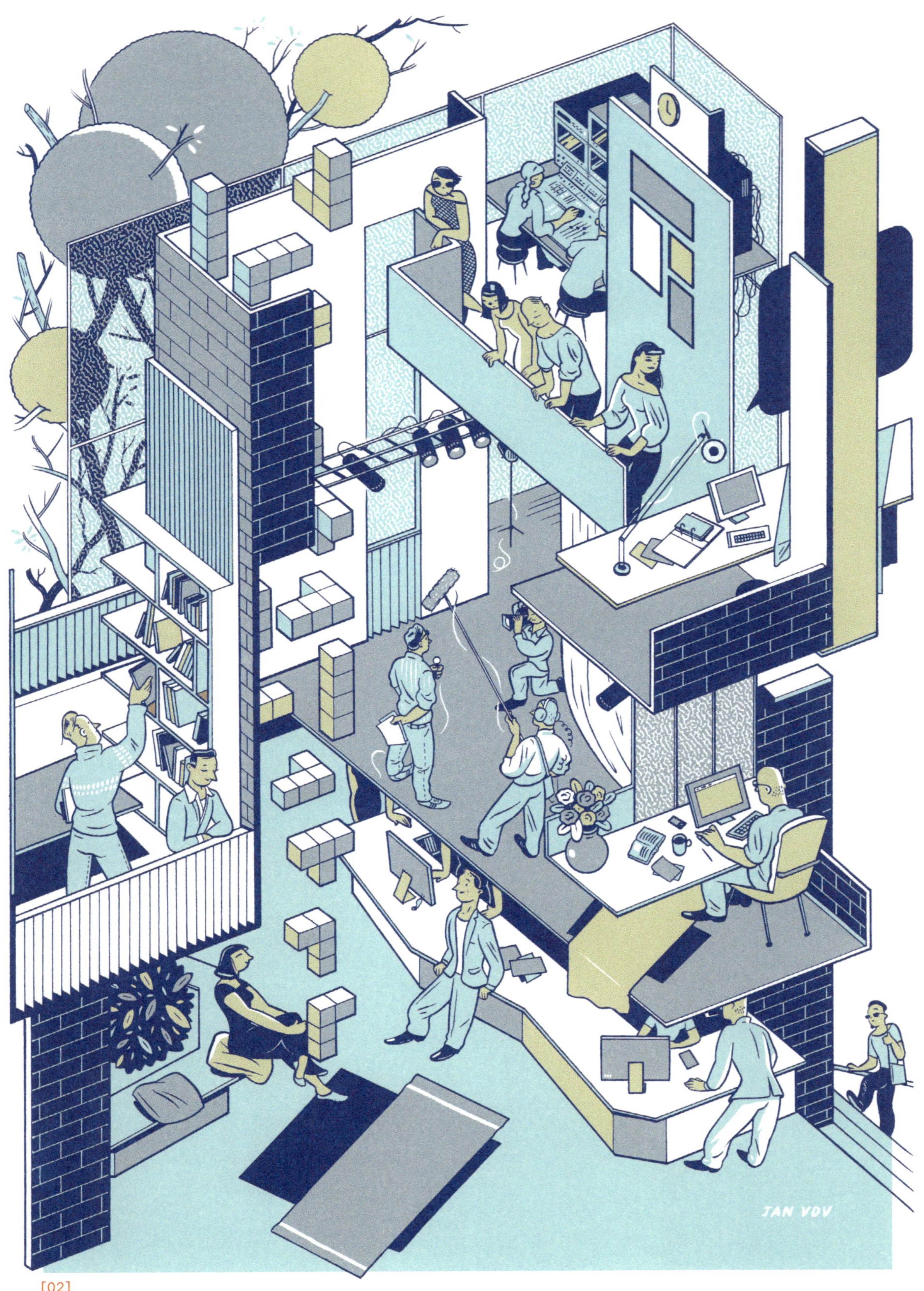
JAN VDV

Contra. Magazine
✳ 2009

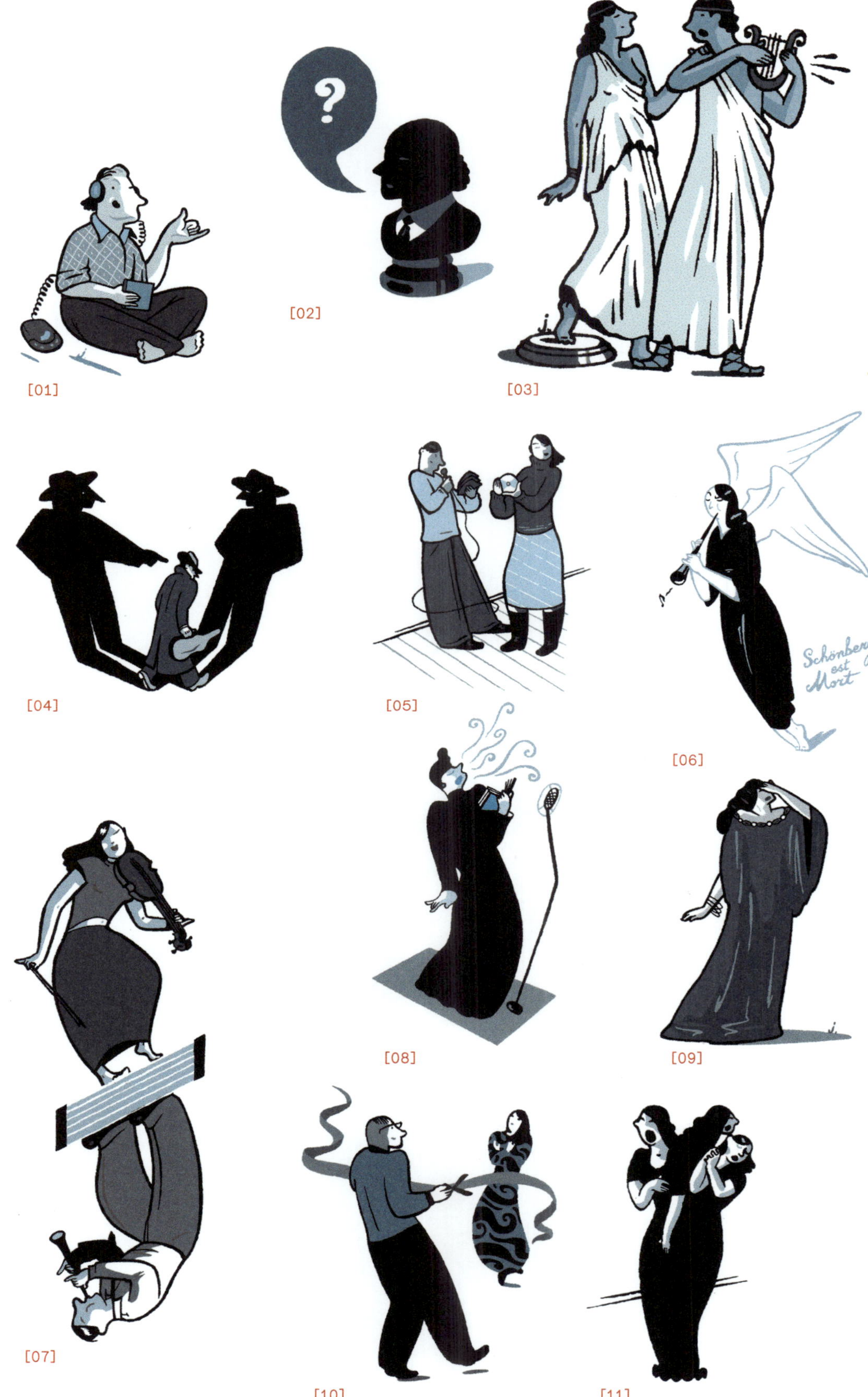

[01]
[02]
[03]
[04]
[05]
[06]
[07]
[08]
[09]
[10]
[11]

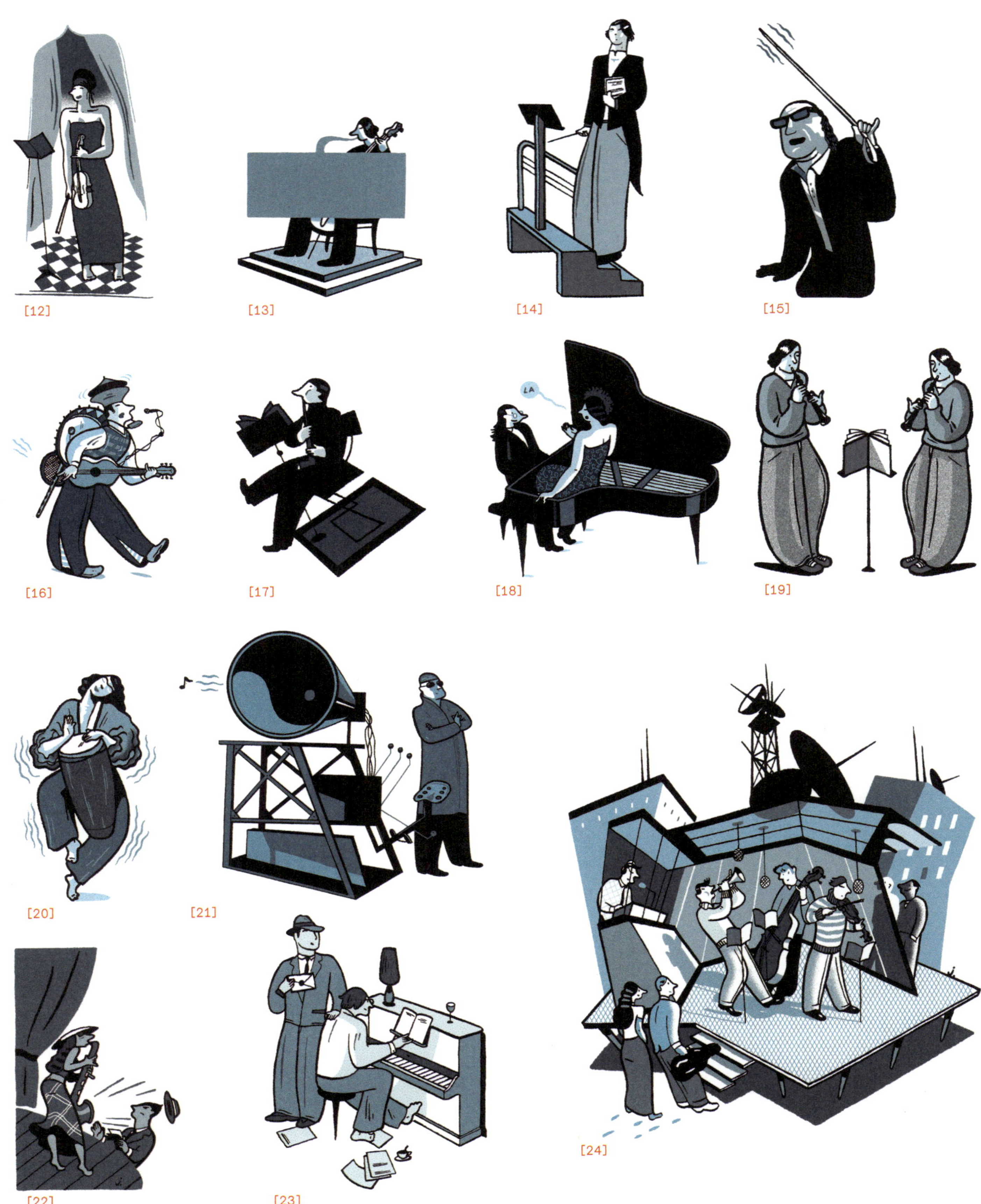

LA

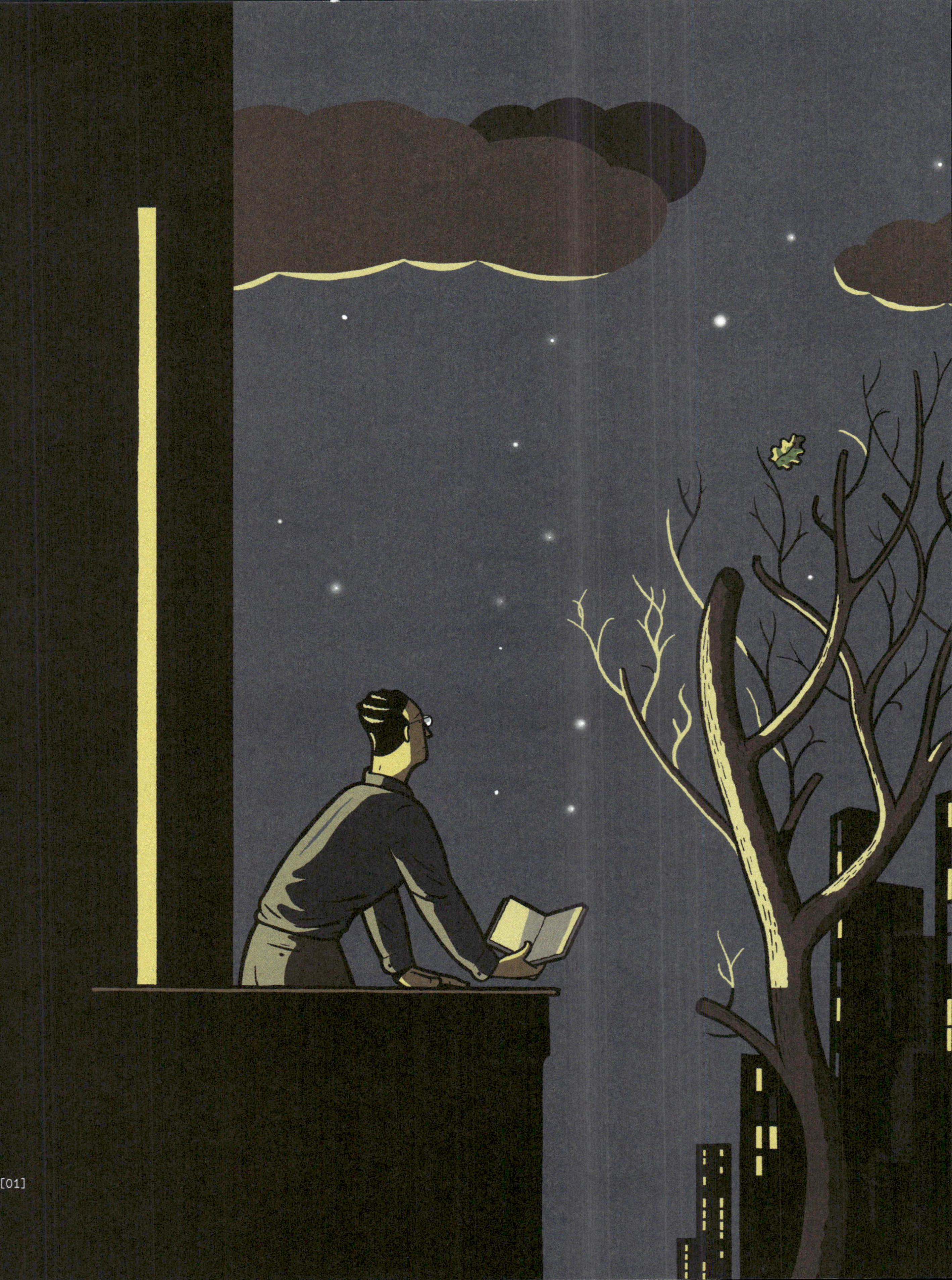

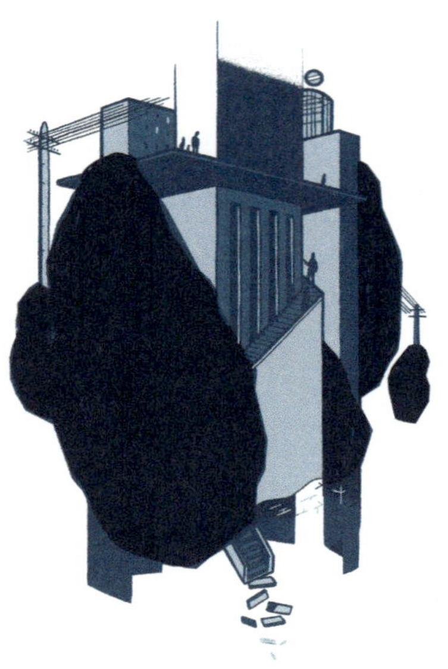

[02]

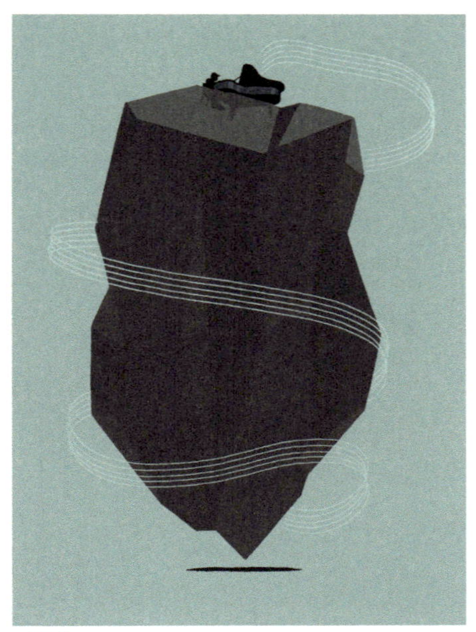

[03]

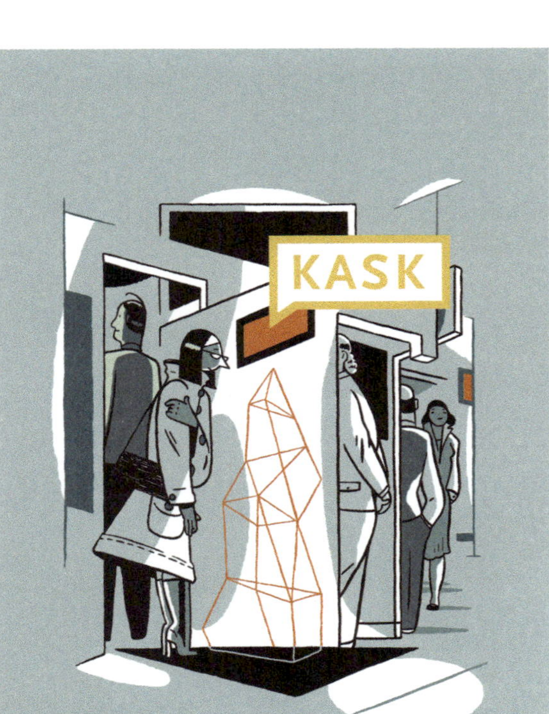

[04]

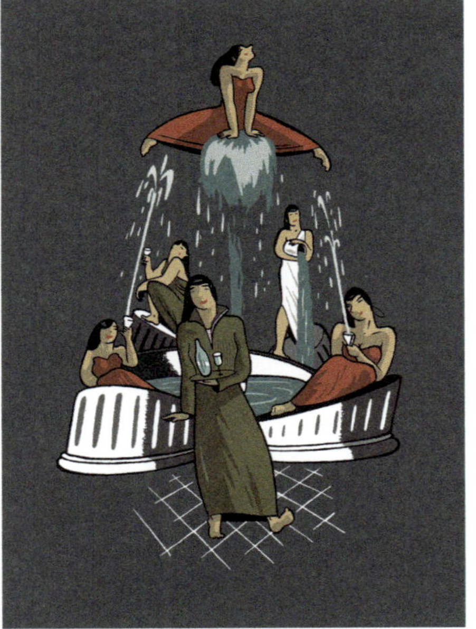

[05]

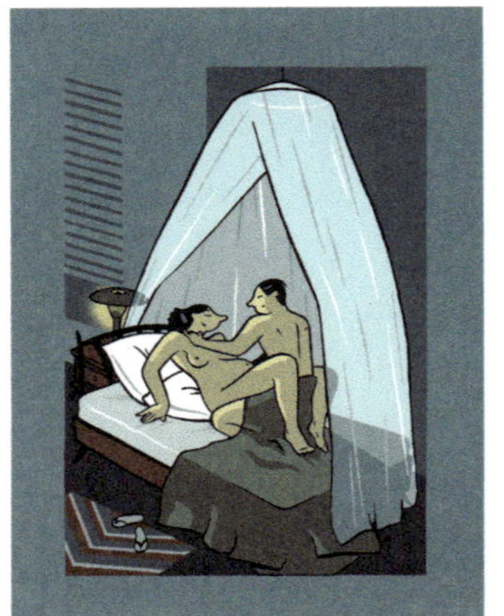

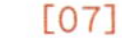

[06]

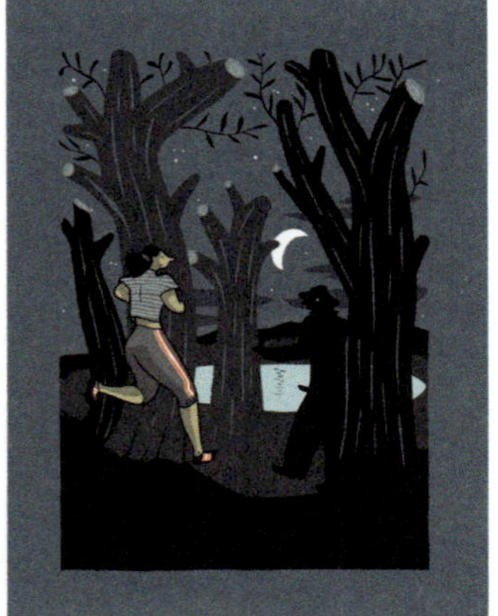

[07]

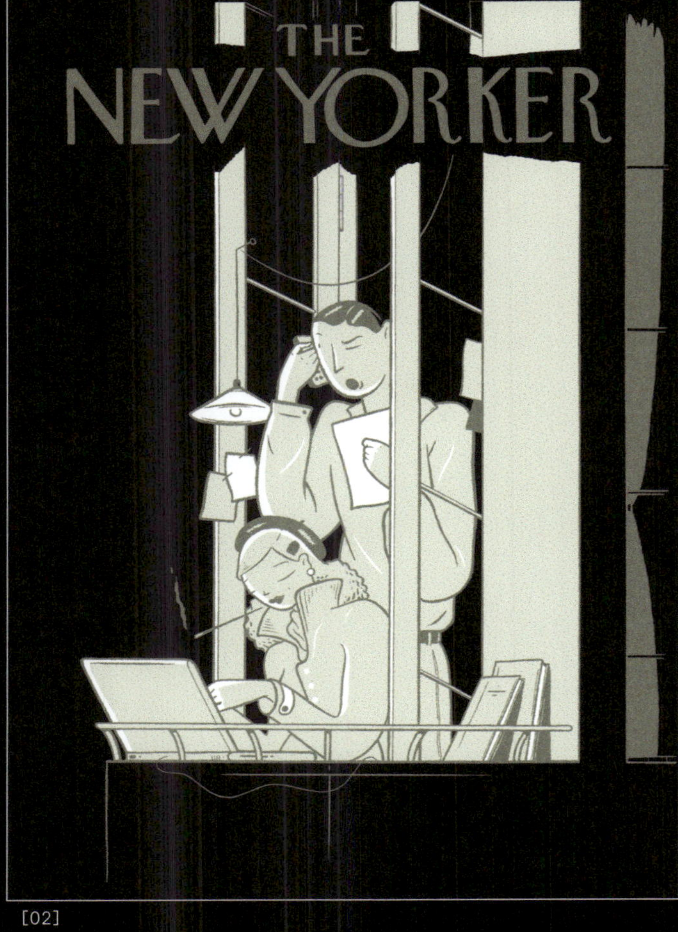

[02]

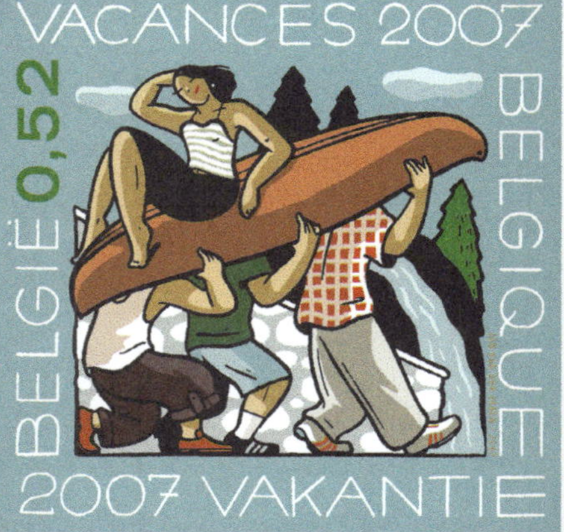

[01]

[03]

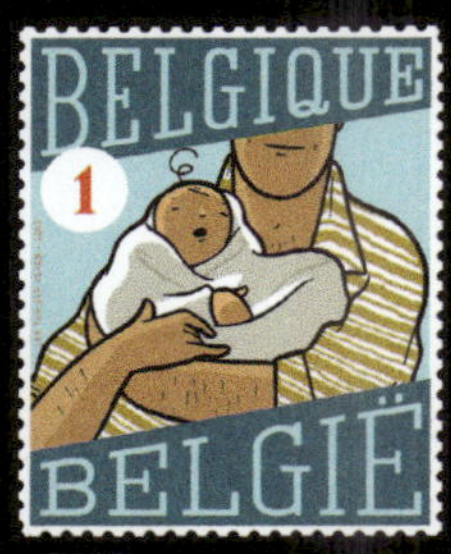

[04]

[05]

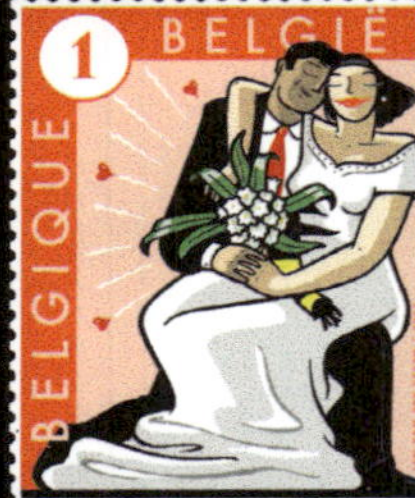

[06]

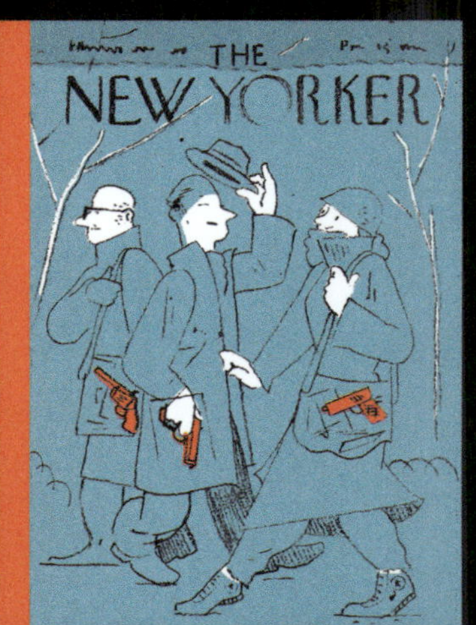

[07]

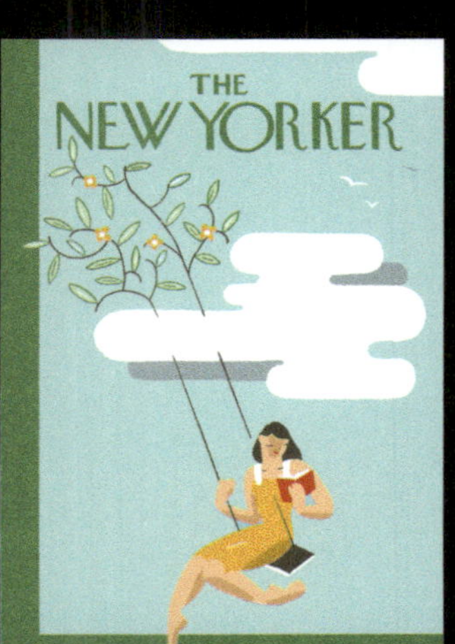

[08]

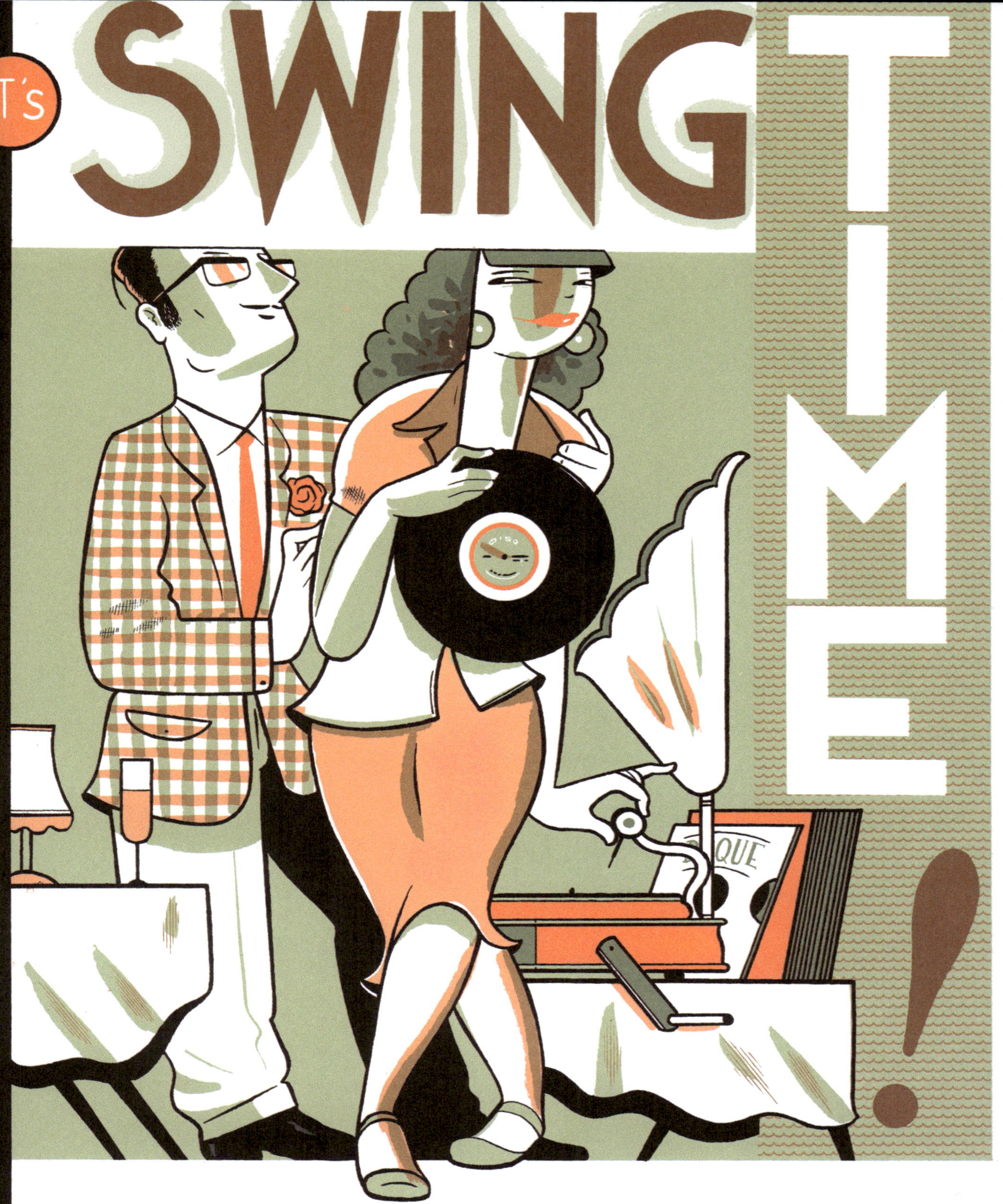
IT's
SWING
TIME!

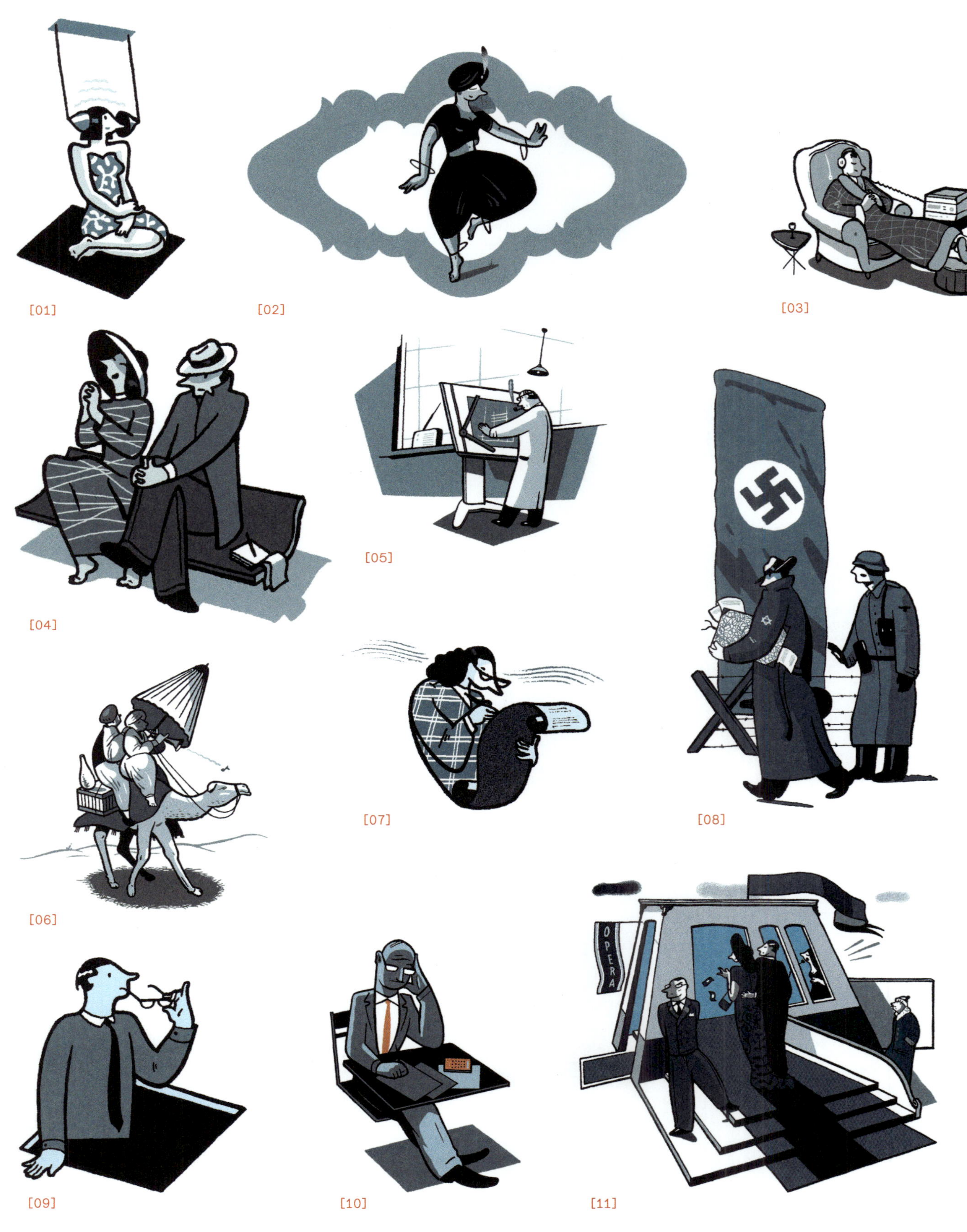

[01]
[02]
[03]
[04]
[05]
[06]
[07]
[08]
[09]
[10]
[11]
OPERA

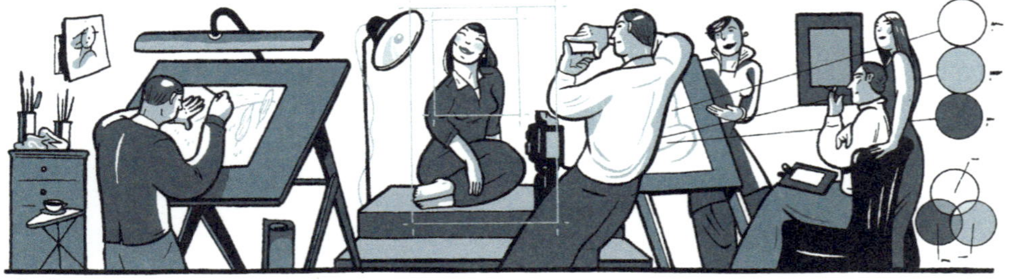

[12]

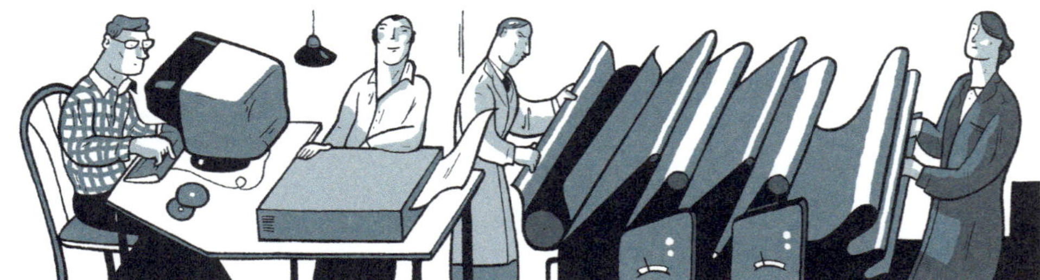

[13]

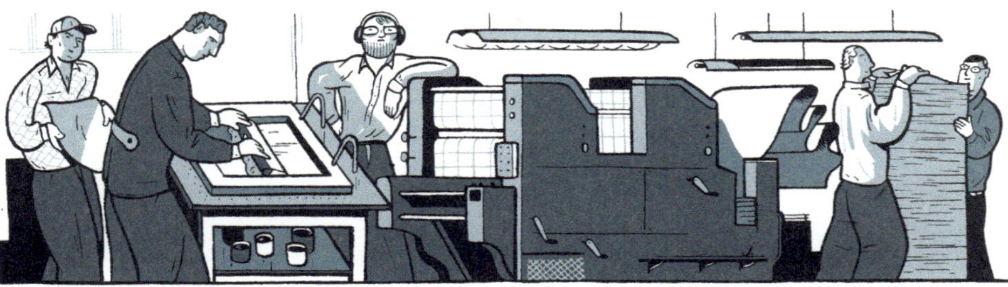

[14]

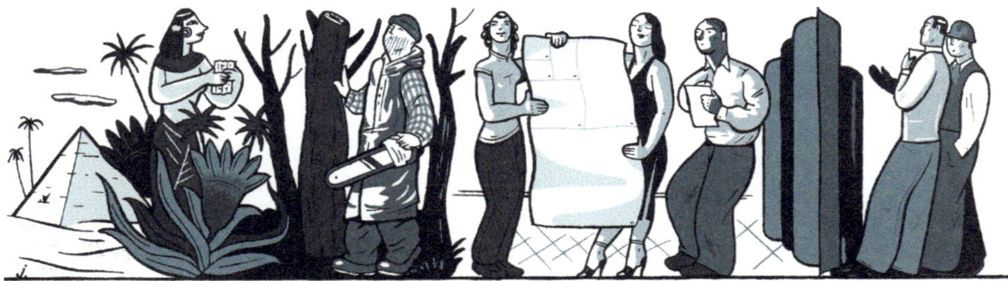

[15]

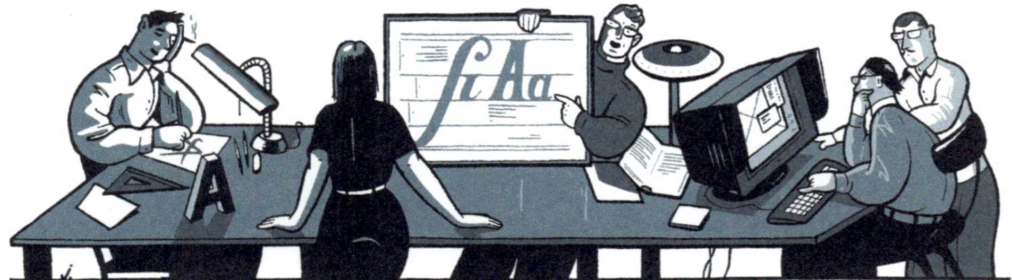

[16]

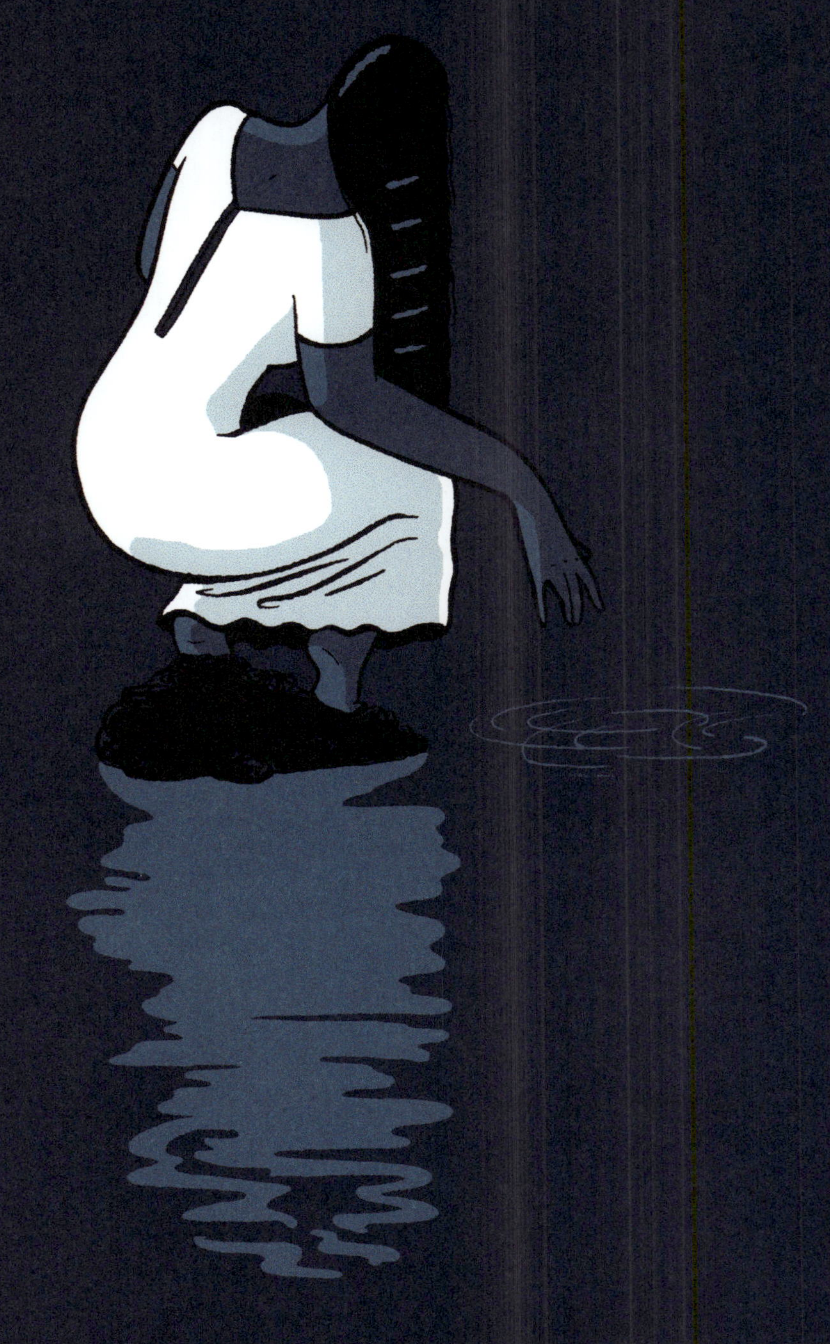

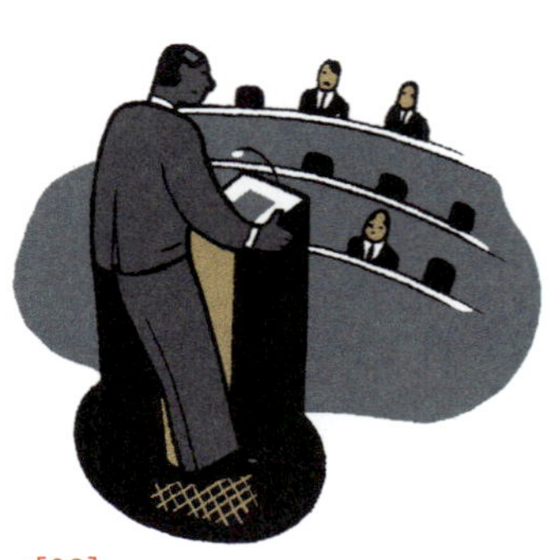

[02]

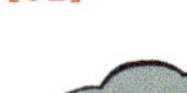

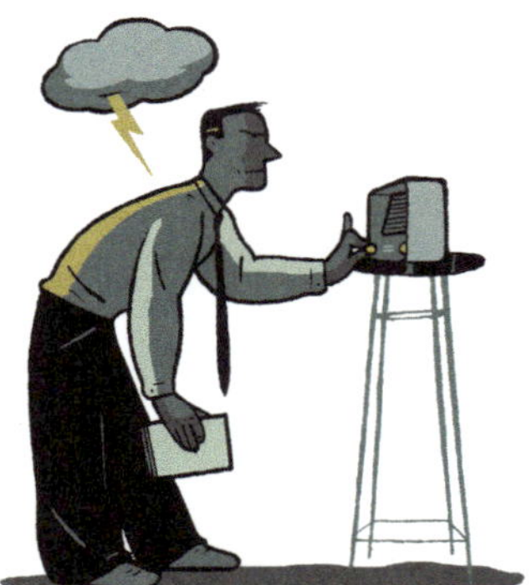

[05]

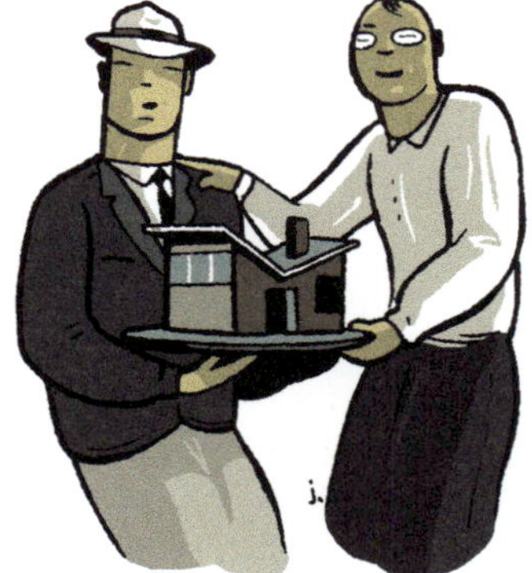

[08]

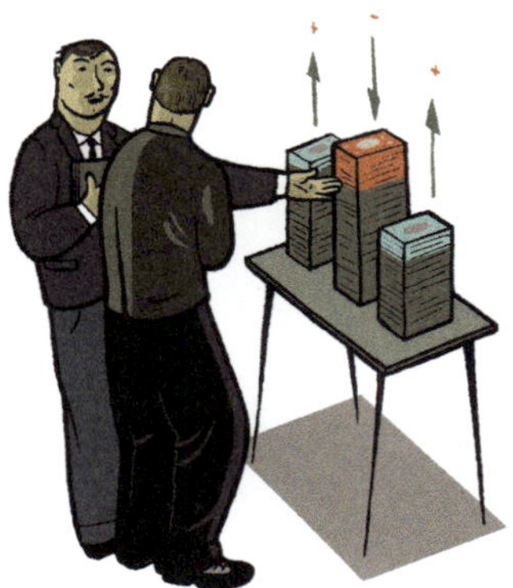

[11]

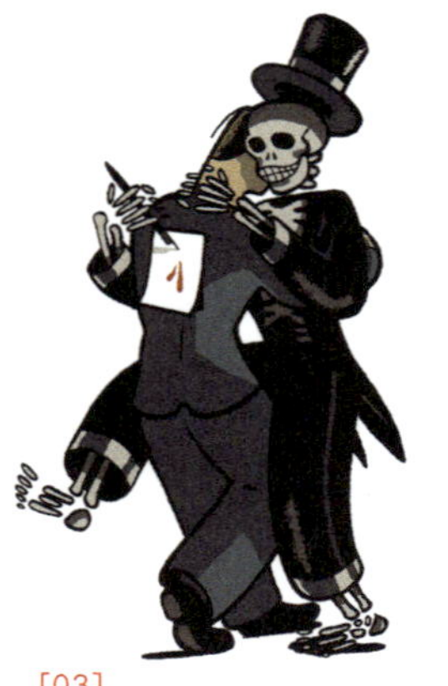

[03]

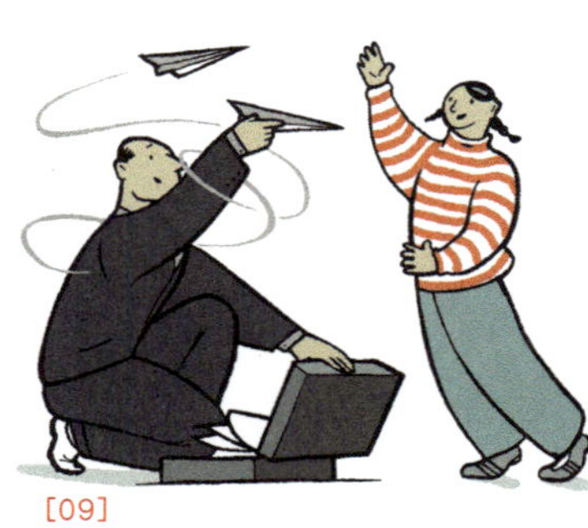

[09]

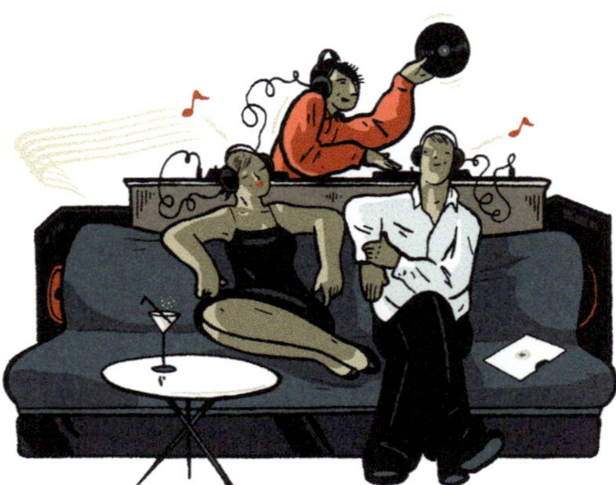

[12]

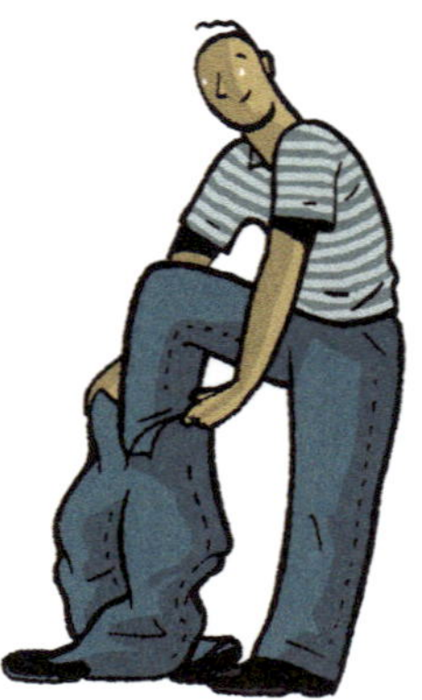

[04]

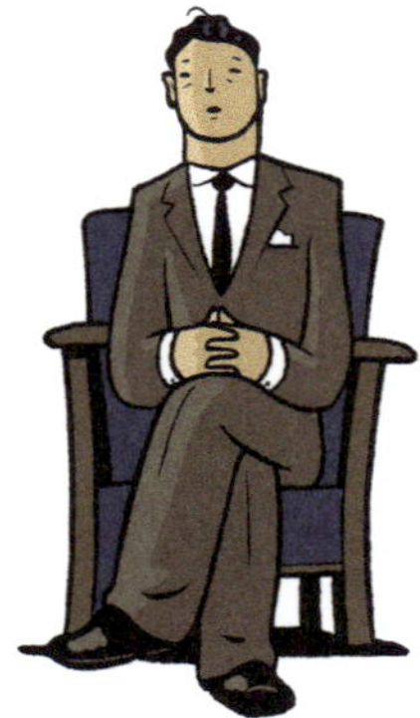

[07]

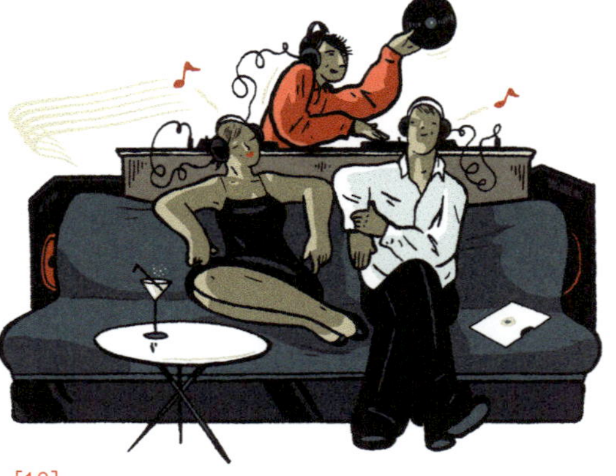

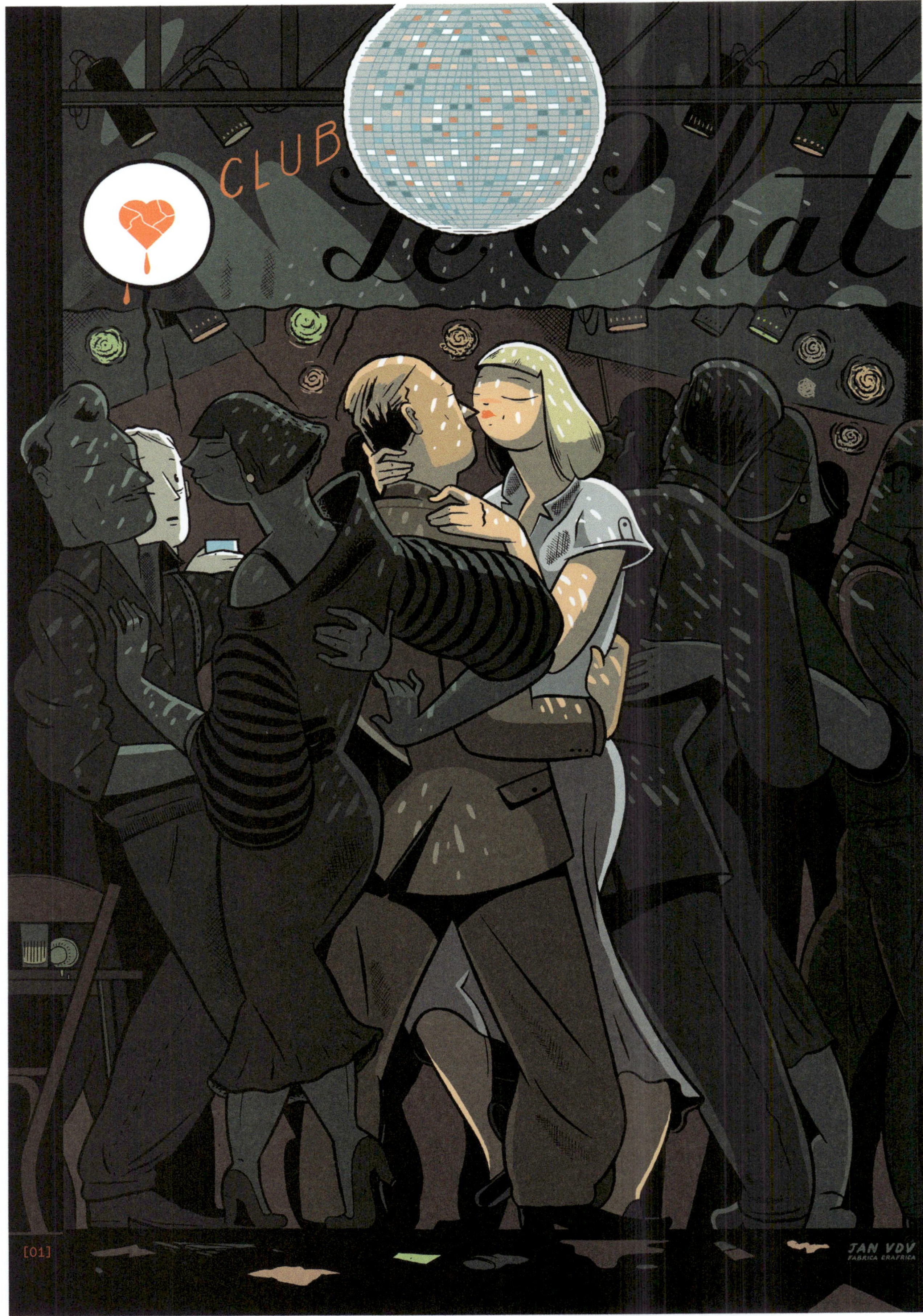

CLUB
Le Chat
[01]
JAN VDV
FABRICA GRAFICA

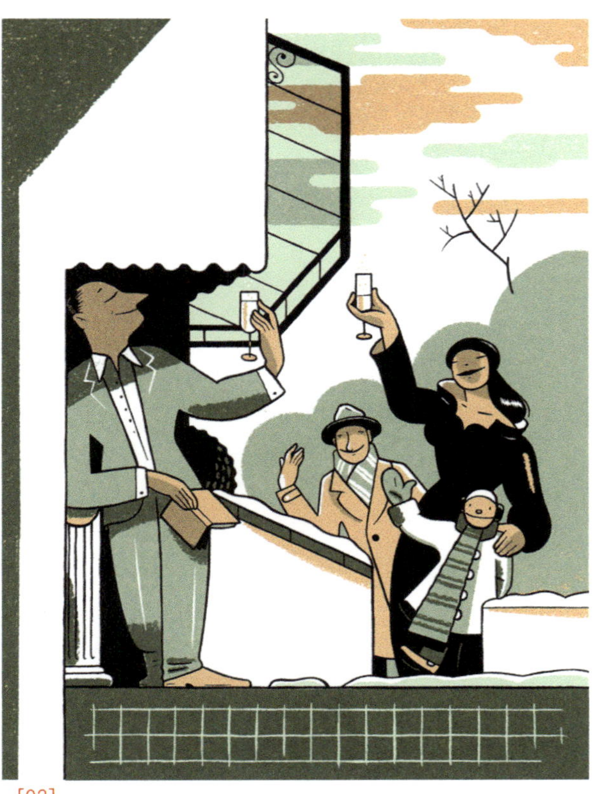

[02]

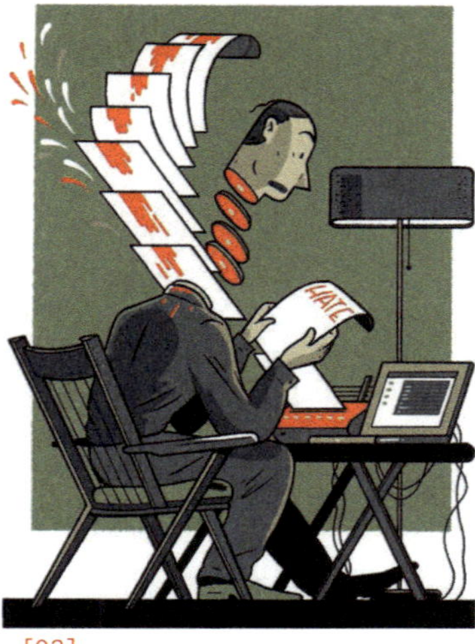

[03]

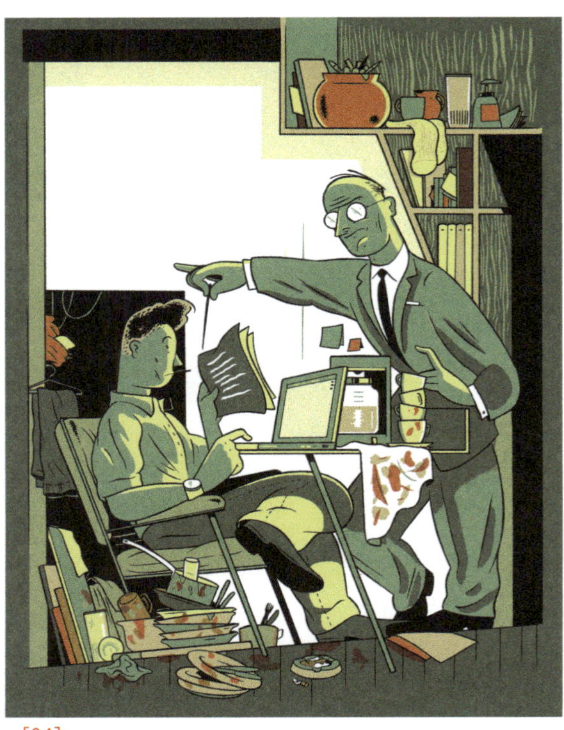

[04]

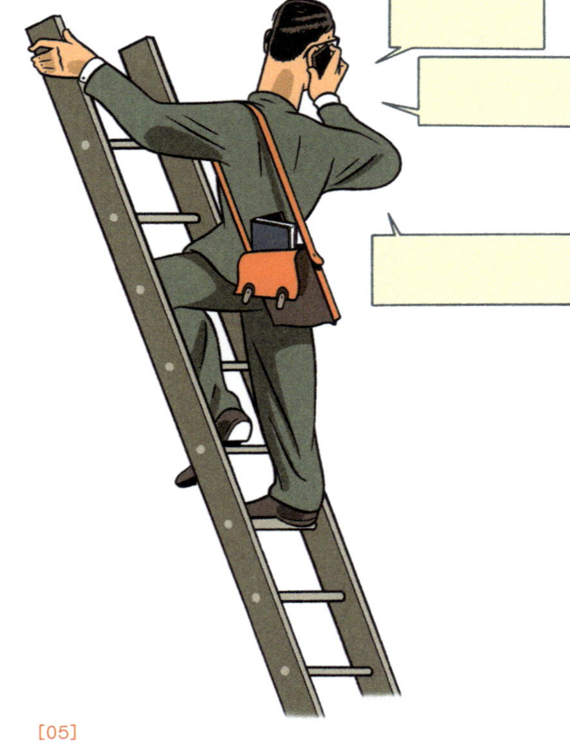

[05]

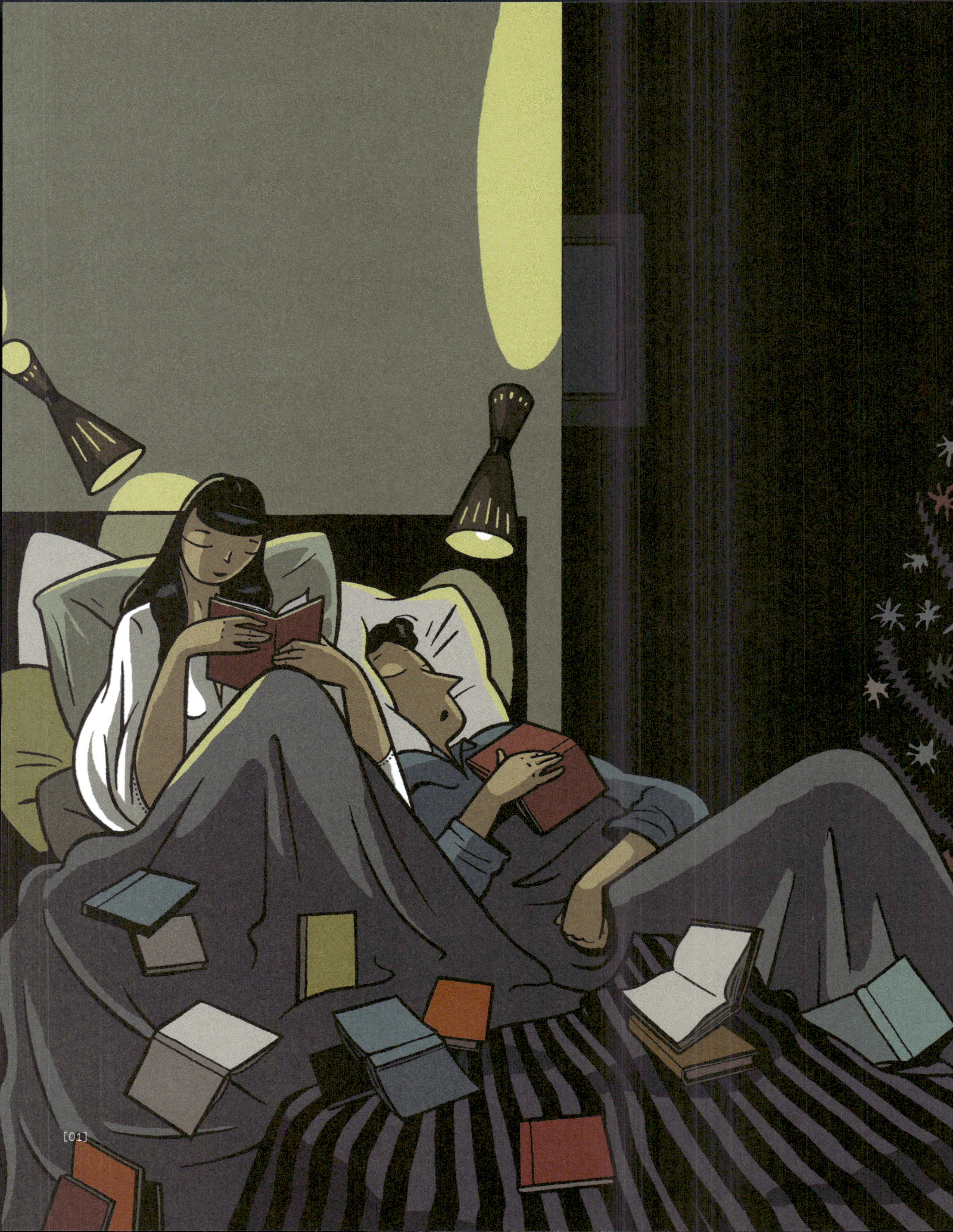

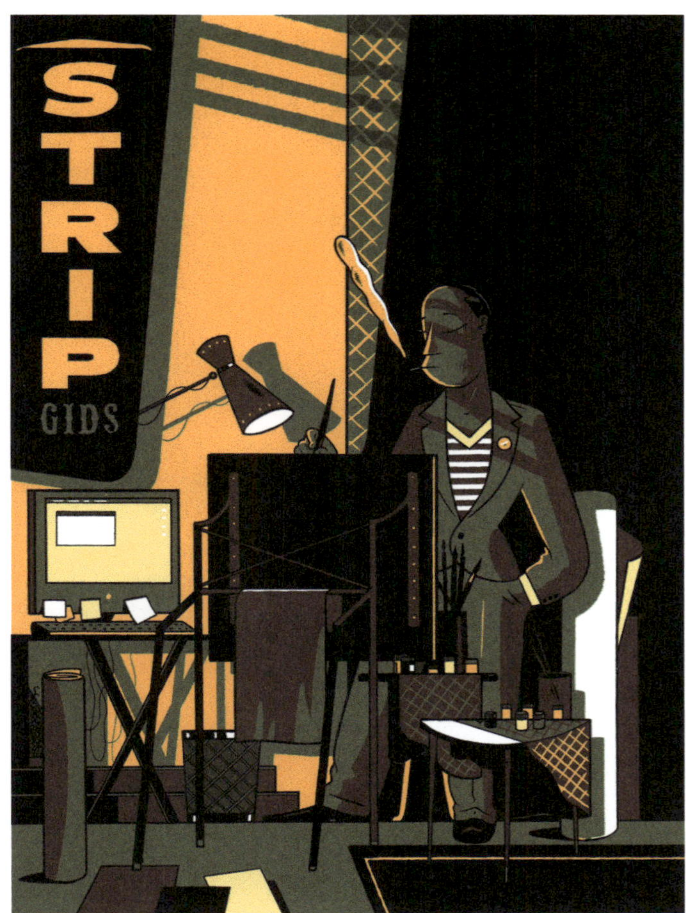

[02]

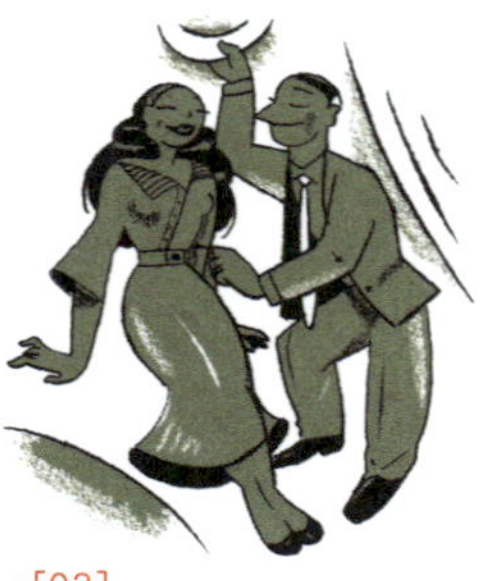

[03]

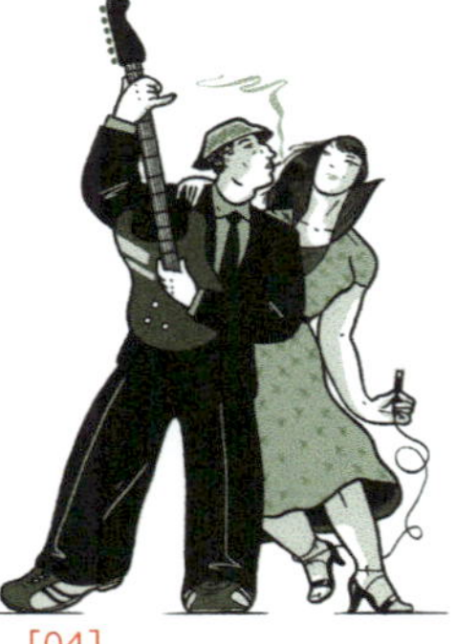

[04]

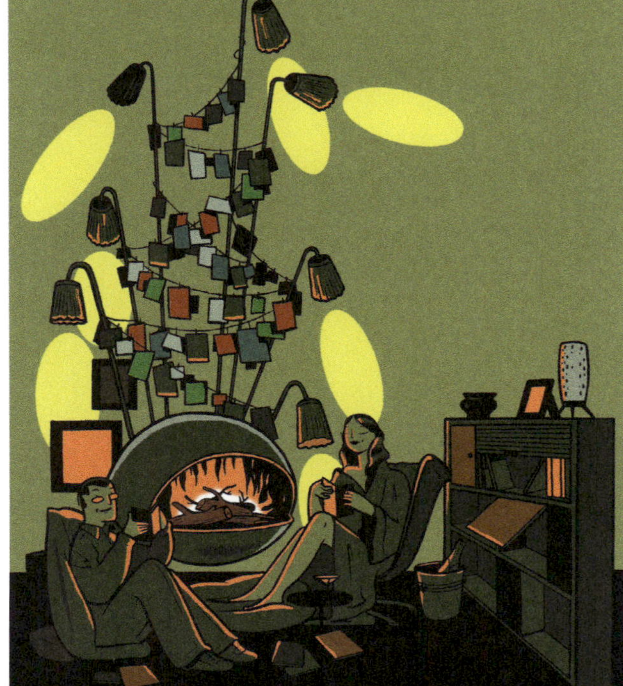
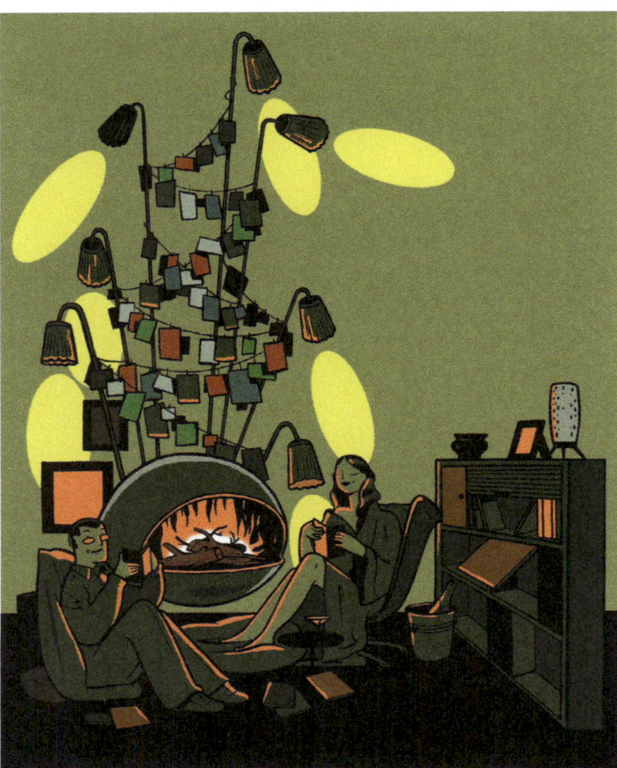

[05]

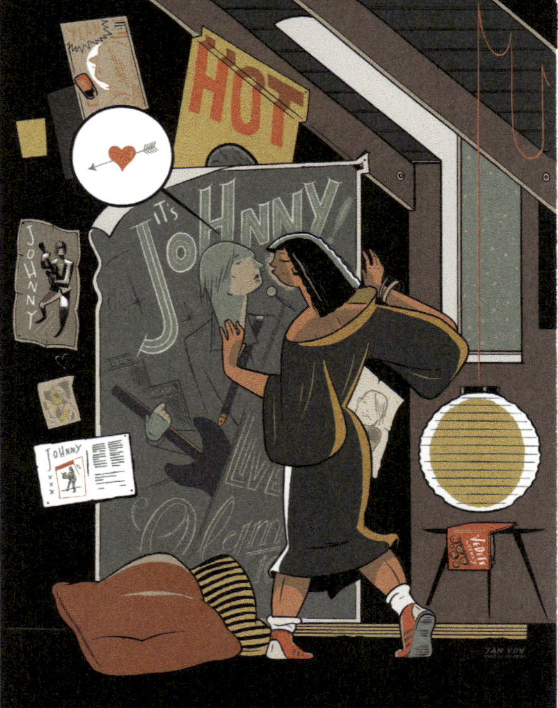

[06]

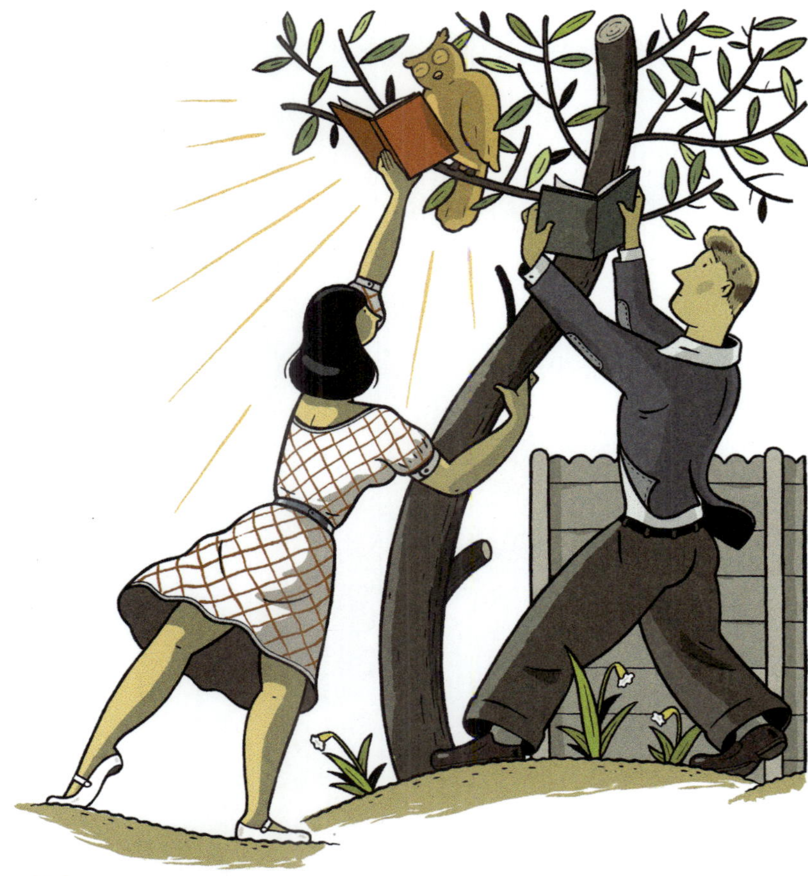

[01]

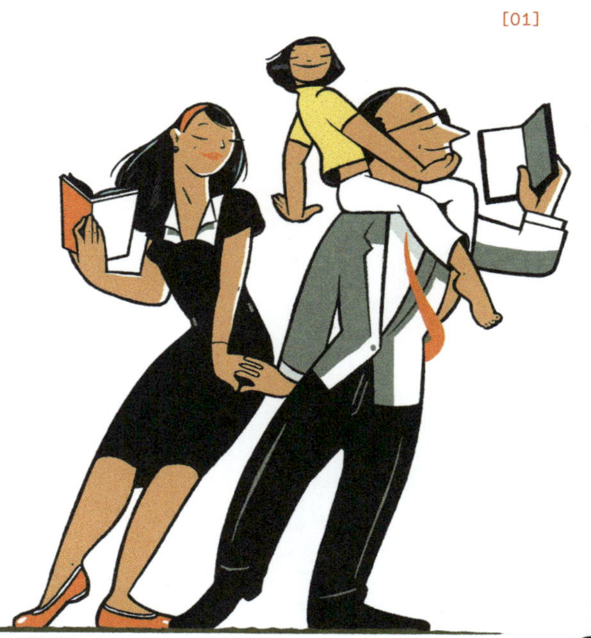

[02]

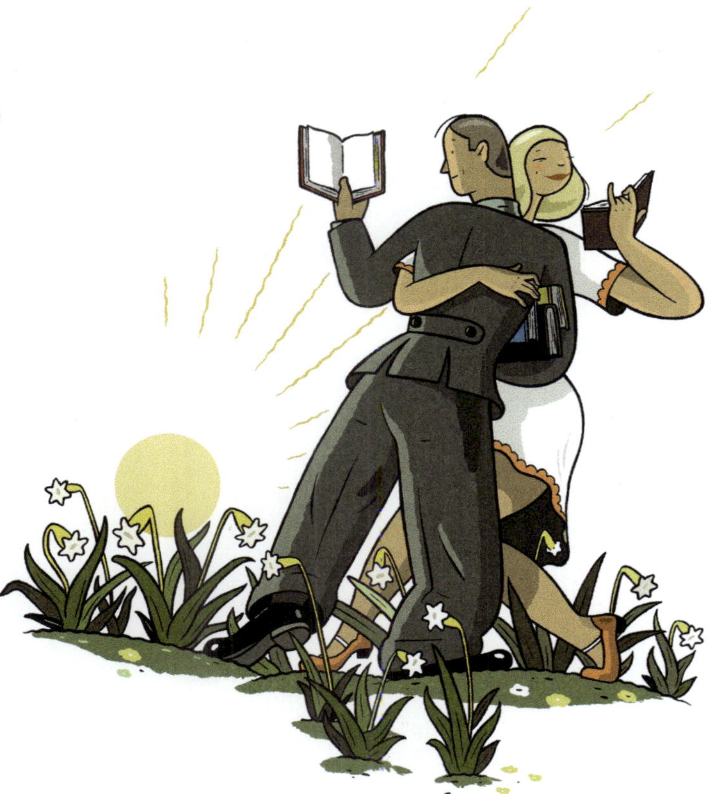

[03]

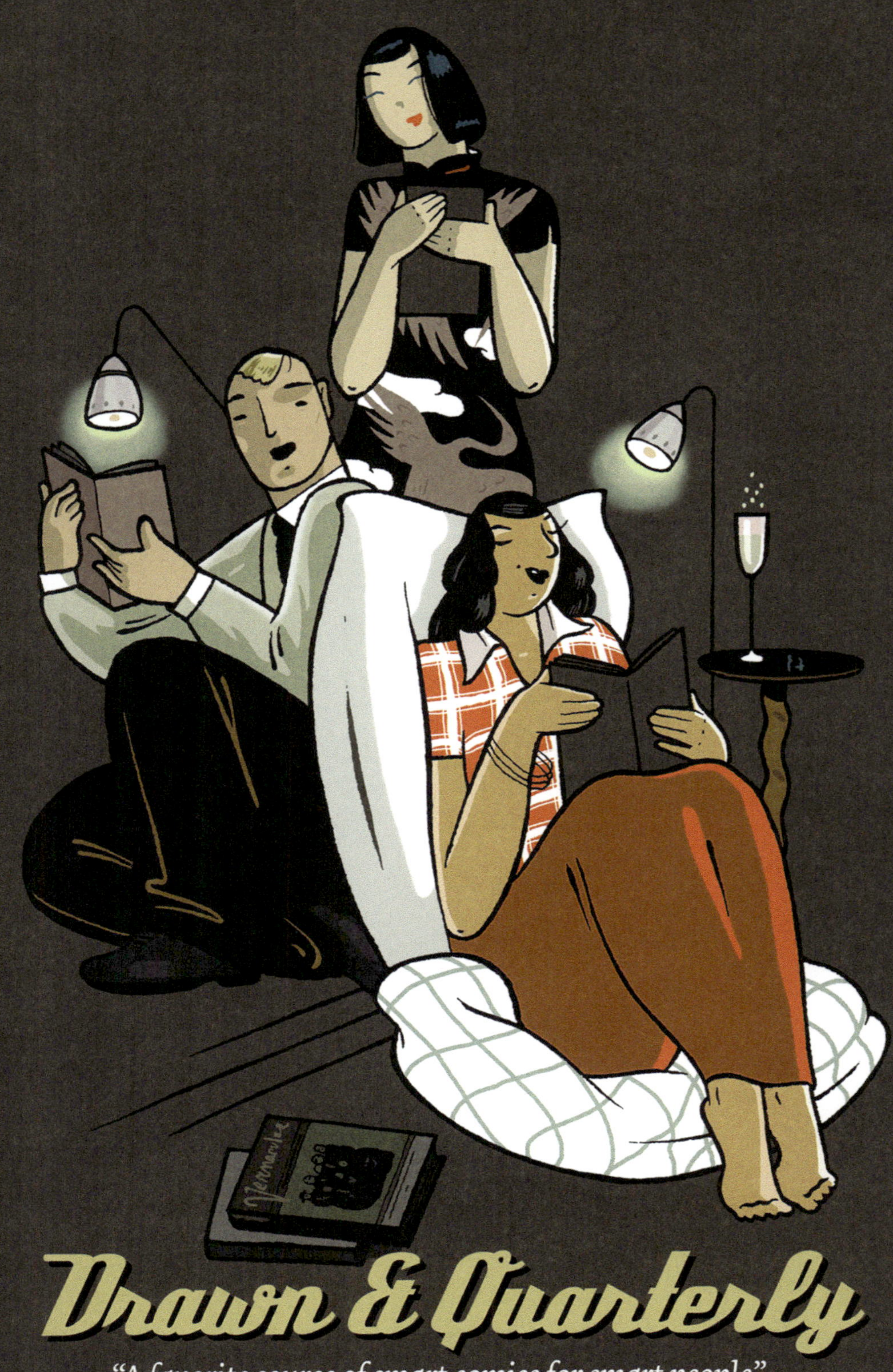

Drawn & Quarterly
"A favorite source of smart comics for smart people"
– THE HARTFORD ADVOCATE –

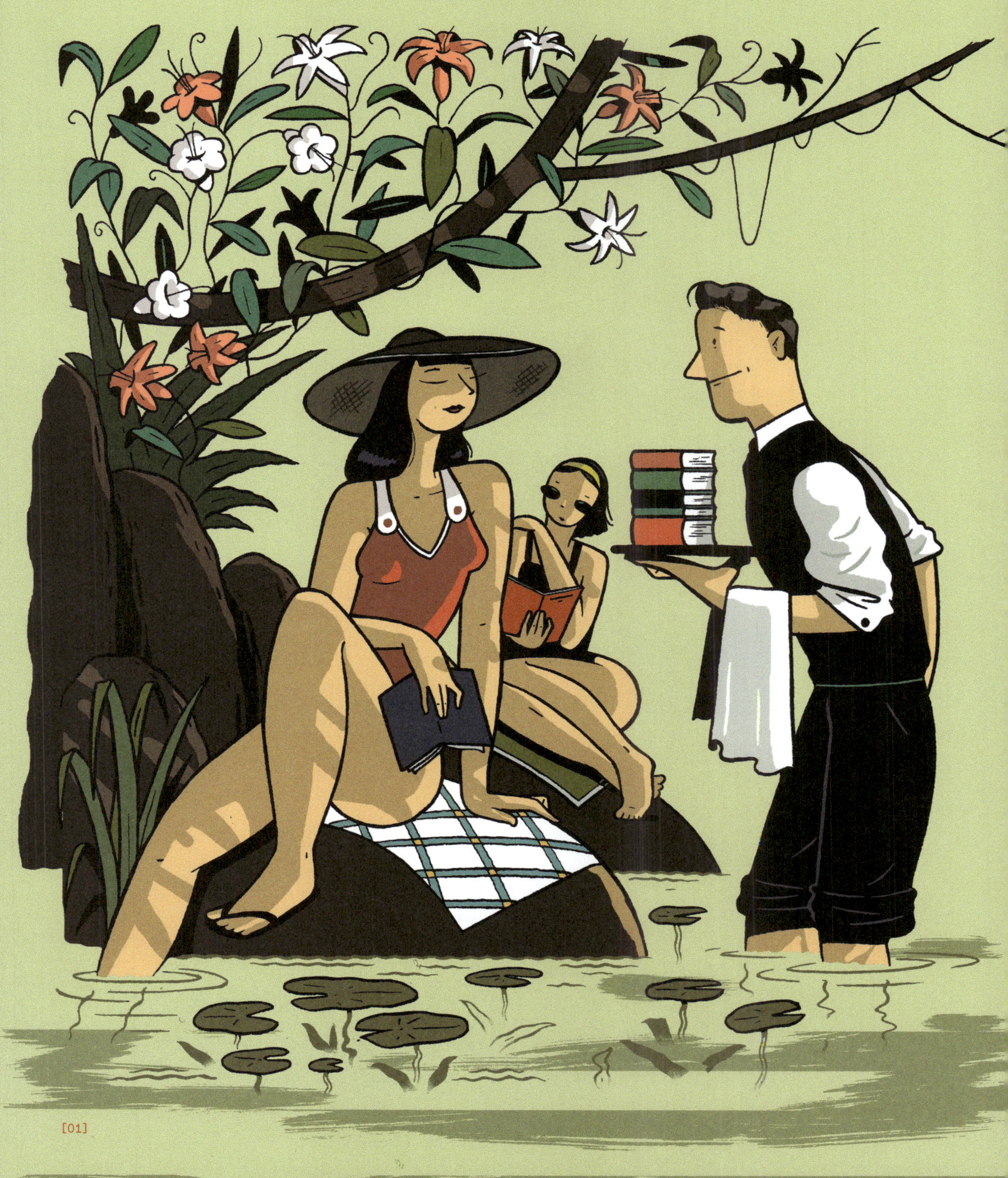
[01]

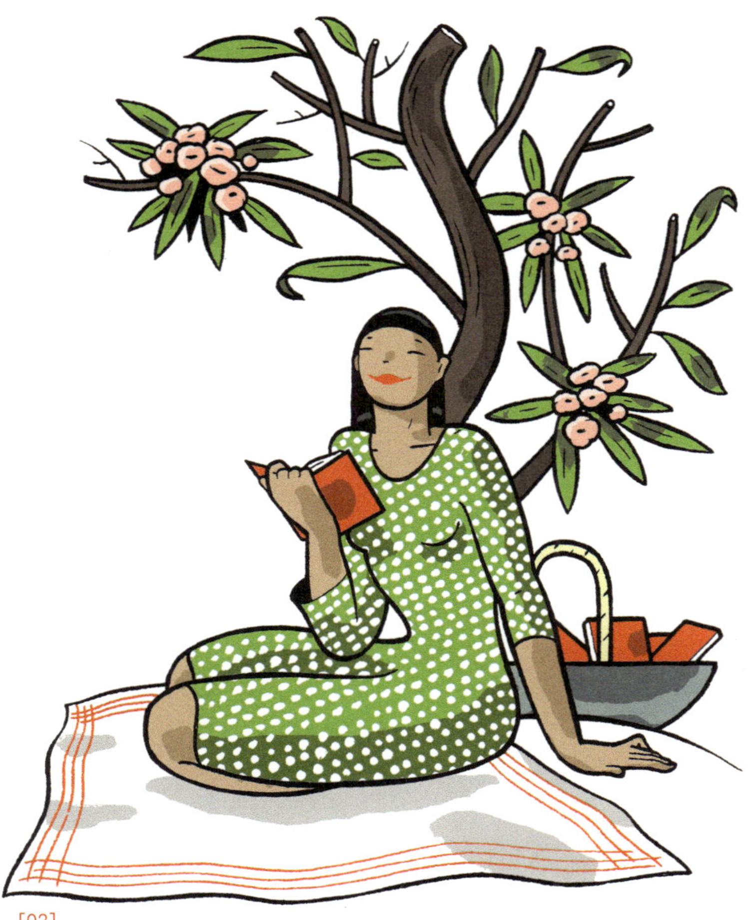

[02]

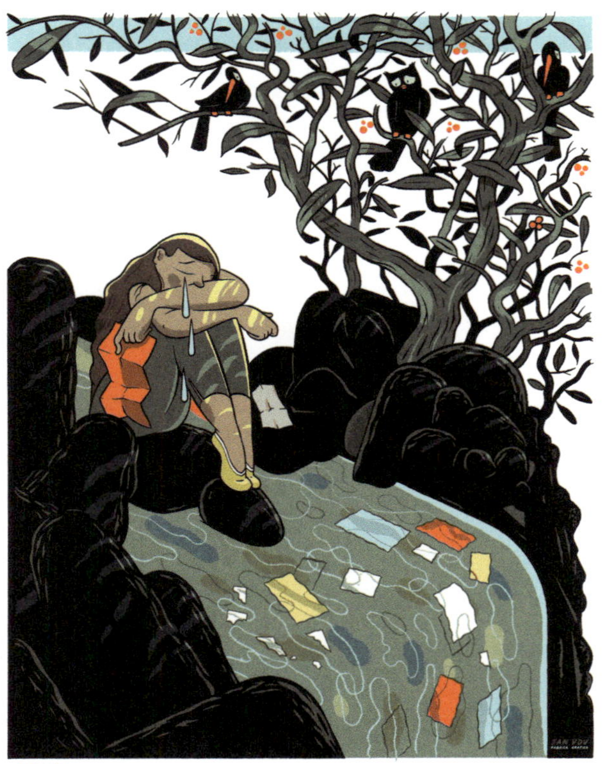

[03]

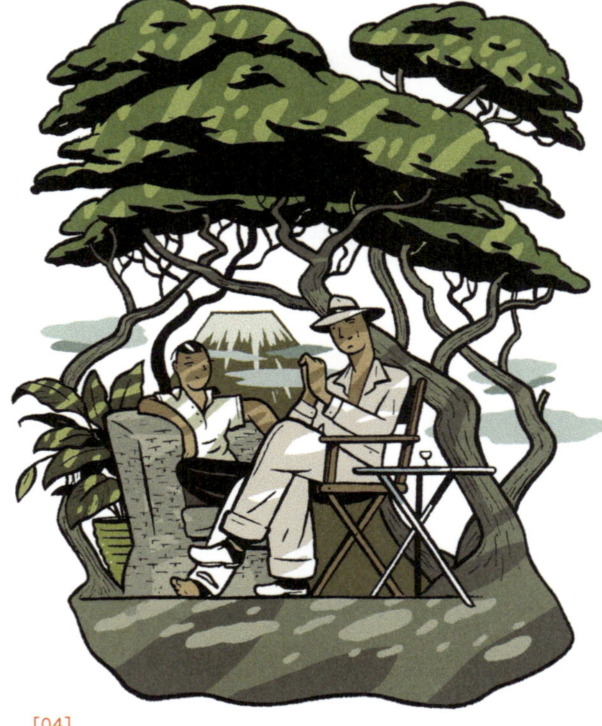

[04]

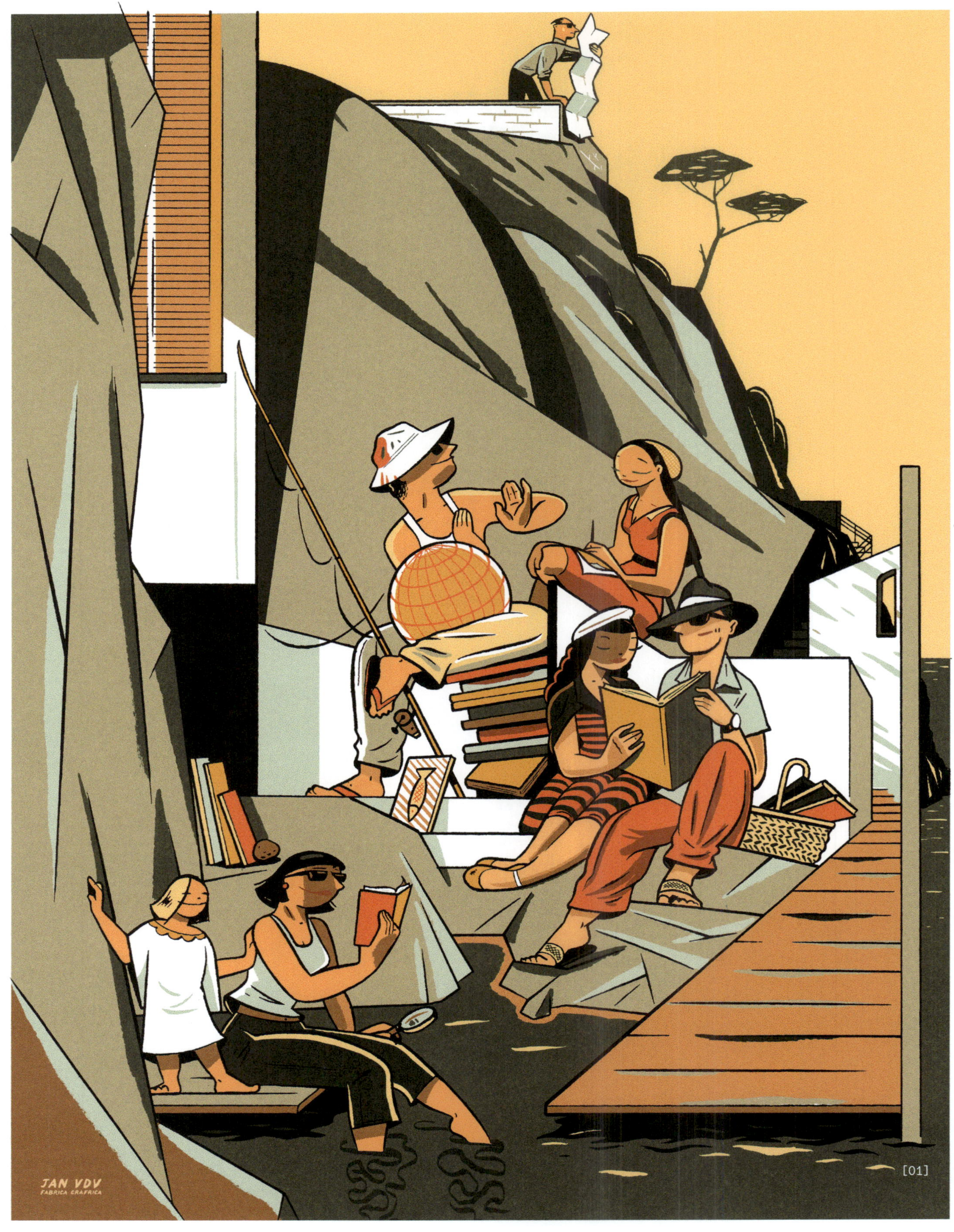

JAN VDV
FABRICA GRAFICA
[01]

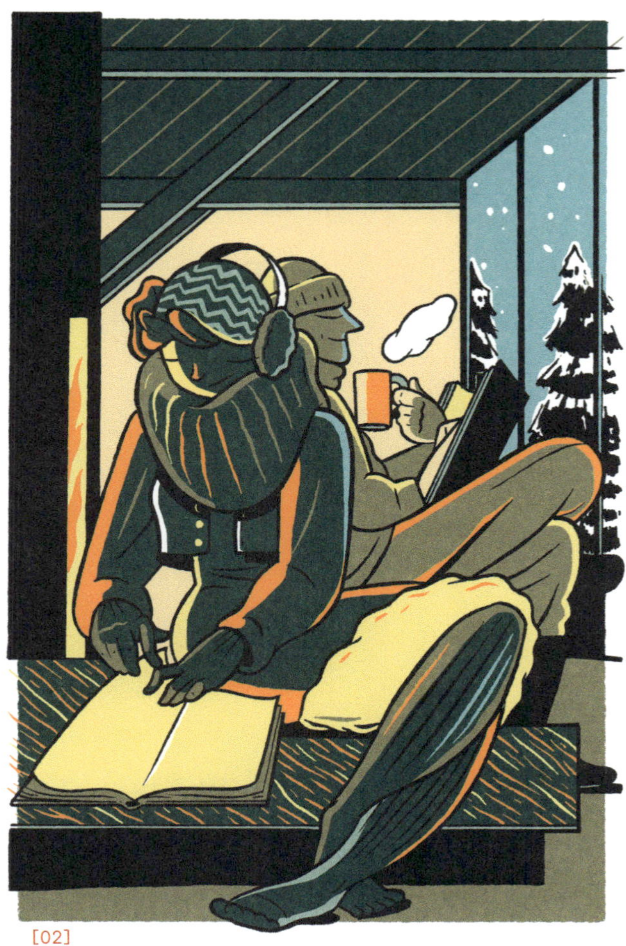

[02]

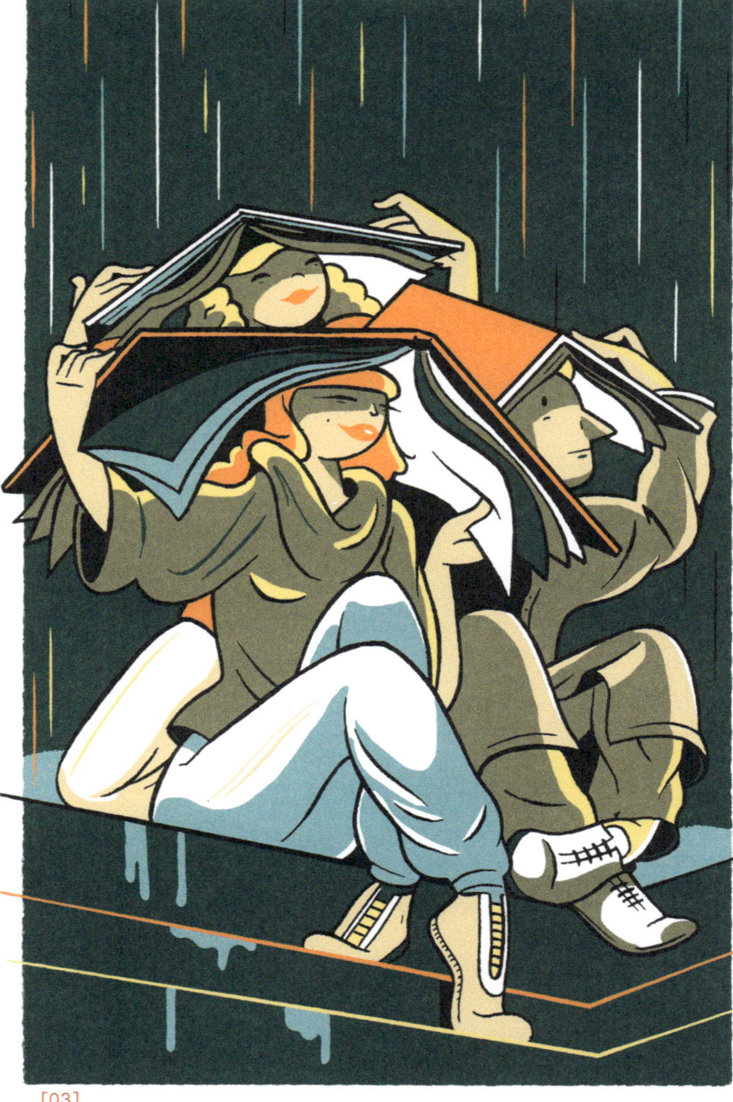

[03]

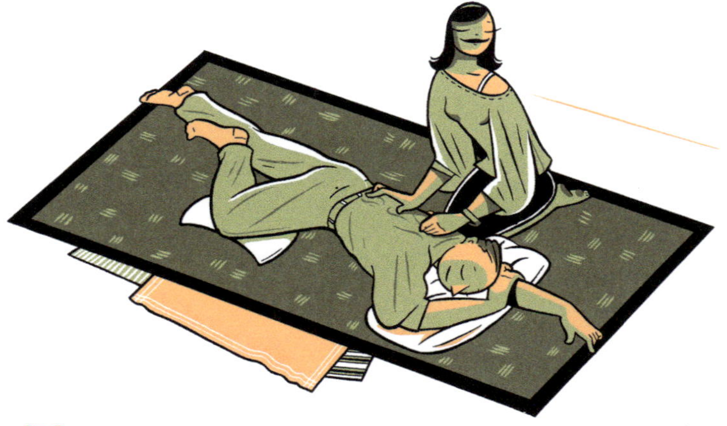

[04]

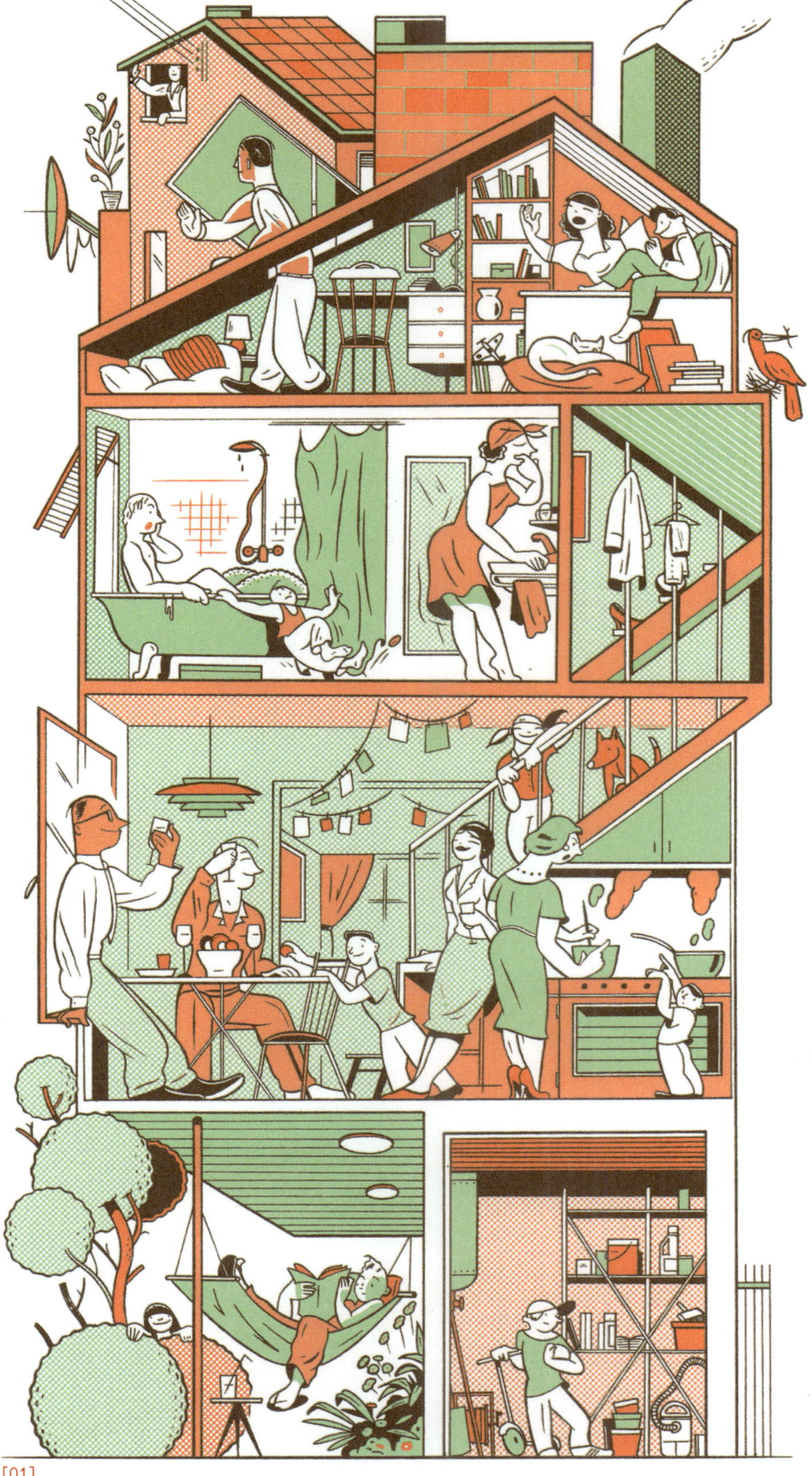

[01]

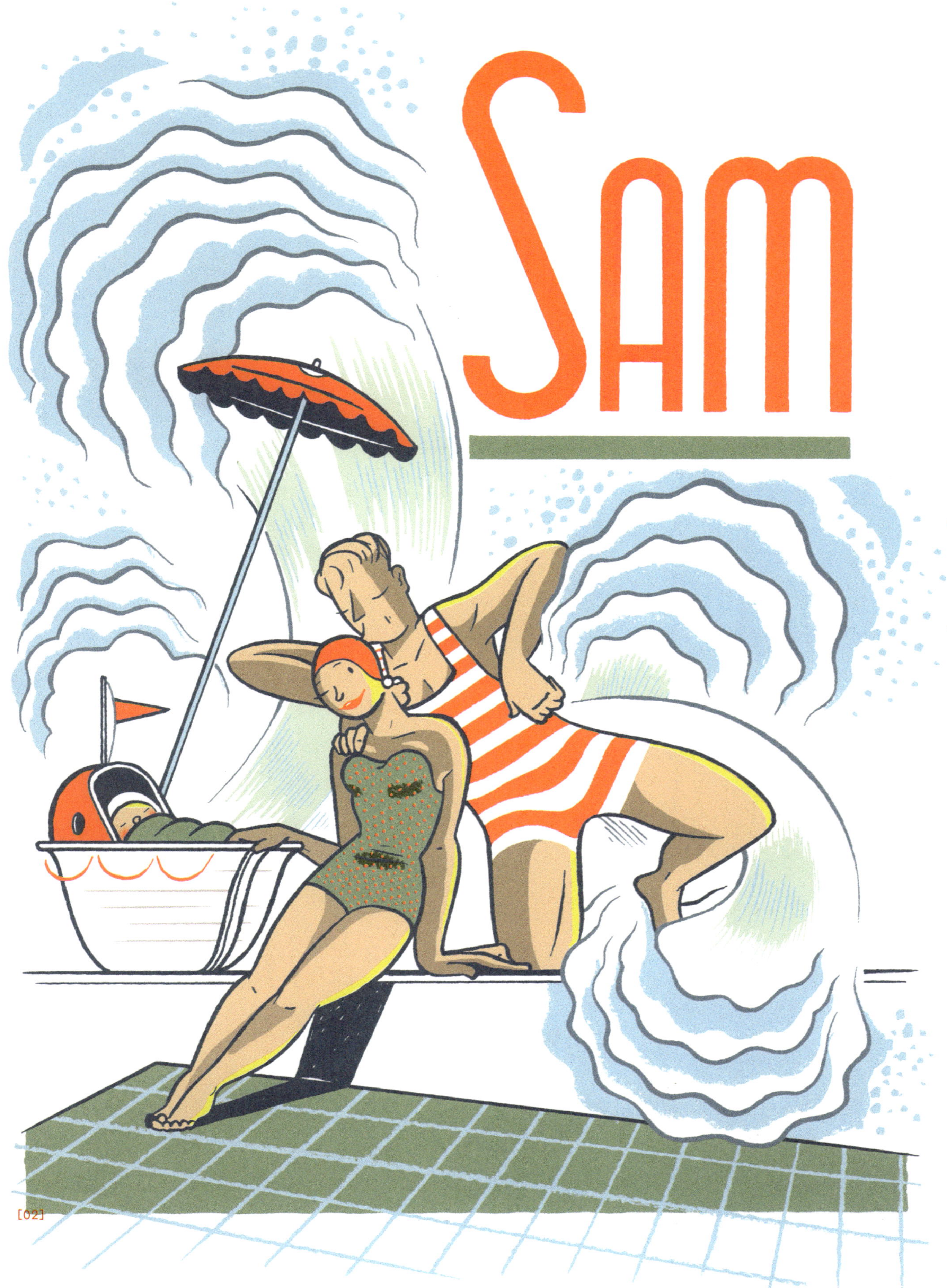

Sam
[02]

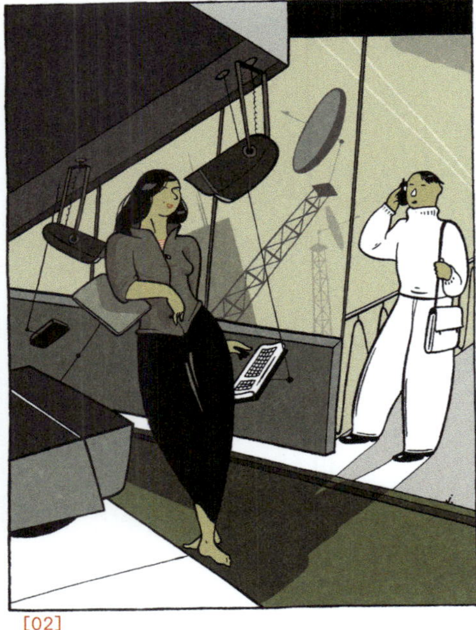

[02]

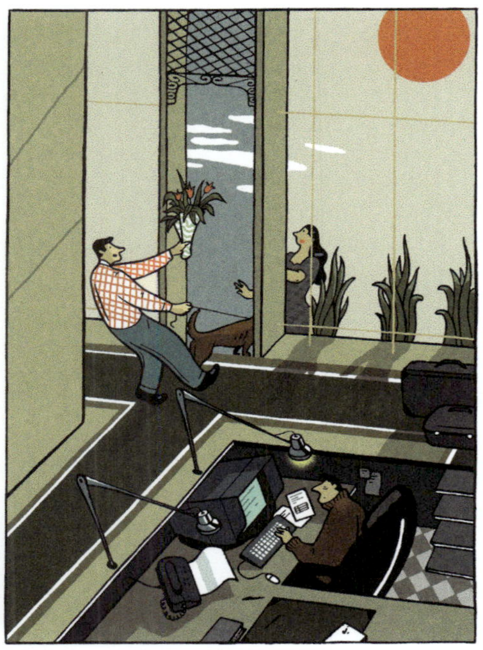

[03]

[01]

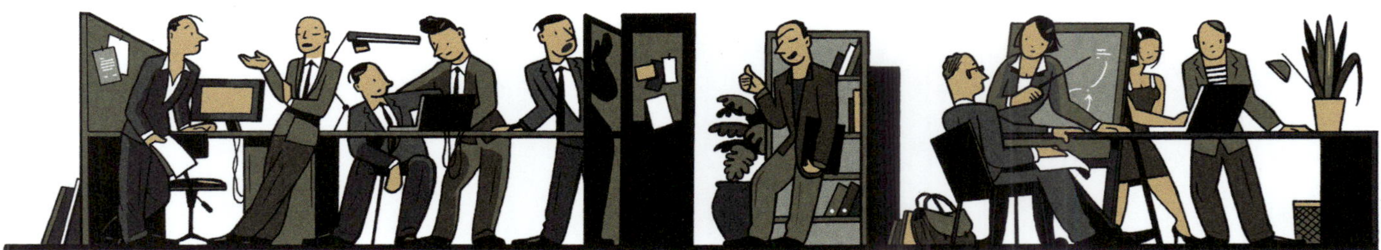

[04]

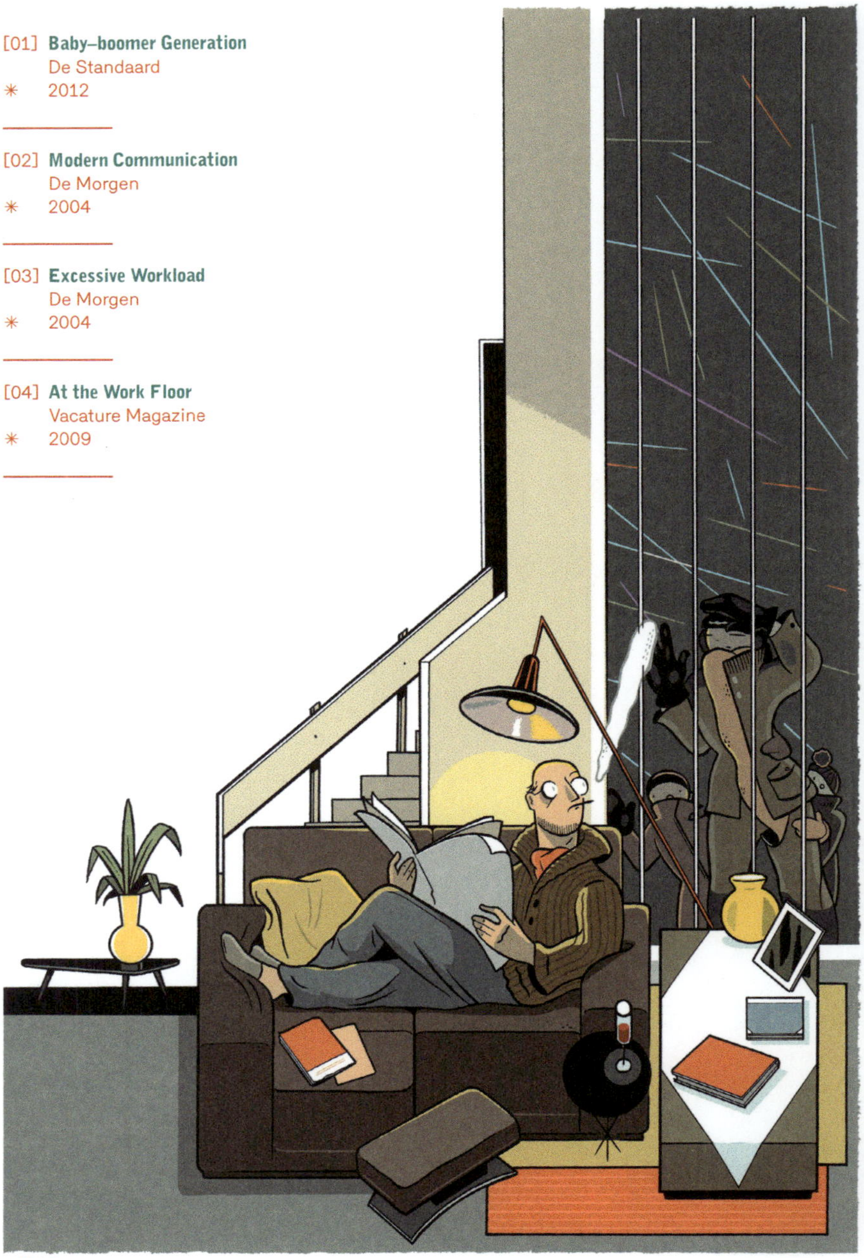

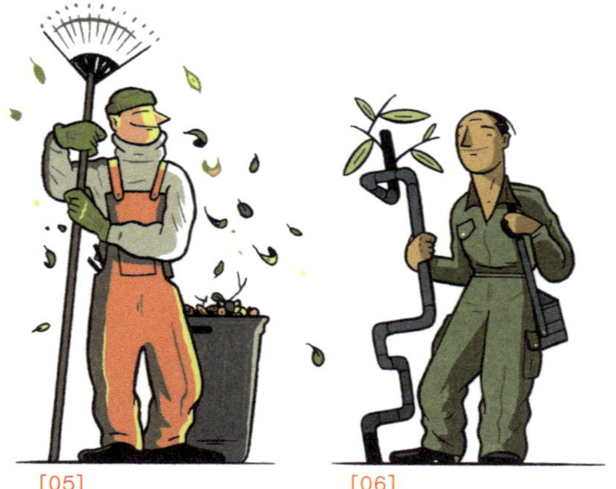

[05]   [06]

ARTHUR

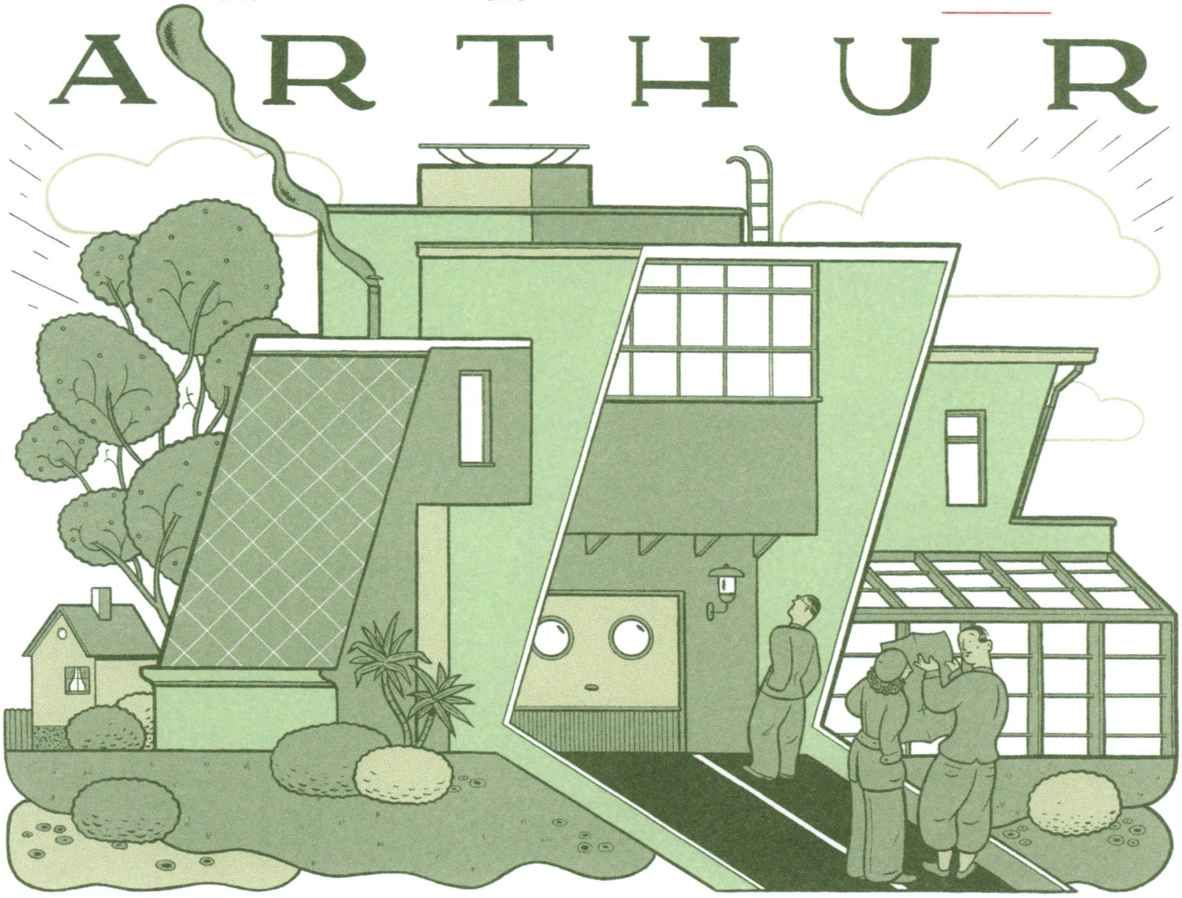

[07]

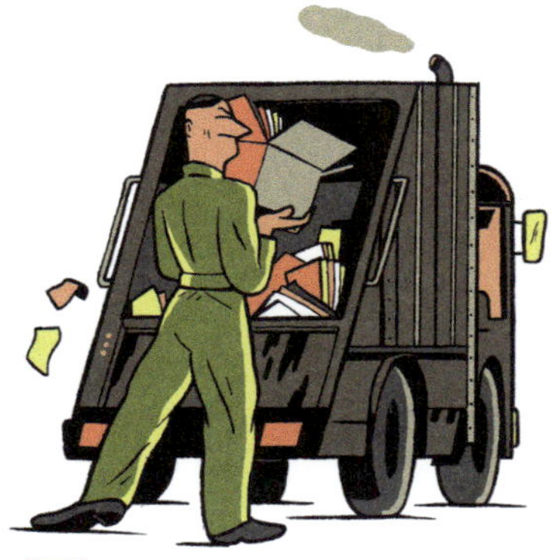

[08]

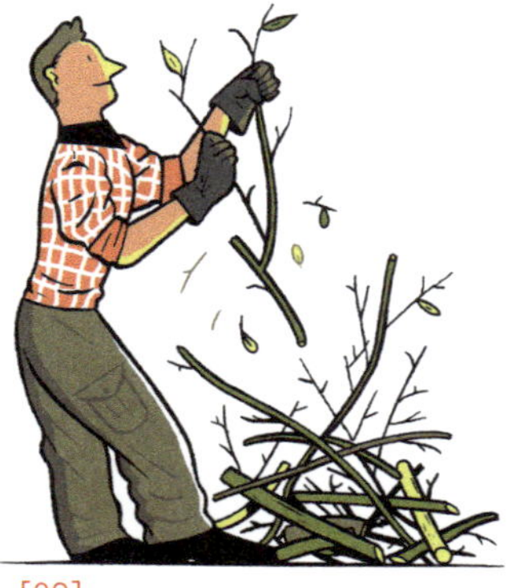

[09]

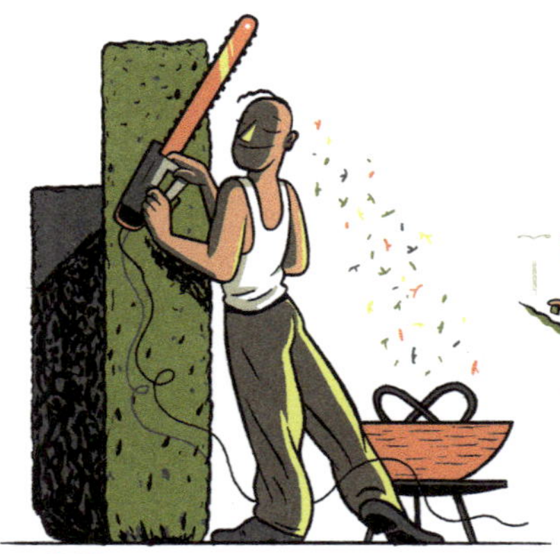

[10]

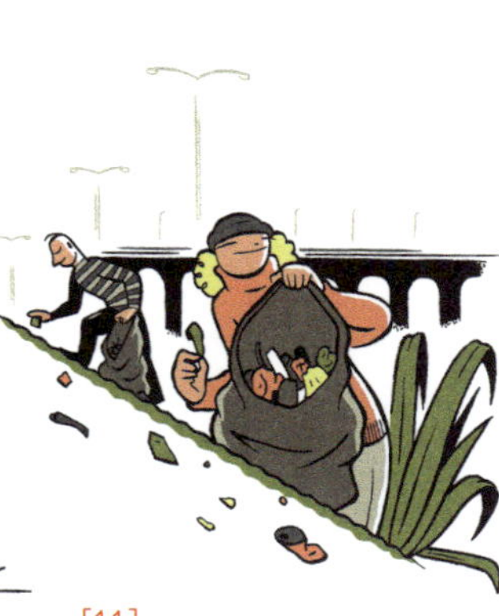

[11]

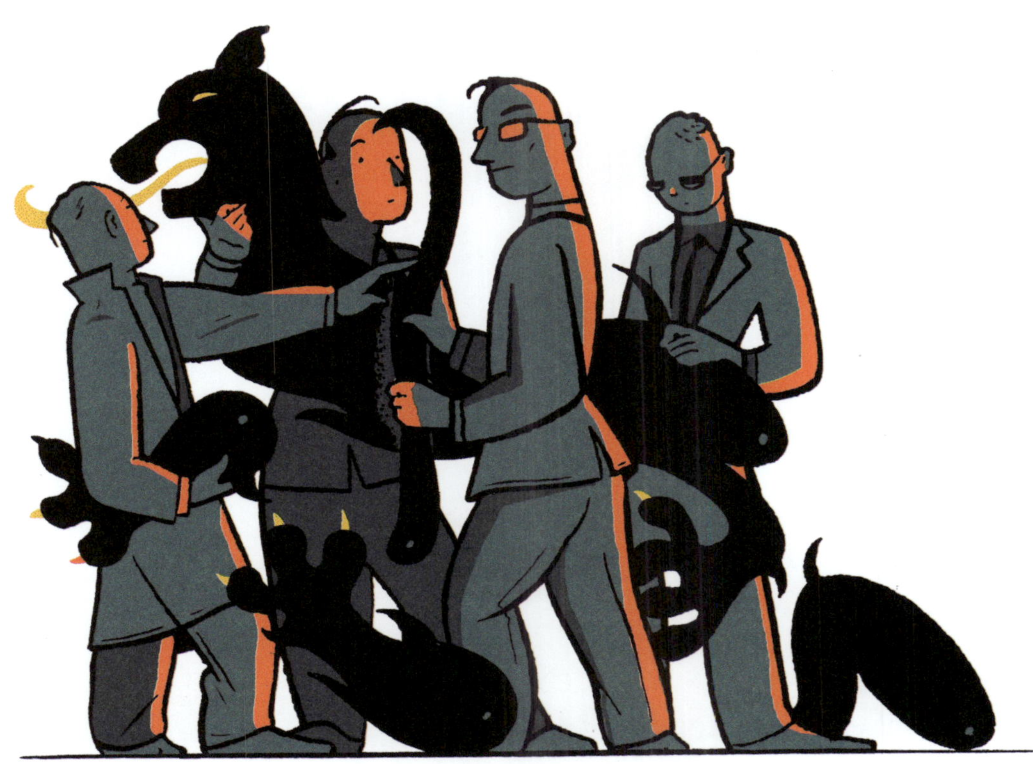

[01]

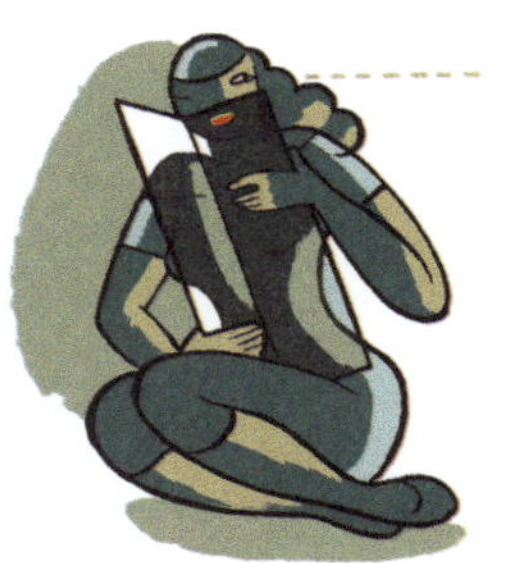
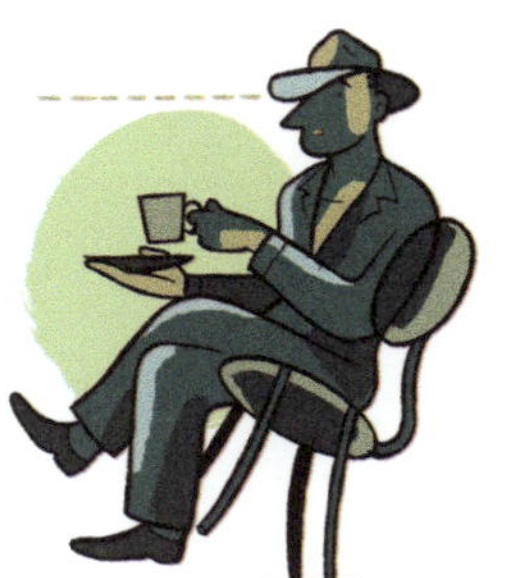
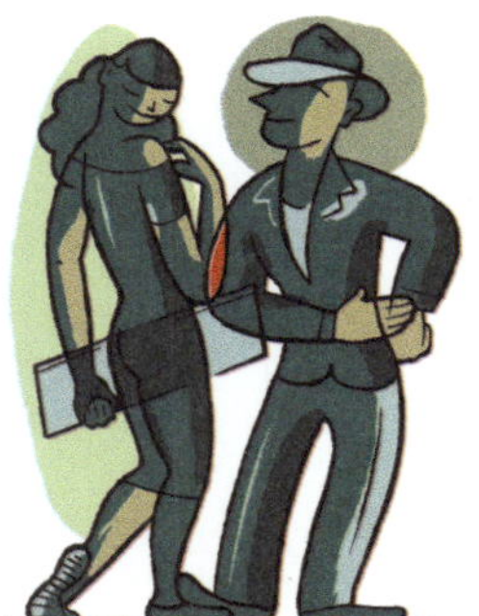
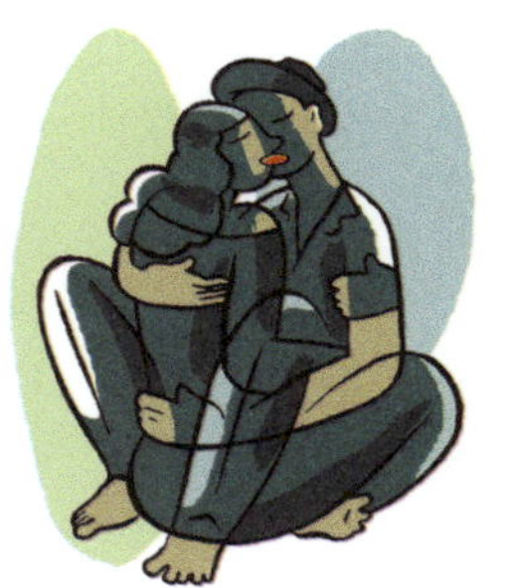

[02]

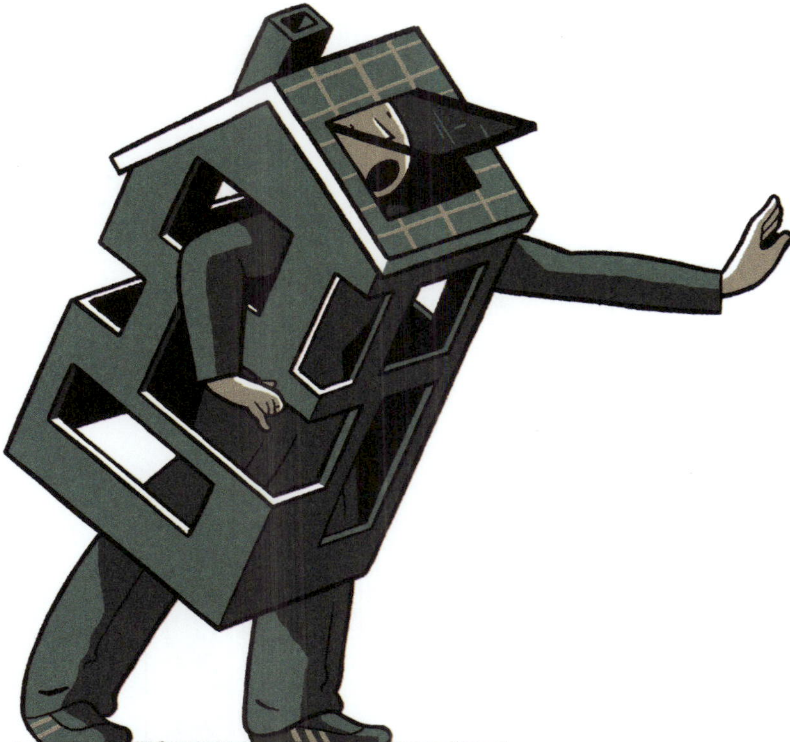

[03]

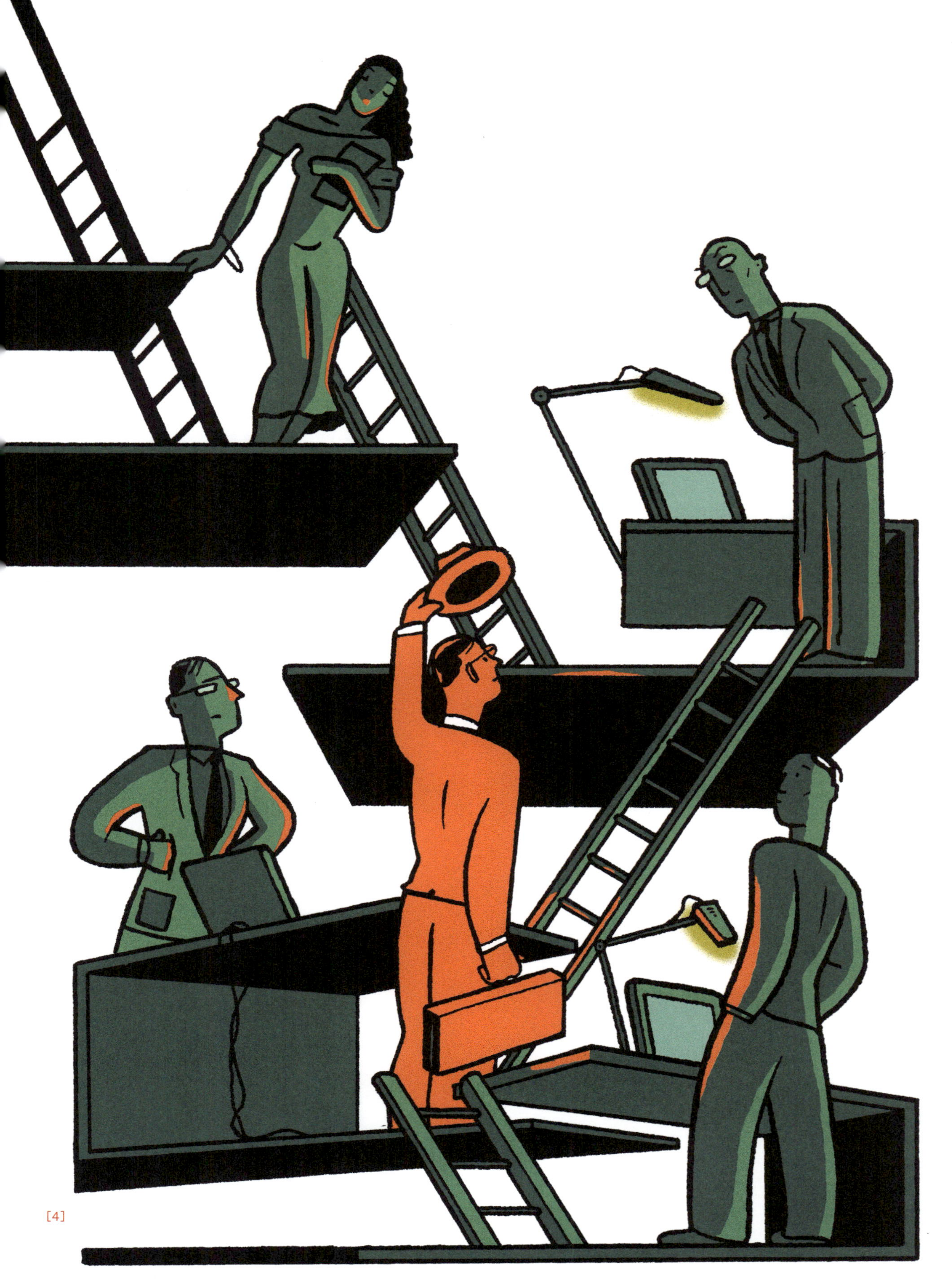

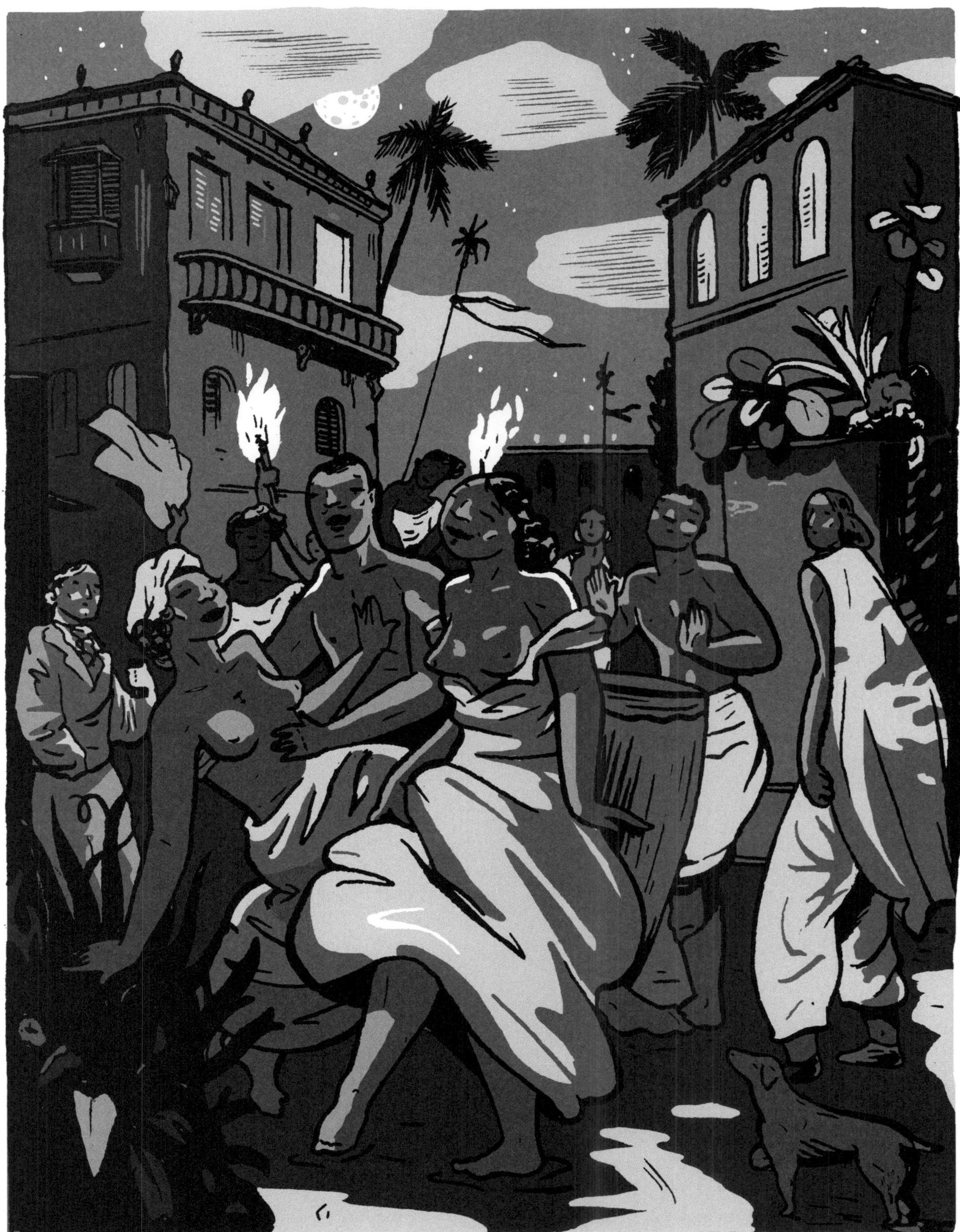

[01]

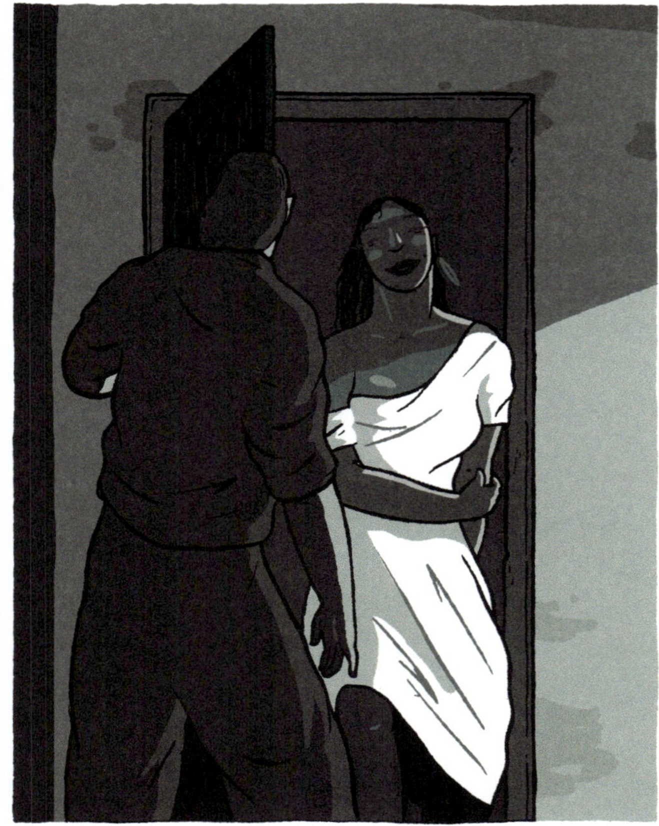
[02]

All Demons' Day –
Hernan Portocarero
✳ 2004

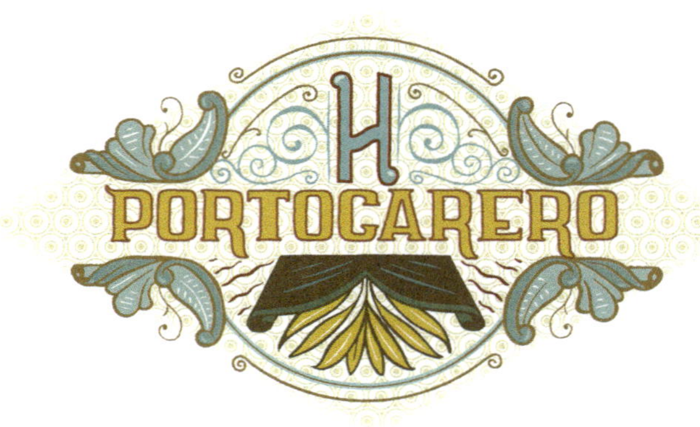
PORTOCARERO

[03]

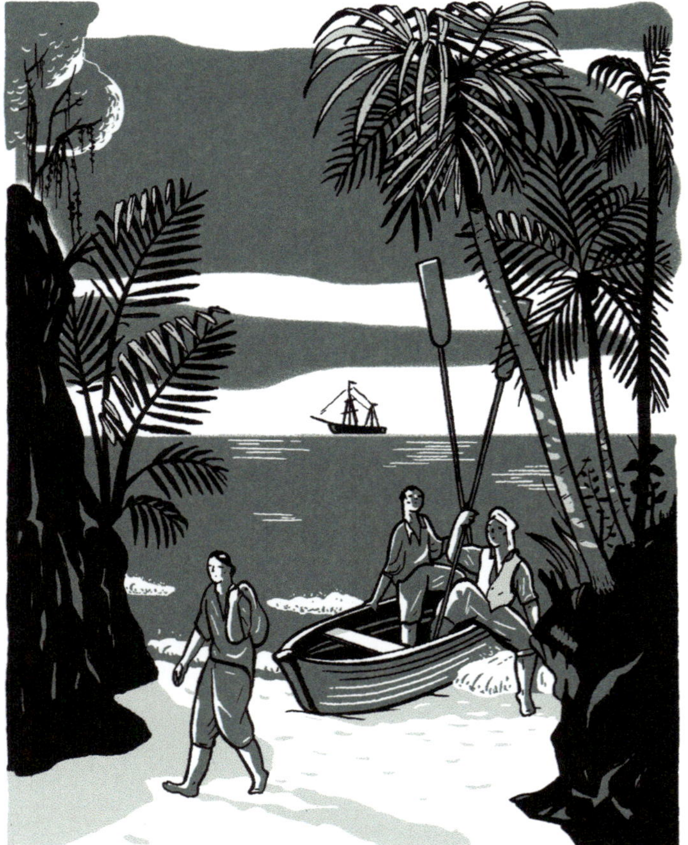
[04]

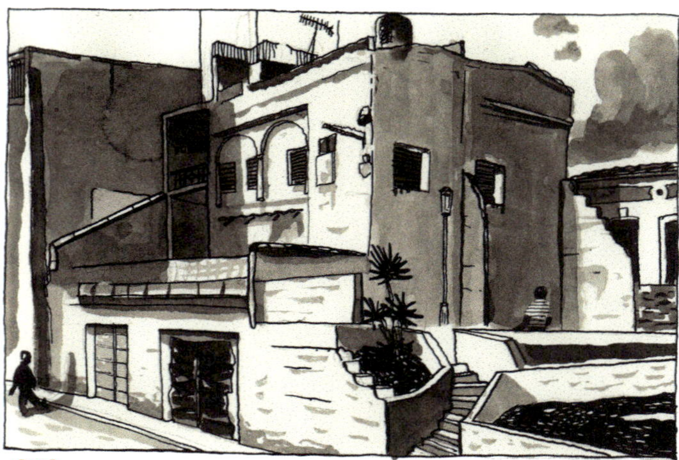
[05]

TOT AMSTERDAM
A
NIGHT IN
THE SULTAN'S
SERAGLIO
TURCO
MAGNIFICO

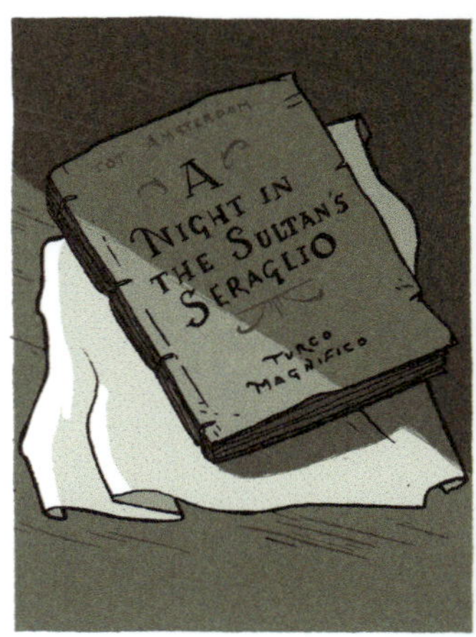

[01]

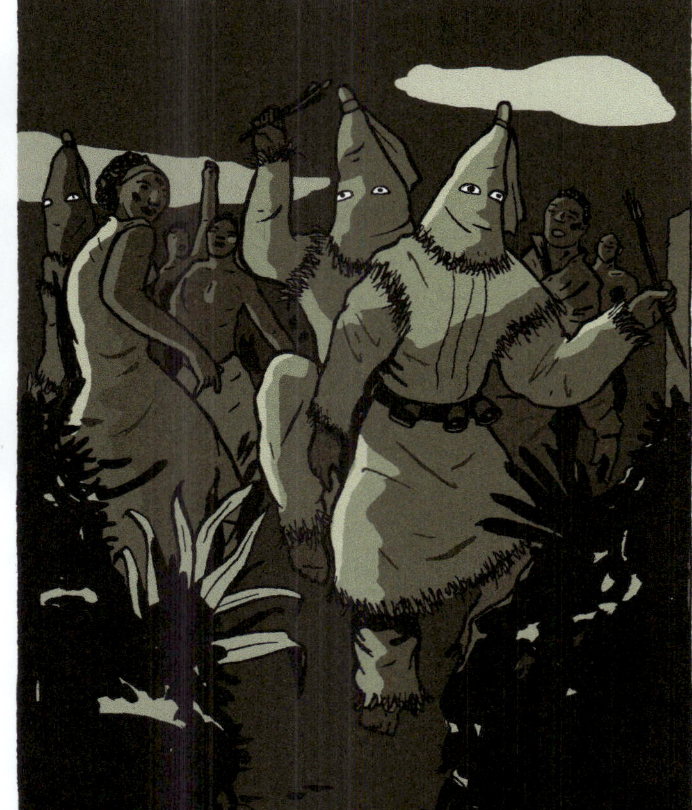

[02]

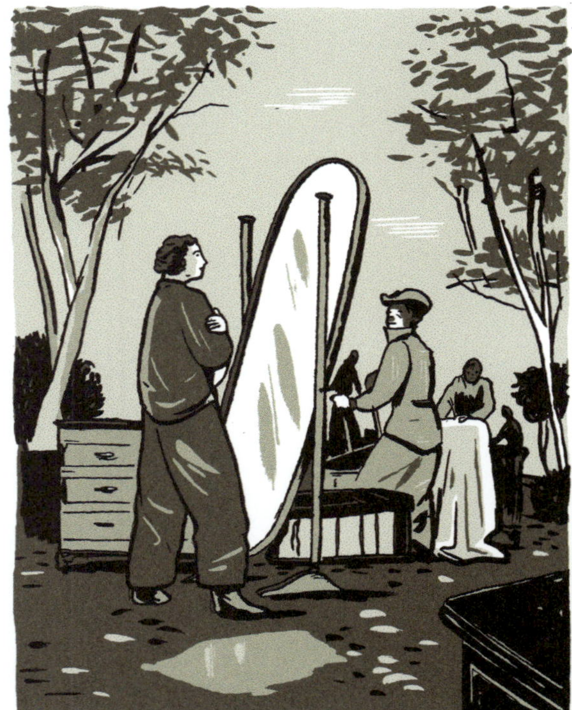

[03]

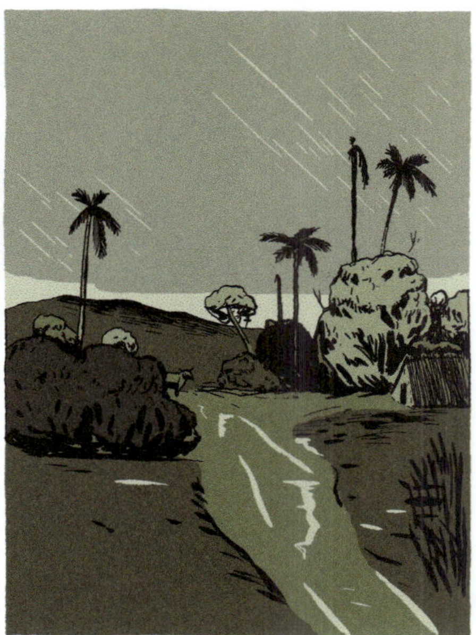

[05]

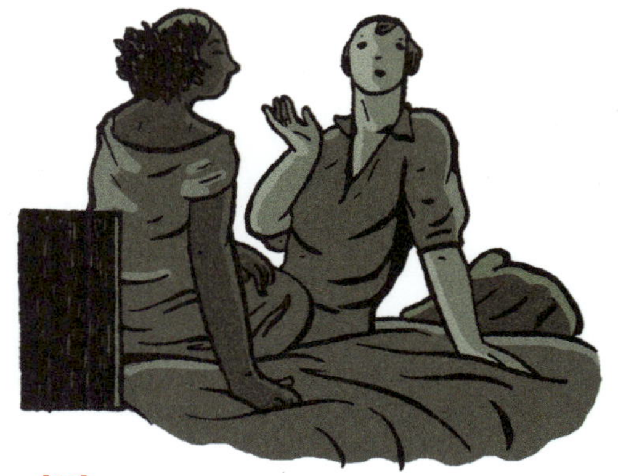

[04]

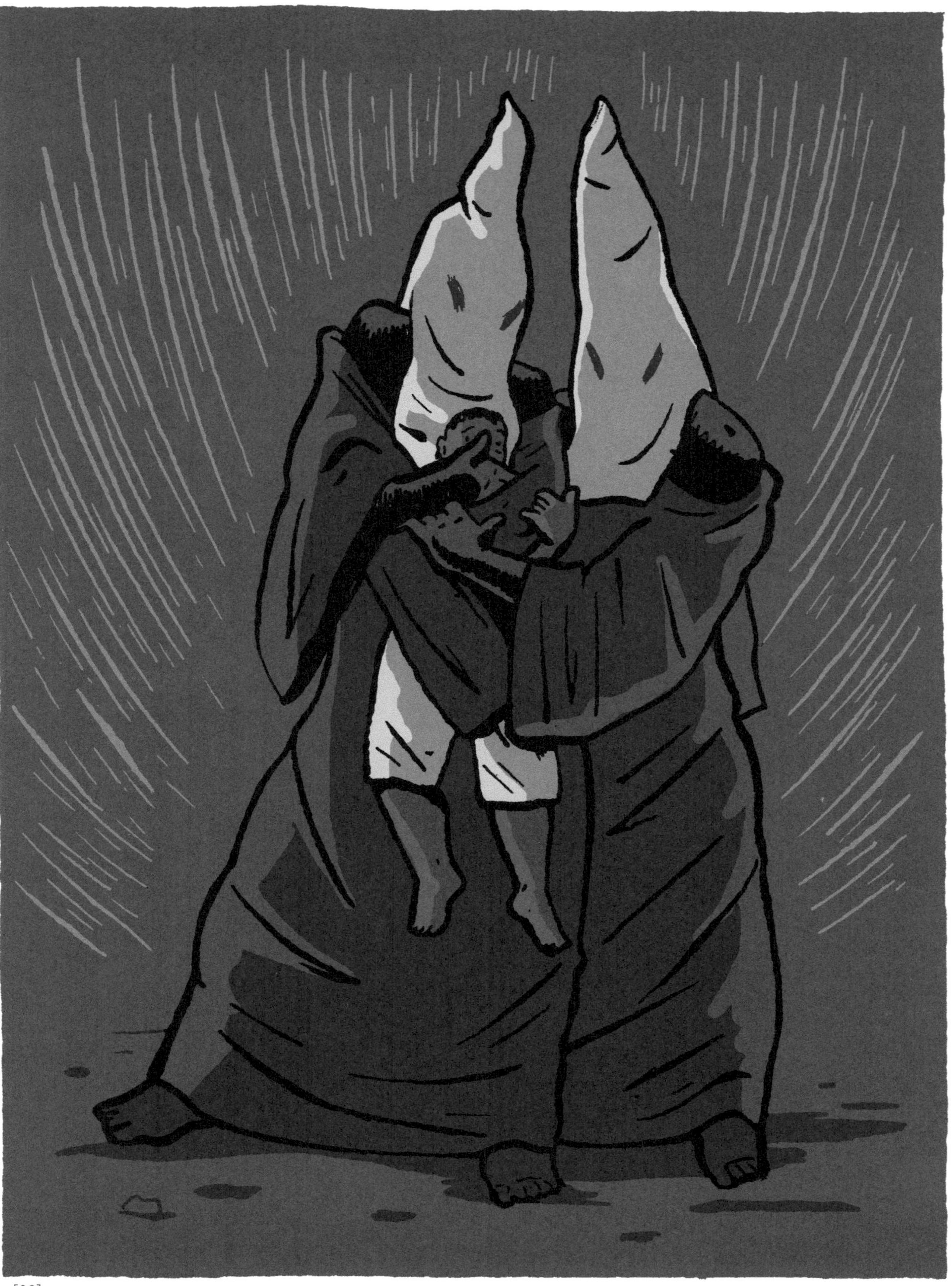

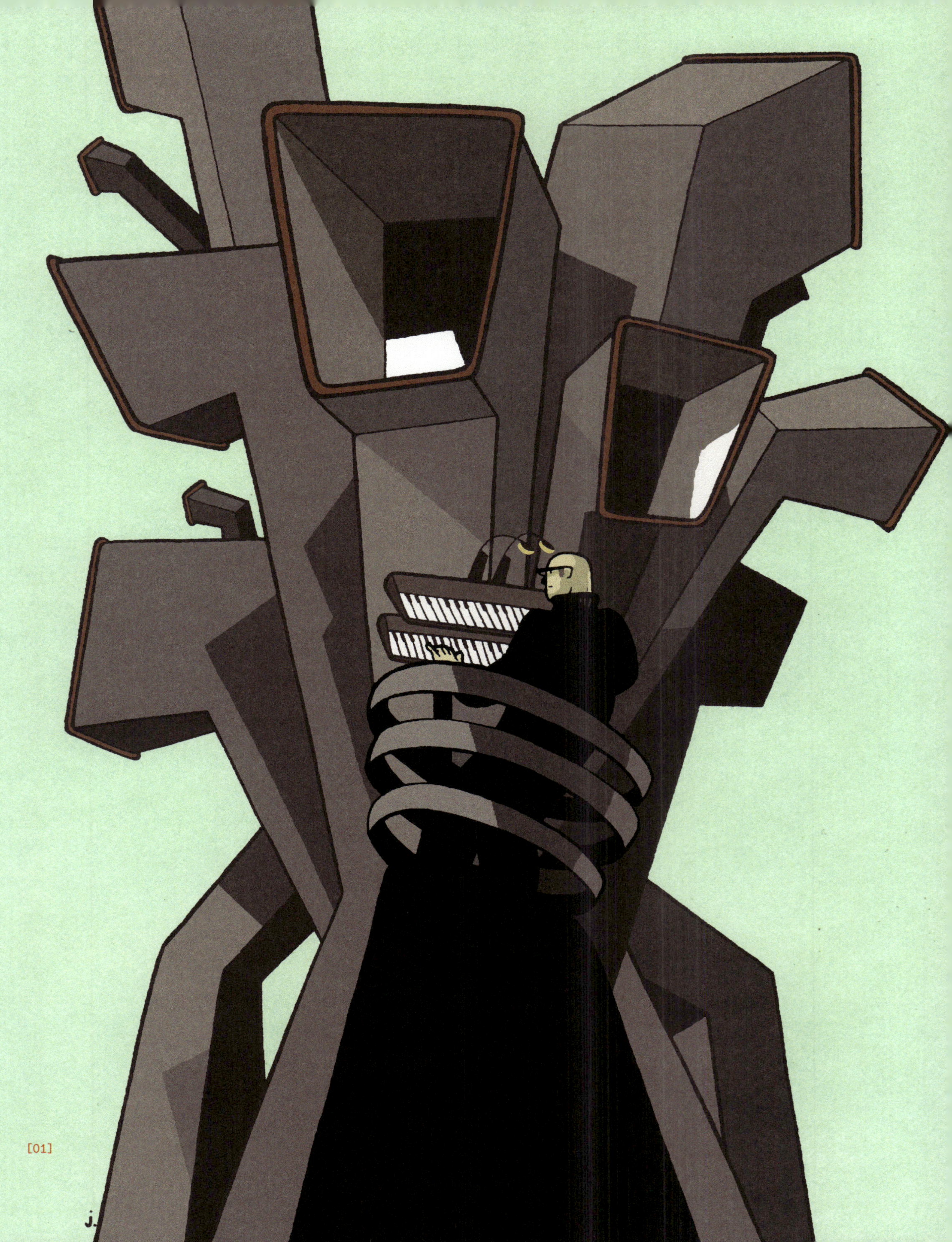

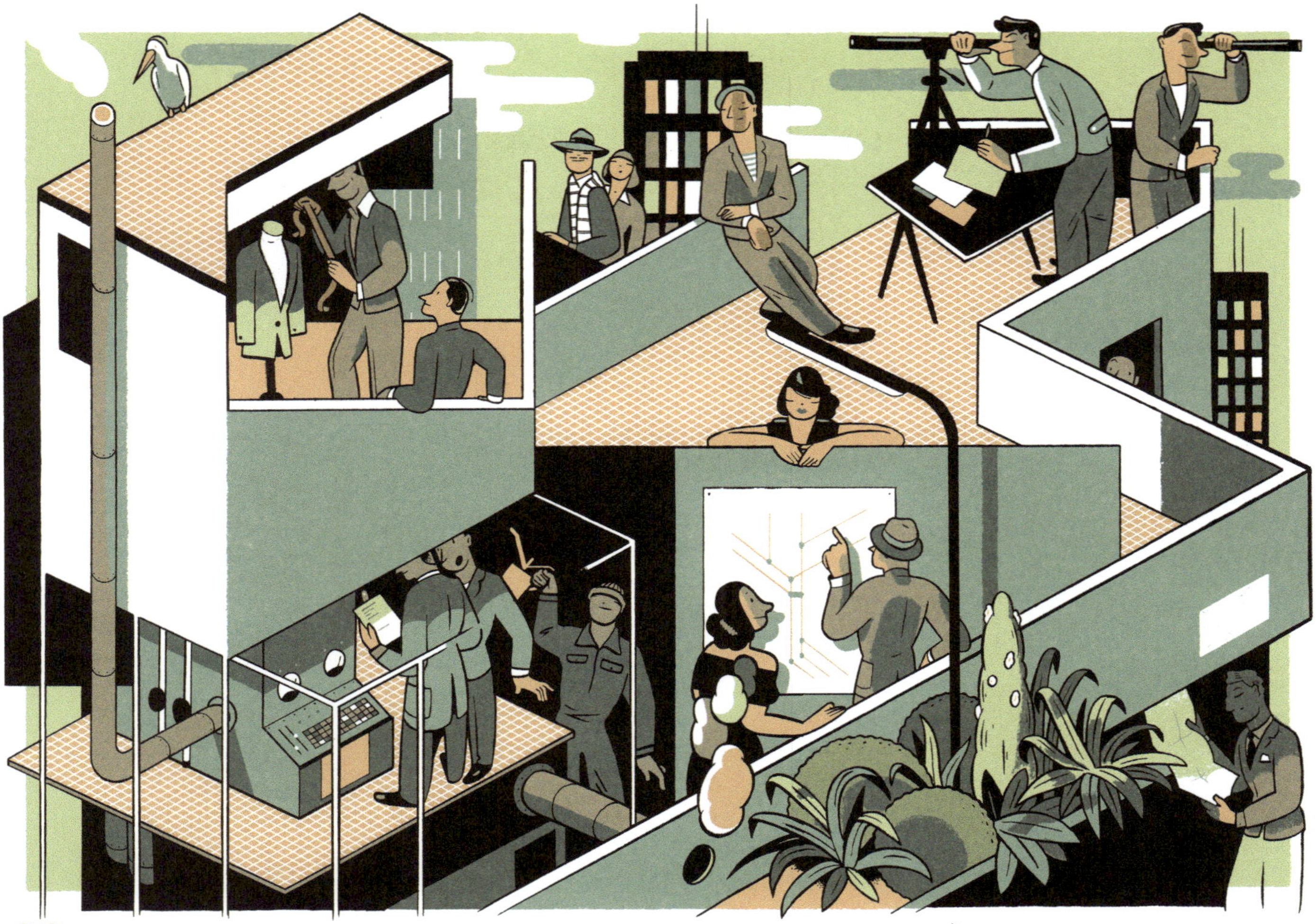

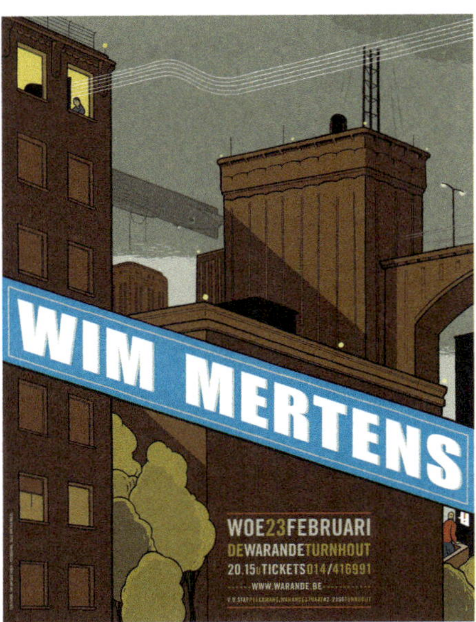

[02]

[03]

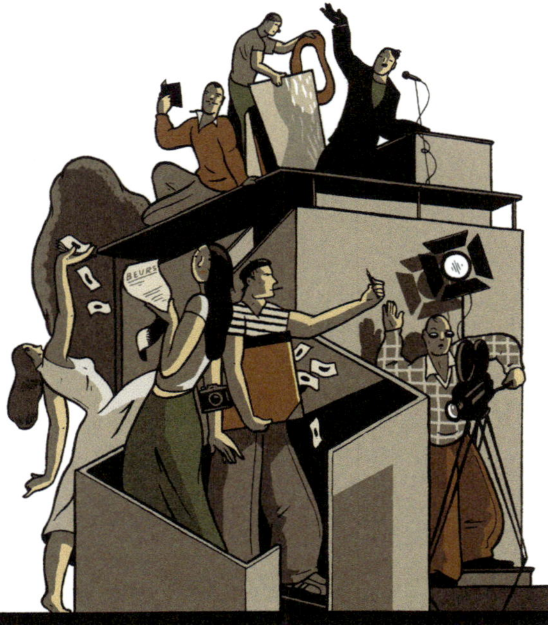

[04]

[01] **The Organ**
Contra. Magazine
2001

[02] **Rooftop View**
Syntigo
2011

[03] **Wim Mertens**
De Warande
2004

[04] **The Arts**
Vpro Gids
2005

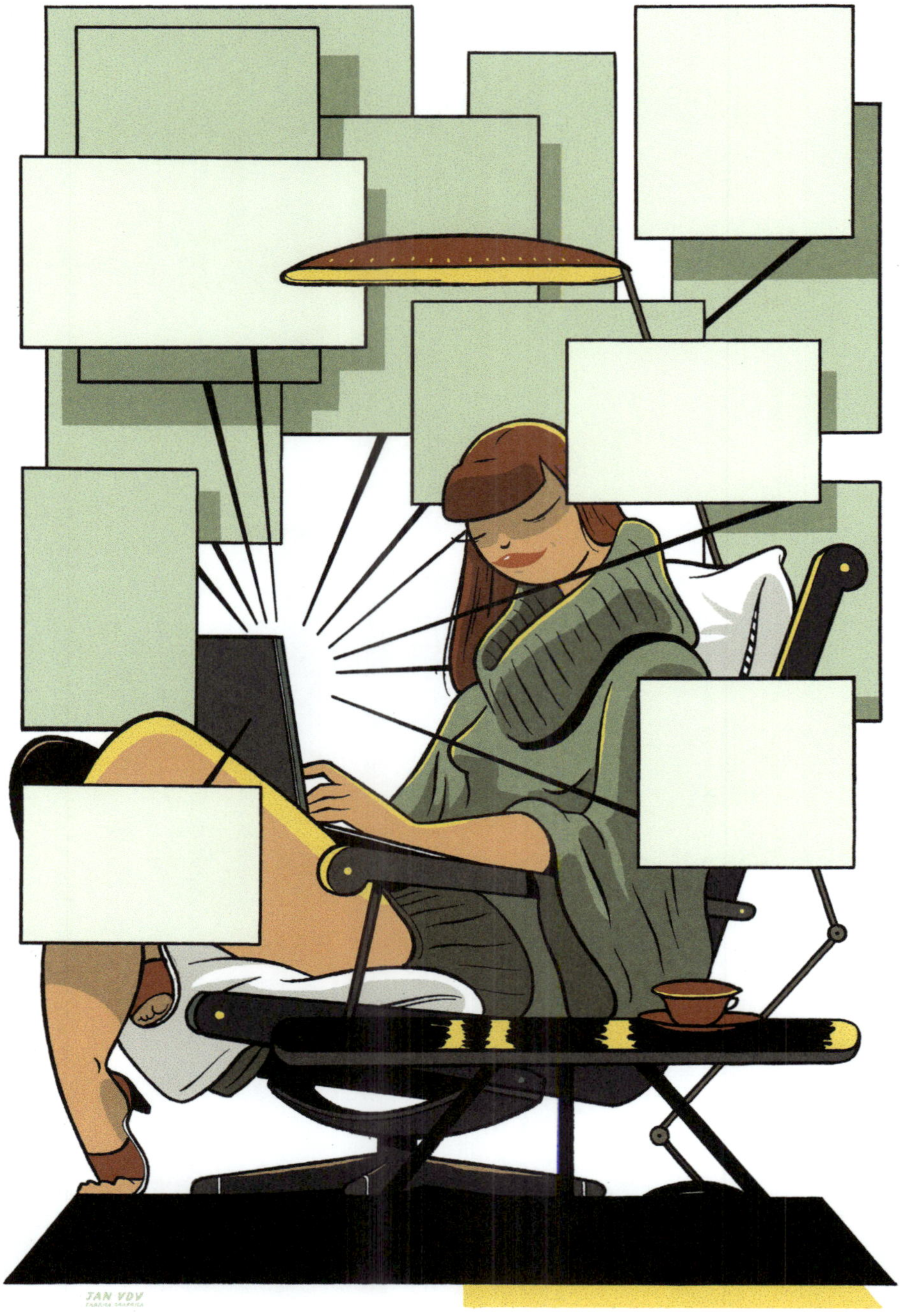

[01]

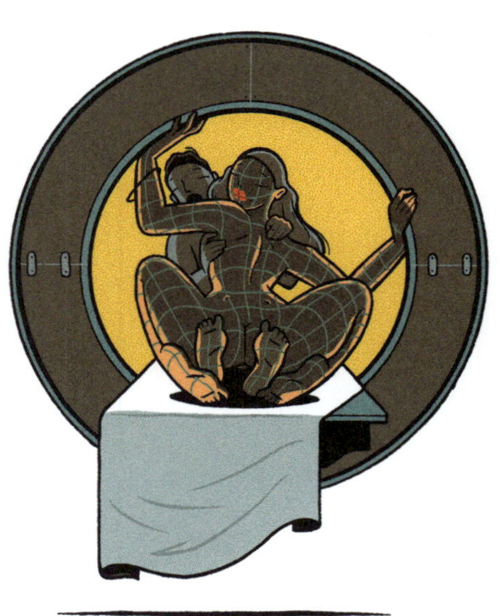

[02]

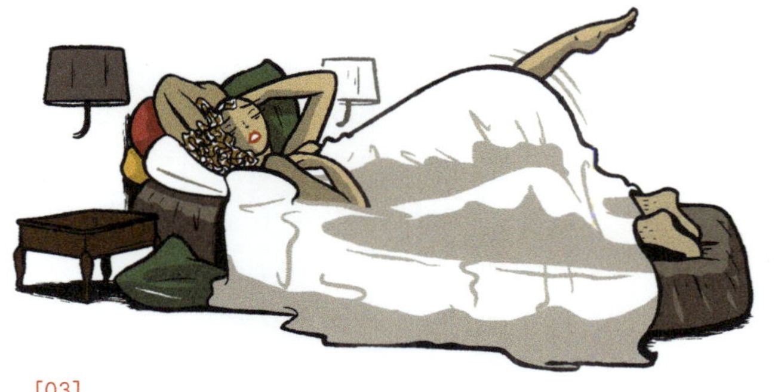

[03]

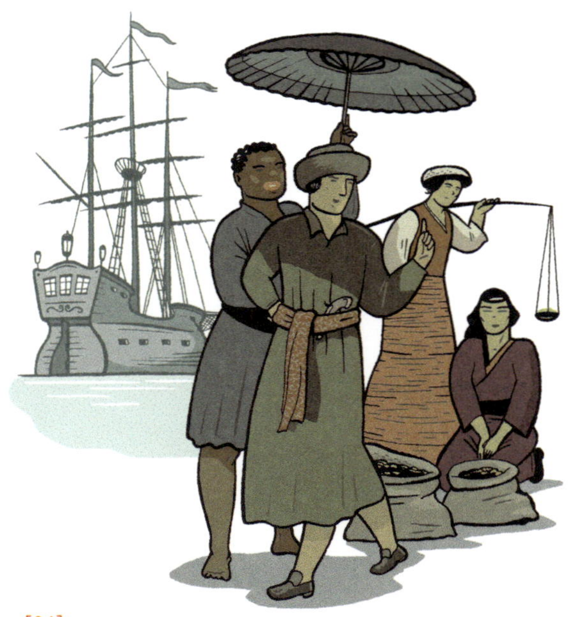

[04]

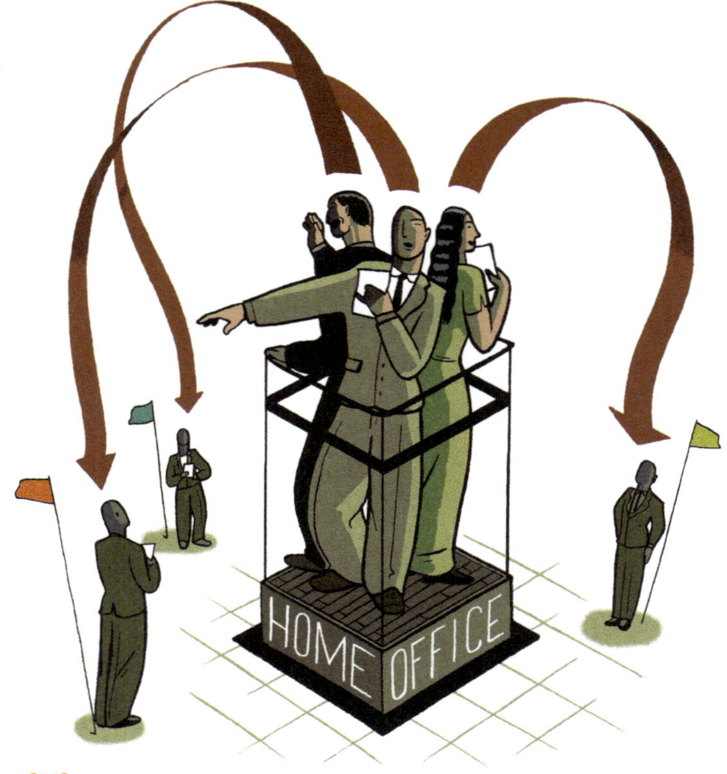

[05]

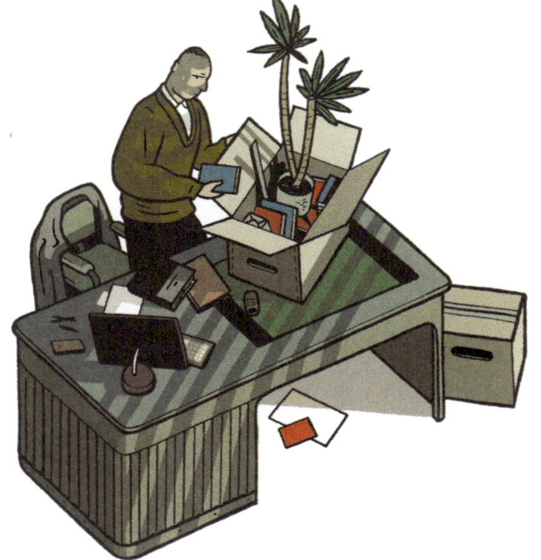

[06]

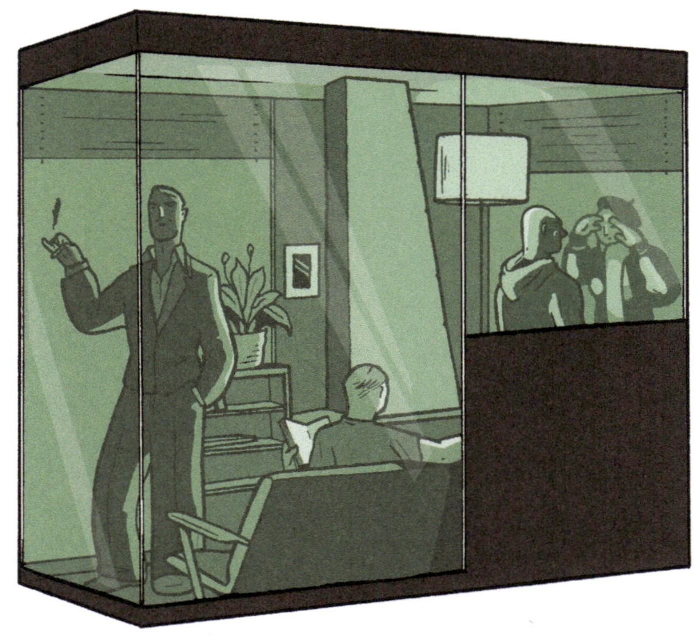

[09]

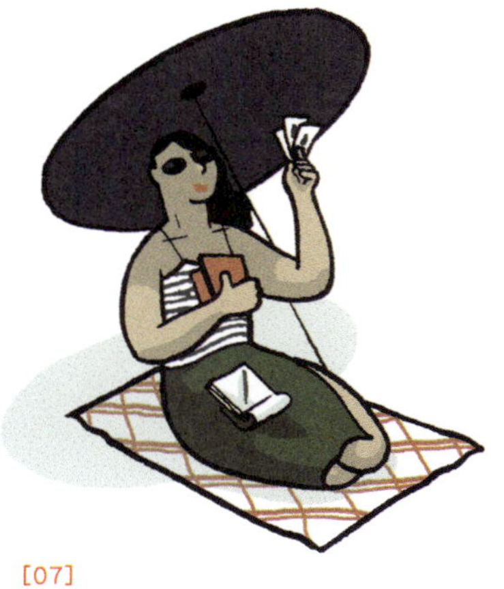

[07]

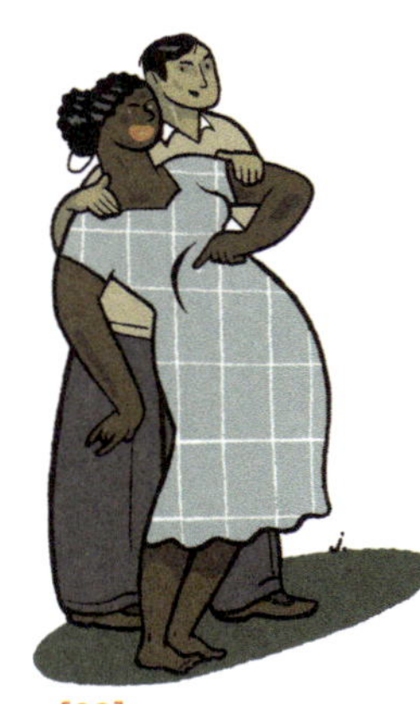

[08]

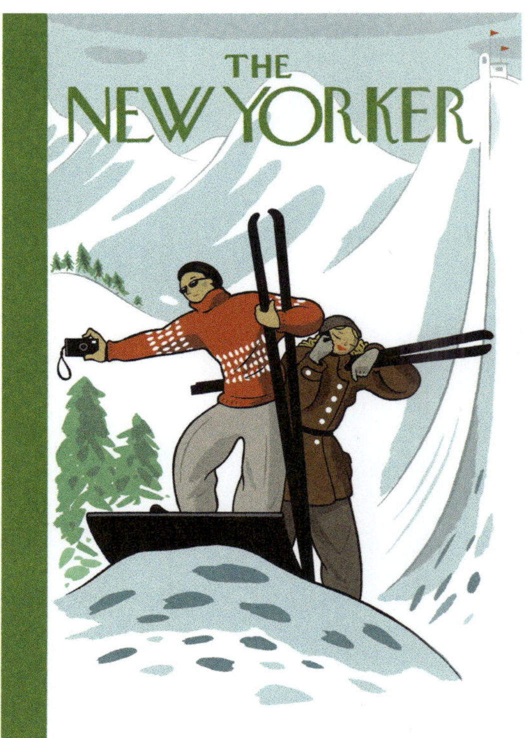

[01]

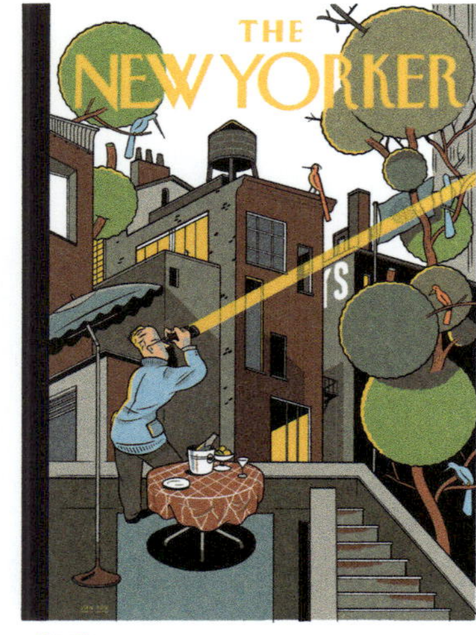

[02]

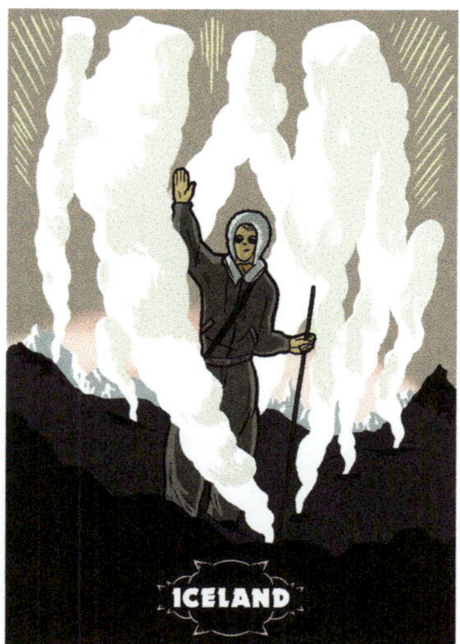

[03]

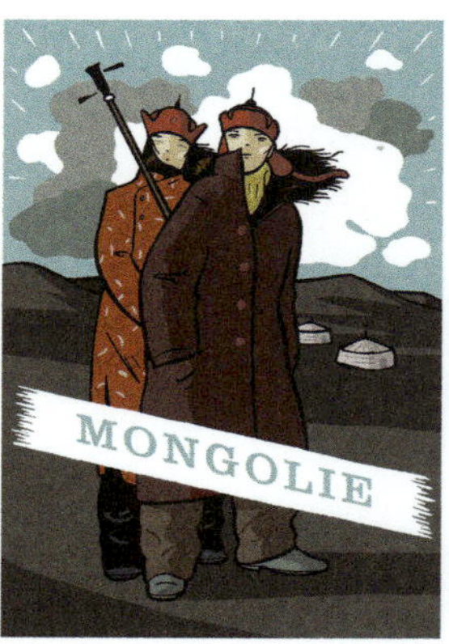

[04]

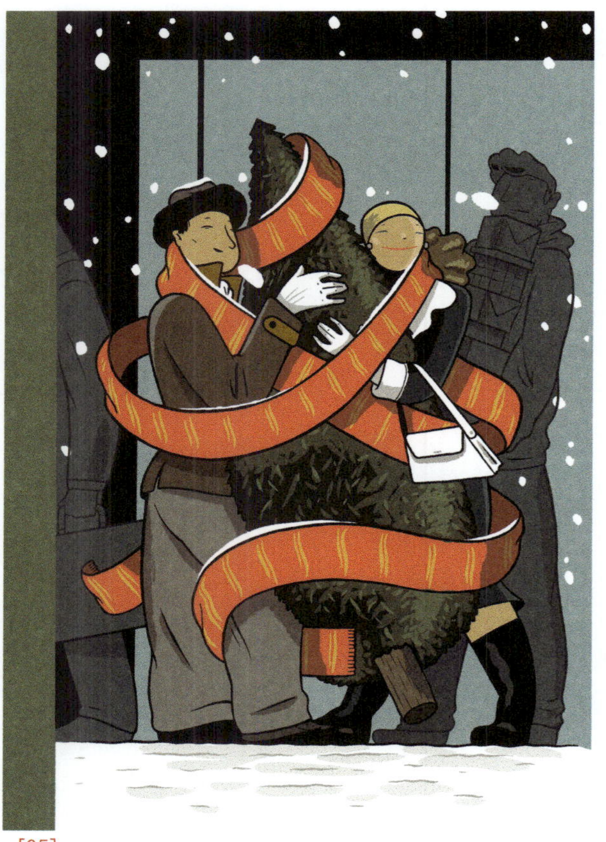

[05]

H O W T O

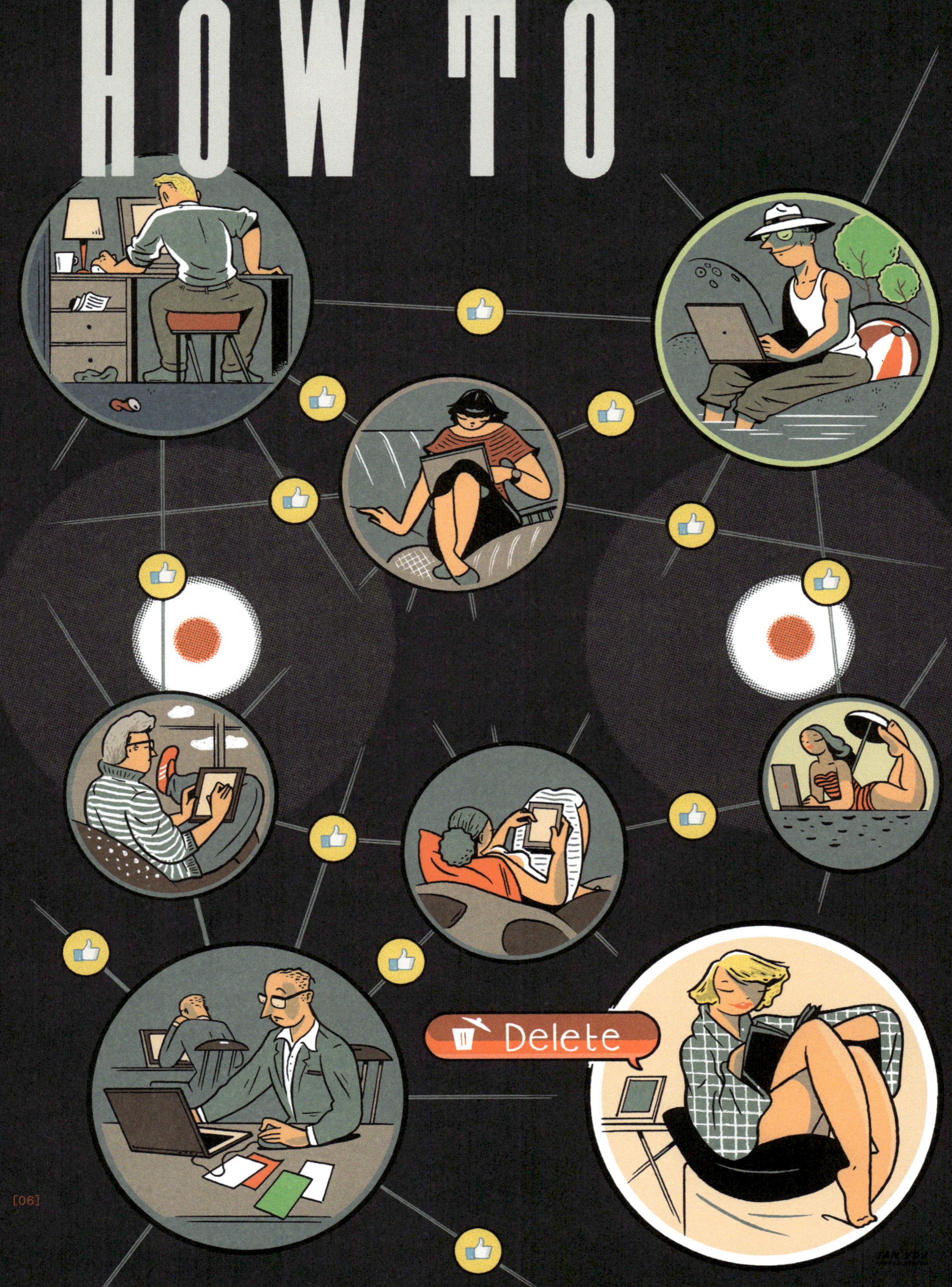

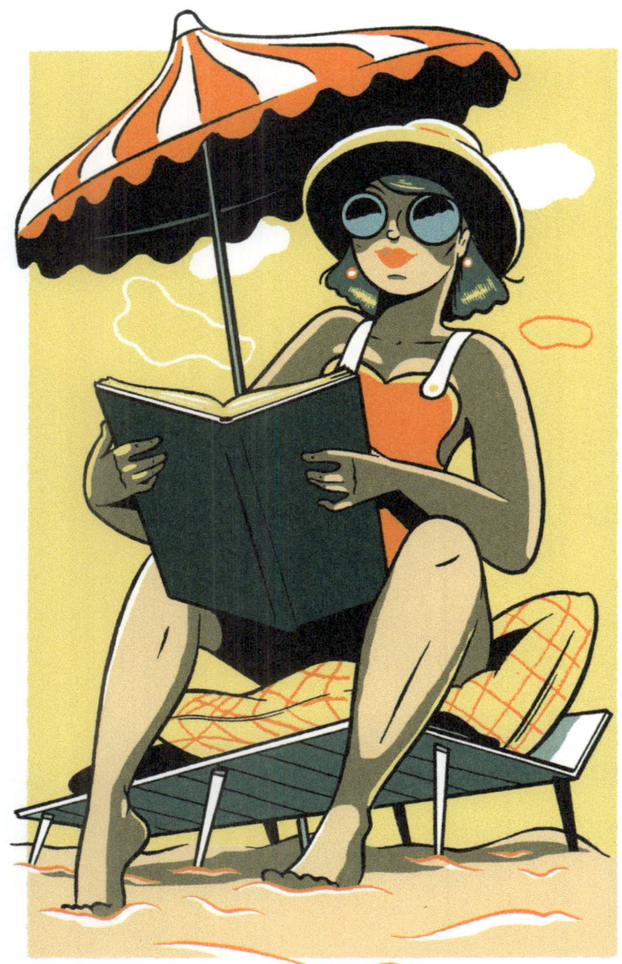
[01]

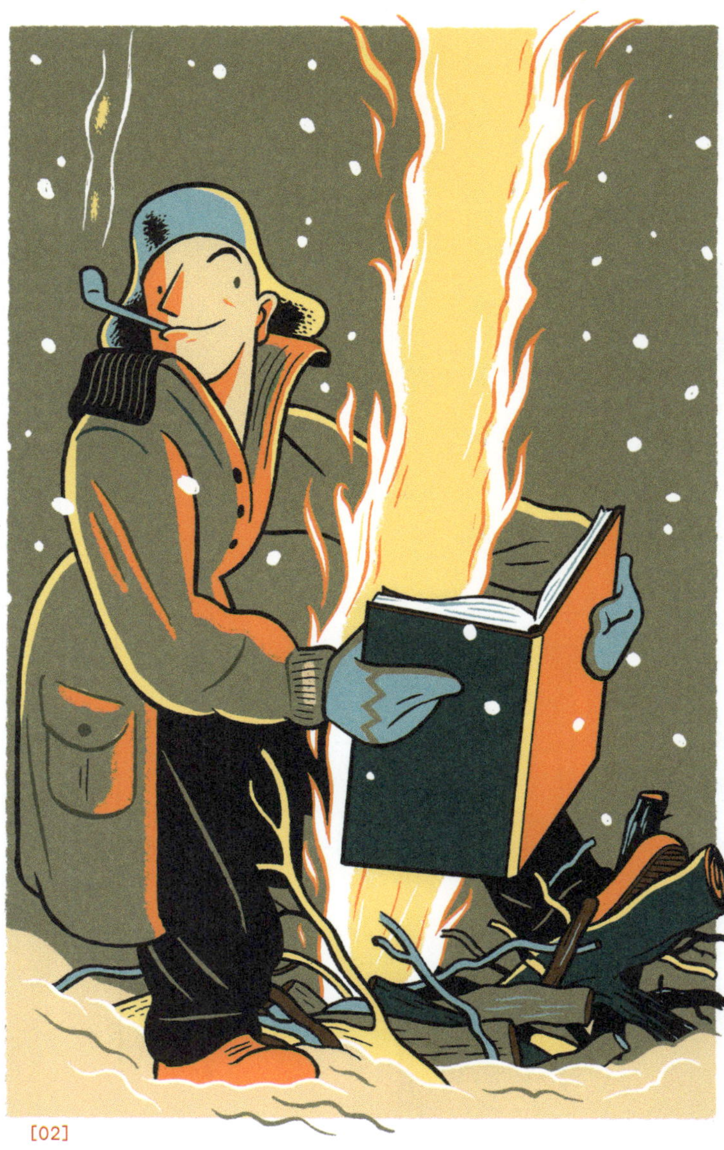
[02]

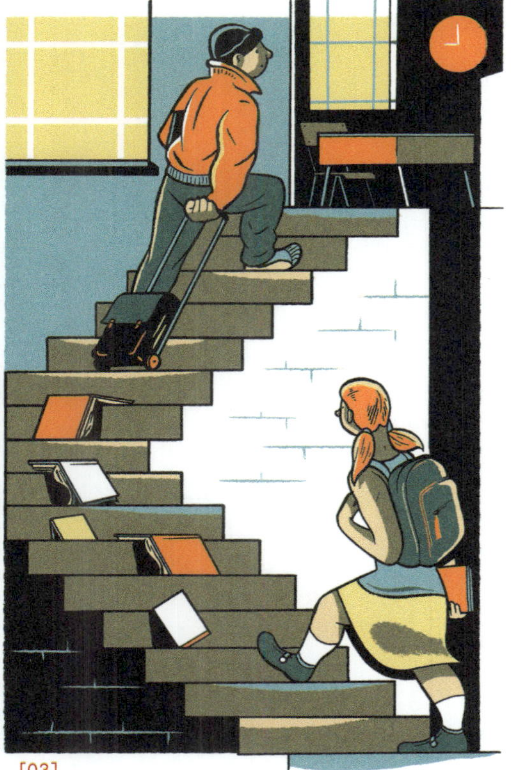
[03]

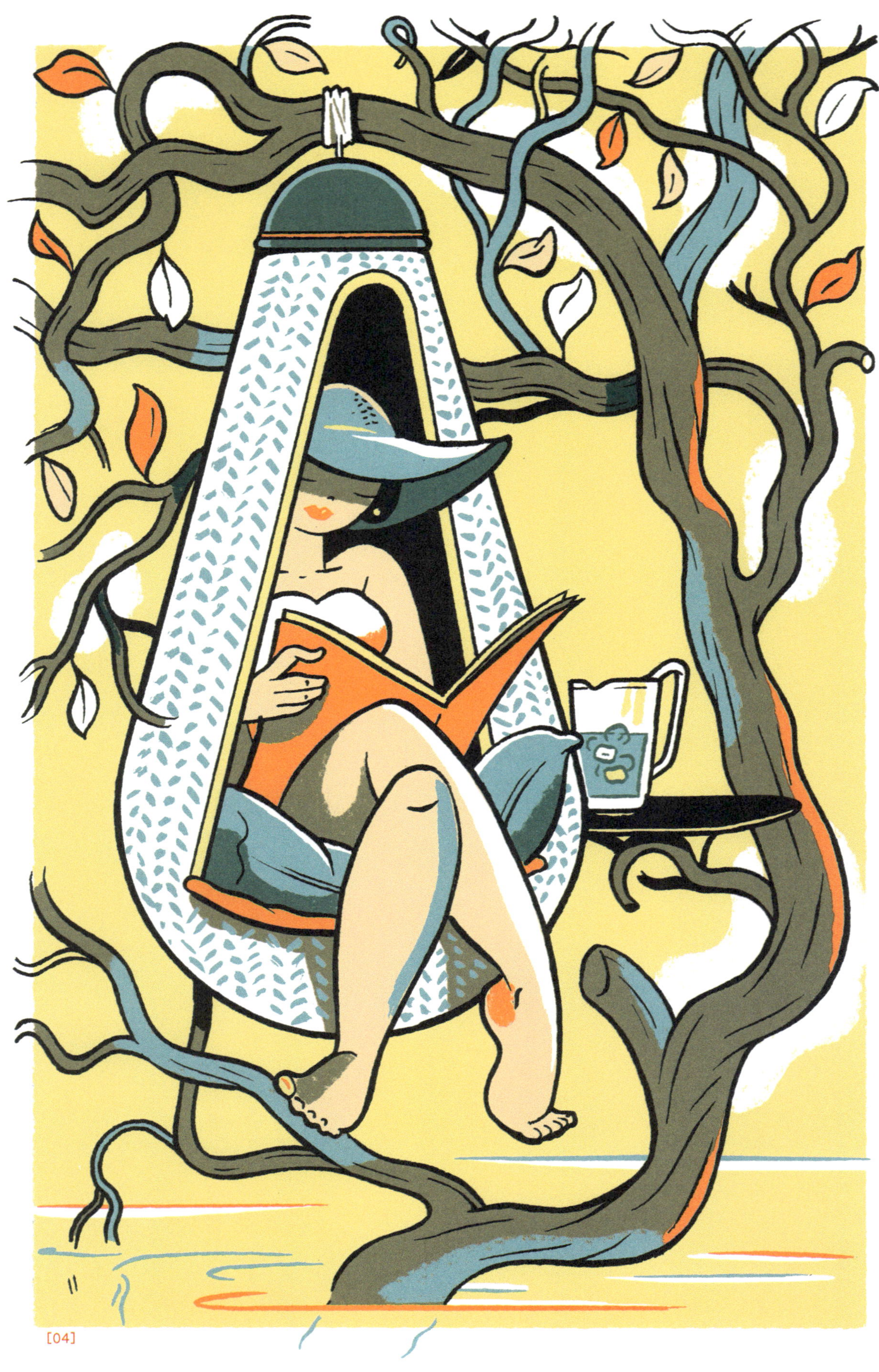

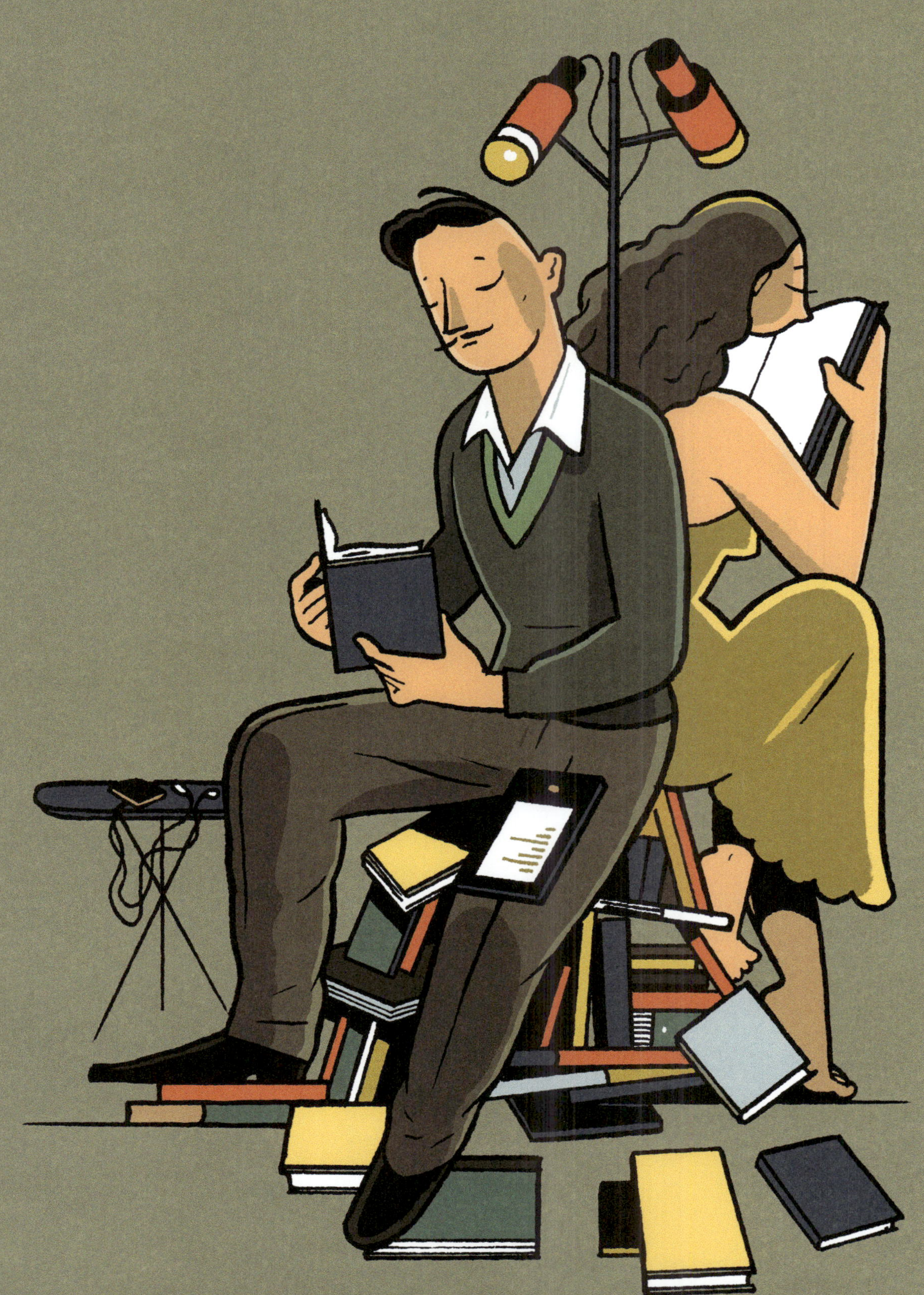

[01]

BOEKEN

[02]

JAN VDV
FABRICA GRAFICA

[03]

LEZEN

[04]

JAN VDV
FABRICA GRAFICA

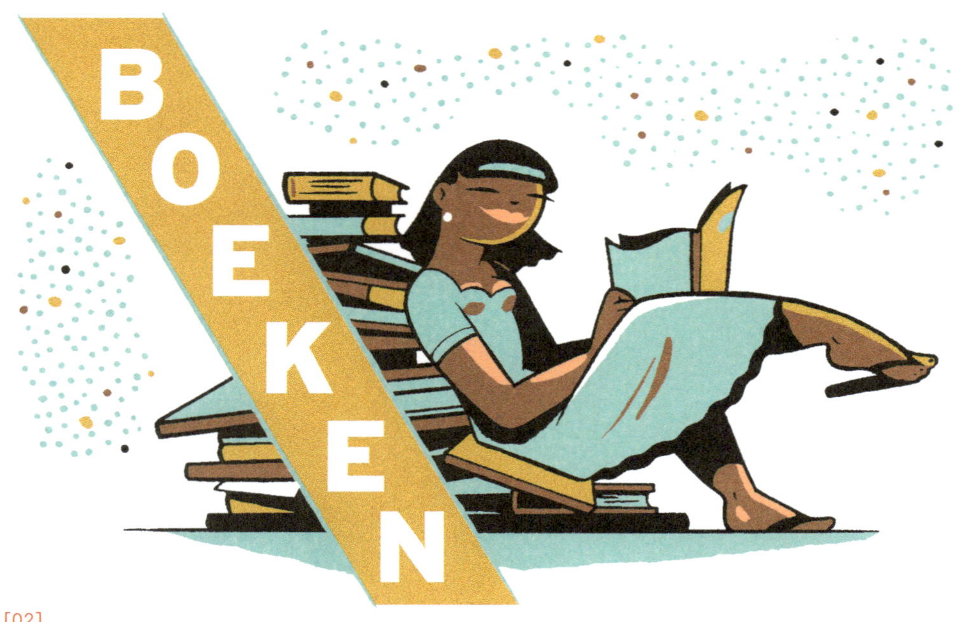

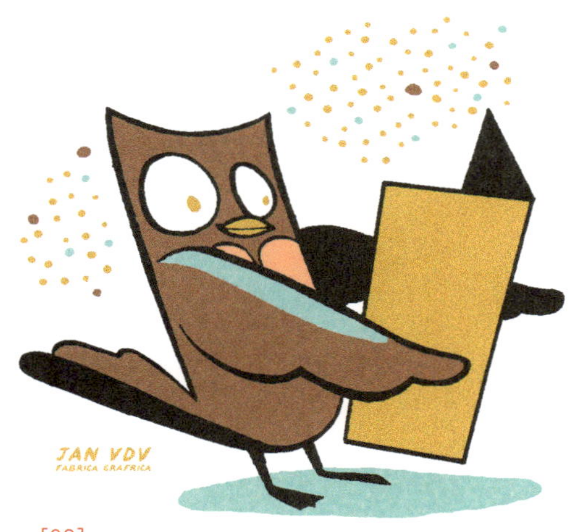

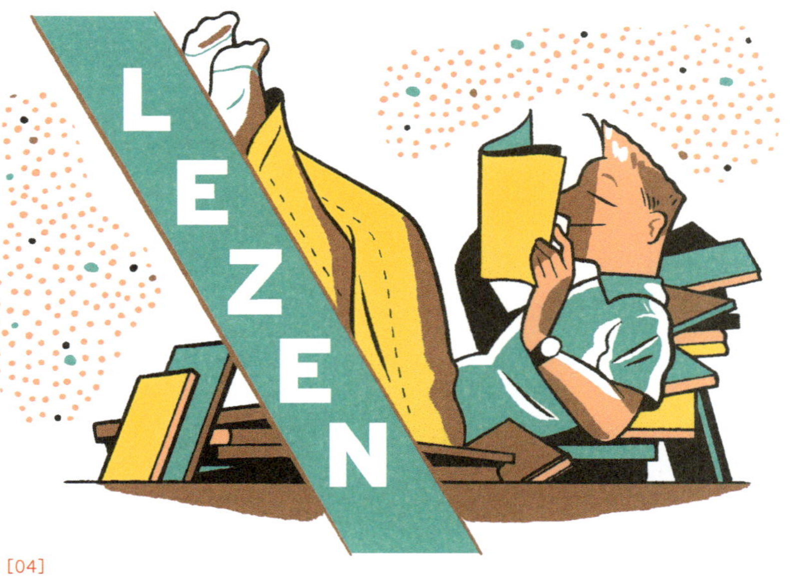

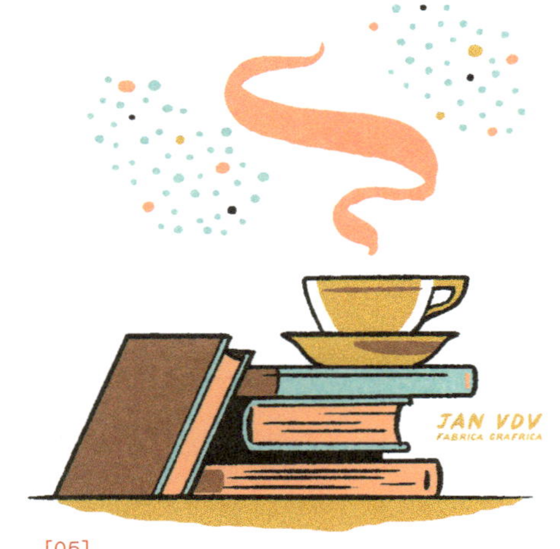

[05]

BATABATA
willem de beersteeg
20 29 JULI
gentse 15 u
feesten 24 u
JAN VDV
FABRICA GRAFICA
Romy
VITAL
gent: zoveel stad
CIRQ

[01]

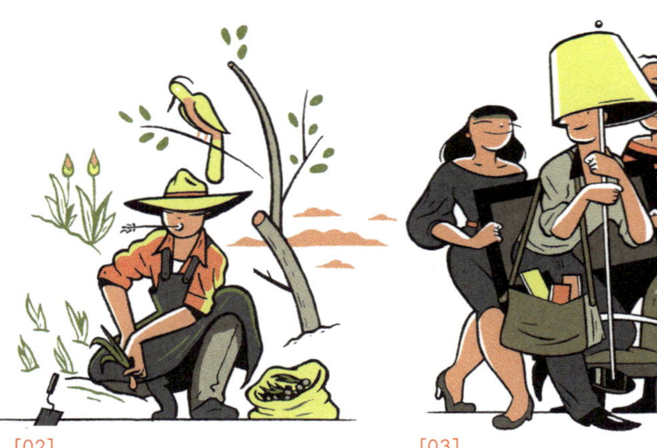

[02]

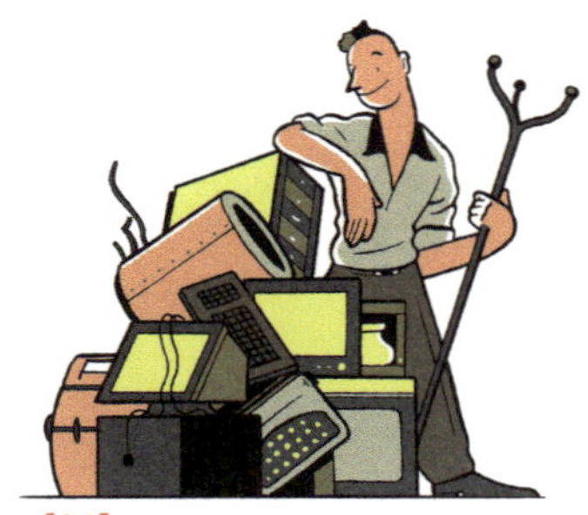

[03]

[04]

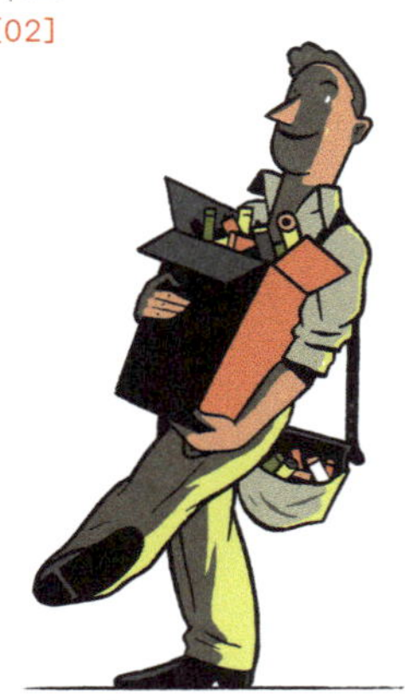

[05]

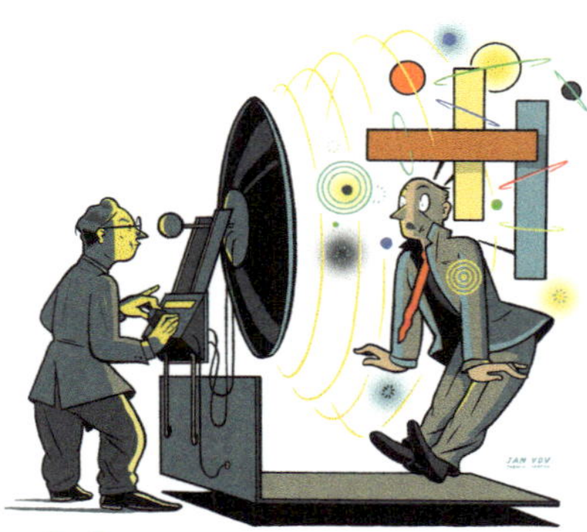

[06]

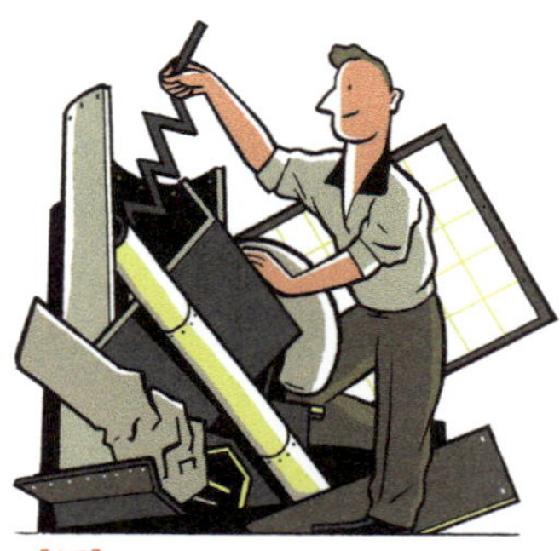

[07]

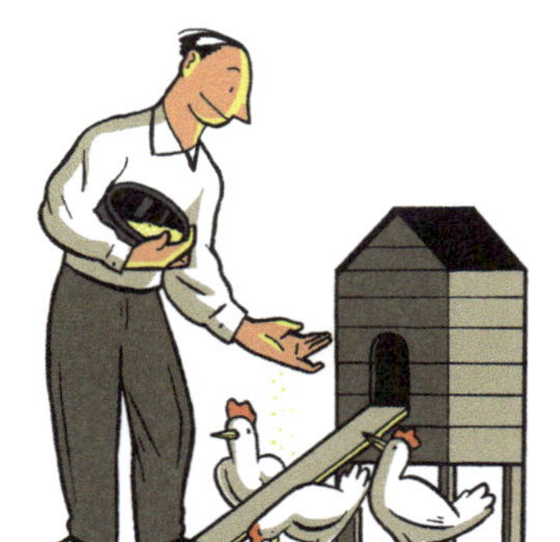

[08]

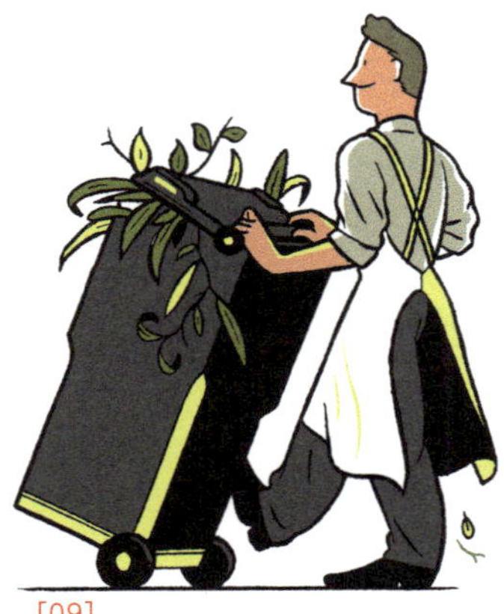

[09]

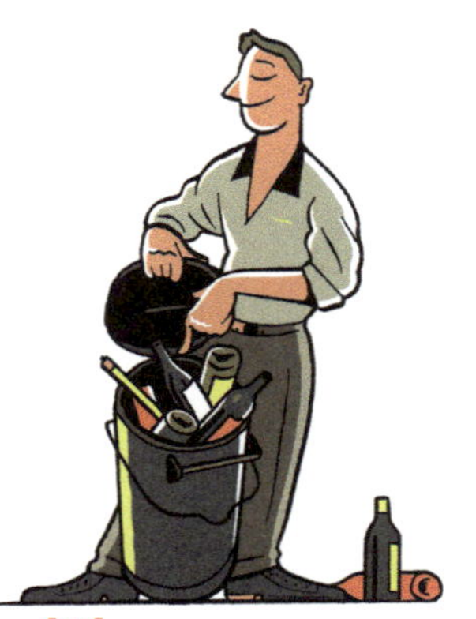

[10]

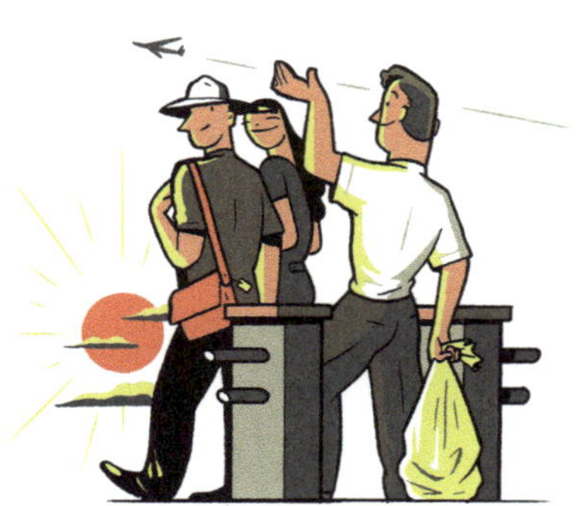

[11]

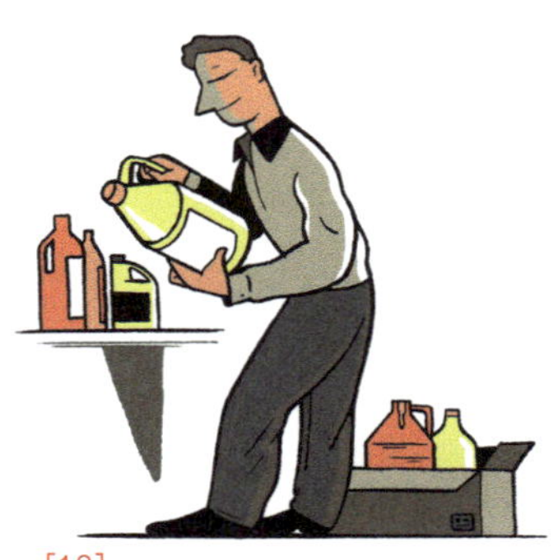

[12]

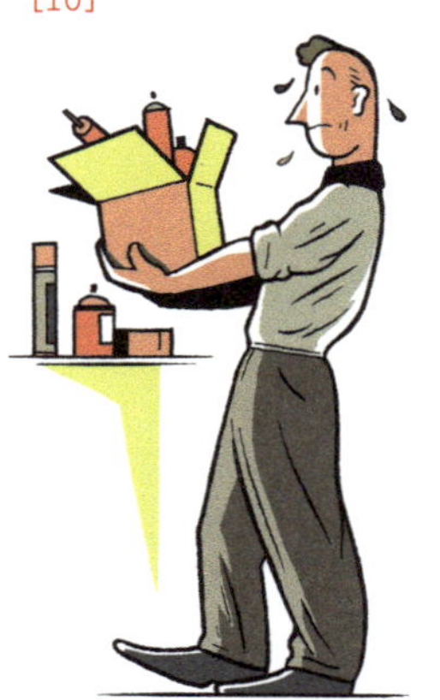

[13]

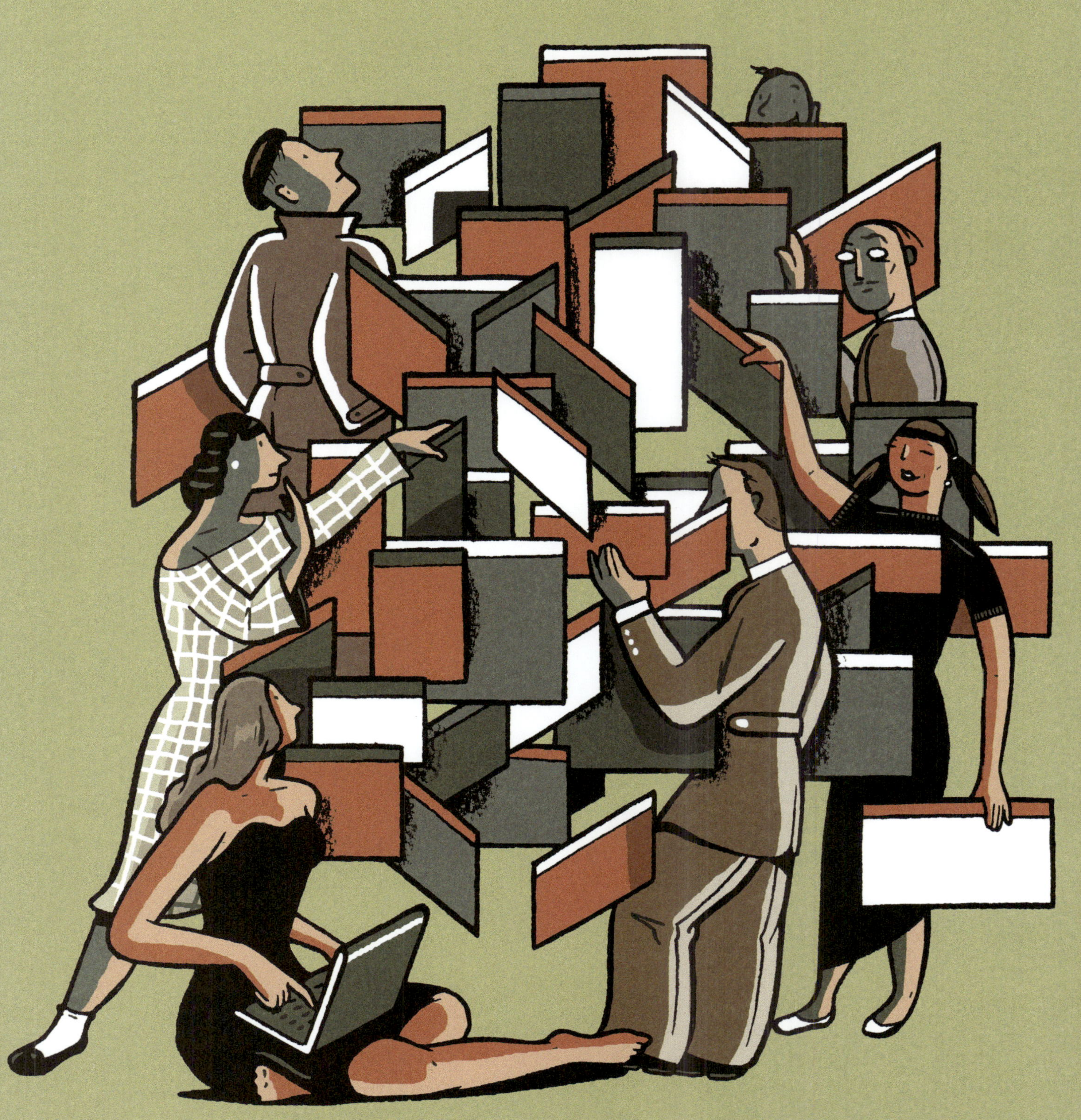

- *Webspace visualised* -

WWW.ATHENEUM-GROENKOUTER.BE

WWW.ATHENEUM-GROENKOUTER.BE
JAN VDV
GO! onderwijs van de
Vlaamse Gemeenschap

WWW.ATHENEUM-GROENKOUTER.BE

[02]

WWW.ATHENEUM-GROENKOUTER.BE

WWW.ATHENEUM-GROENKOUTER.BE

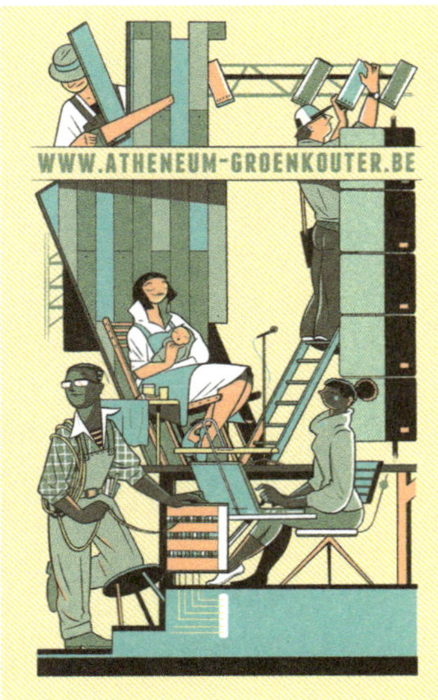

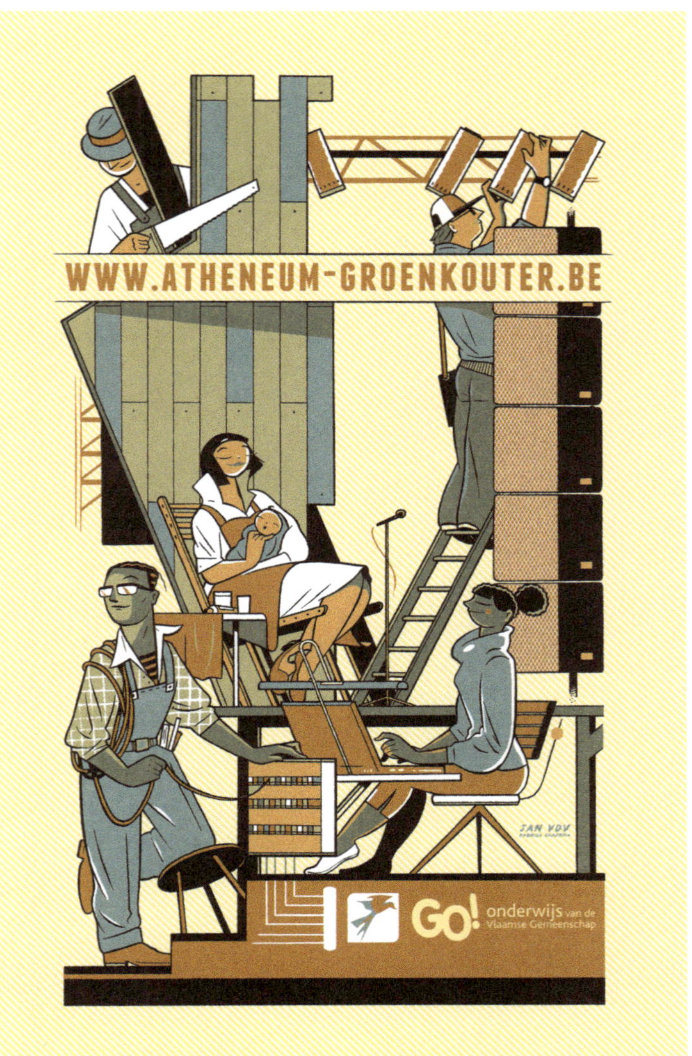

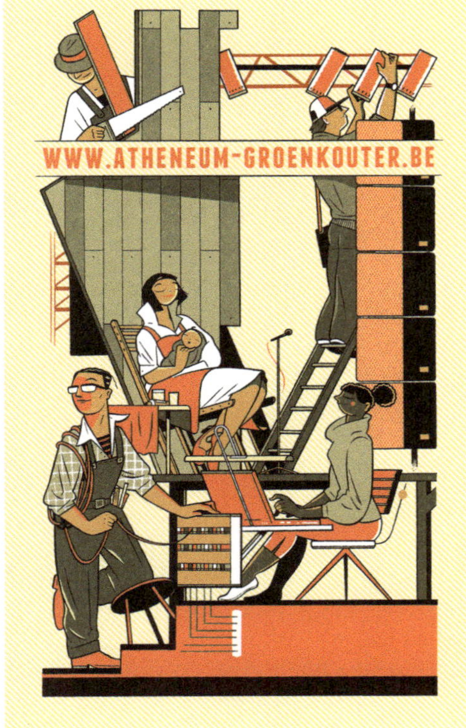

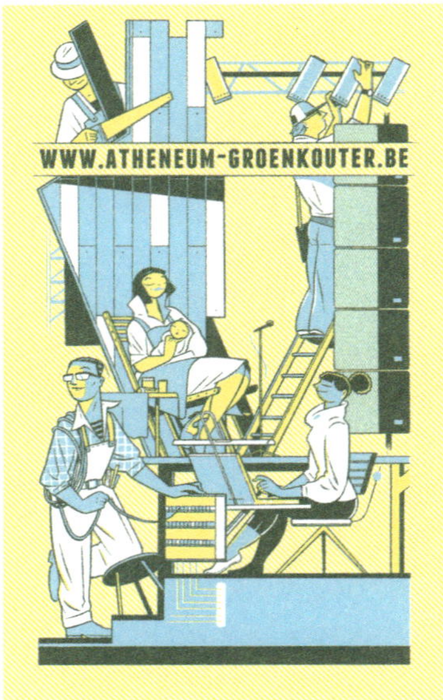

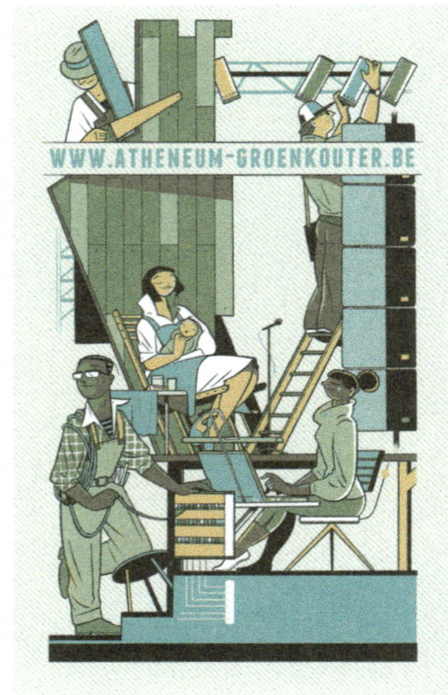

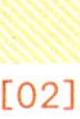

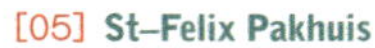

[01]

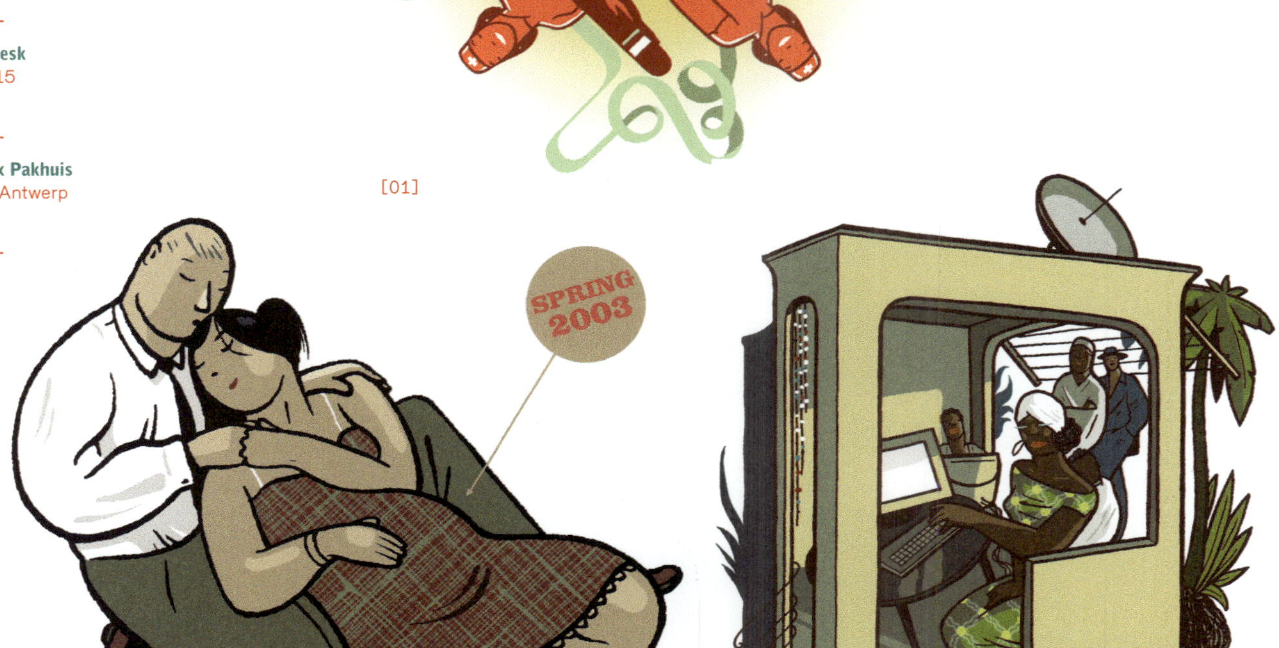

[02]

[03]

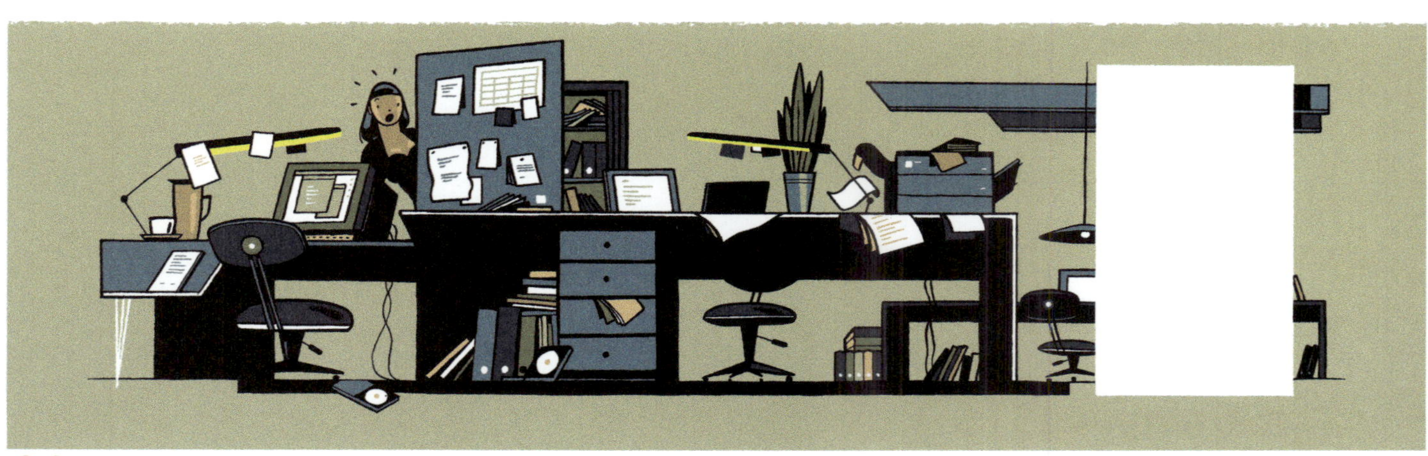

[04]

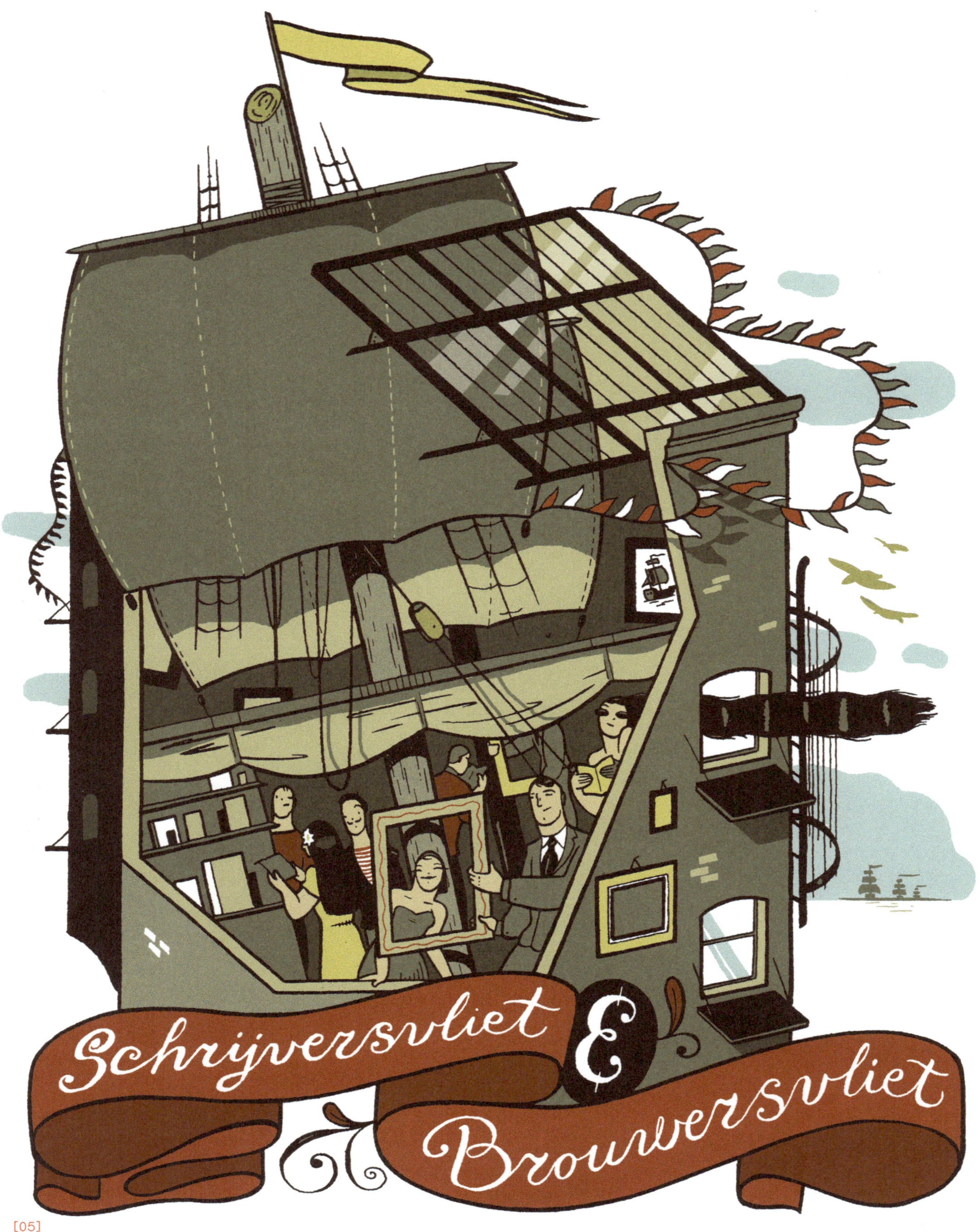Schrijversvliet & Brouwersvliet

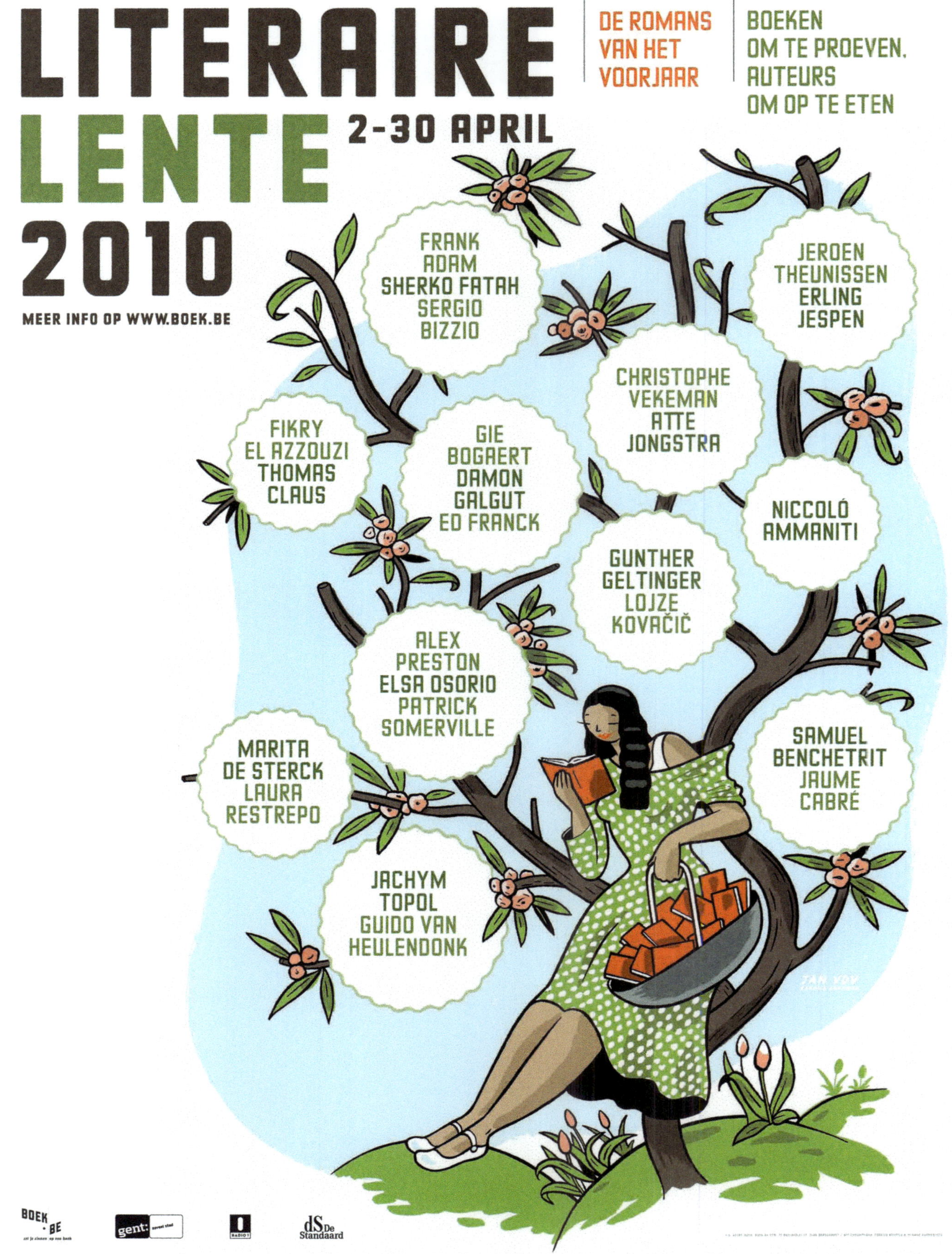

LITERAIRE LENTE 2010
2-30 APRIL
MEER INFO OP WWW.BOEK.BE
DE ROMANS VAN HET VOORJAAR
BOEKEN OM TE PROEVEN. AUTEURS OM OP TE ETEN
FRANK ADAM SHERKO FATAH SERGIO BIZZIO
JEROEN THEUNISSEN ERLING JESPEN
CHRISTOPHE VEKEMAN ATTE JONGSTRA
FIKRY EL AZZOUZI THOMAS CLAUS
GIE BOGAERT DAMON GALGUT ED FRANCK
NICCOLÓ AMMANITI
GUNTHER GELTINGER LOJZE KOVAČIČ
ALEX PRESTON ELSA OSORIO PATRICK SOMERVILLE
MARITA DE STERCK LAURA RESTREPO
SAMUEL BENCHETRIT JAUME CABRÉ
JACHYM TOPOL GUIDO VAN HEULENDONK
BOEK.BE
gent: soweet vind
RADIO 1
dS De Standaard

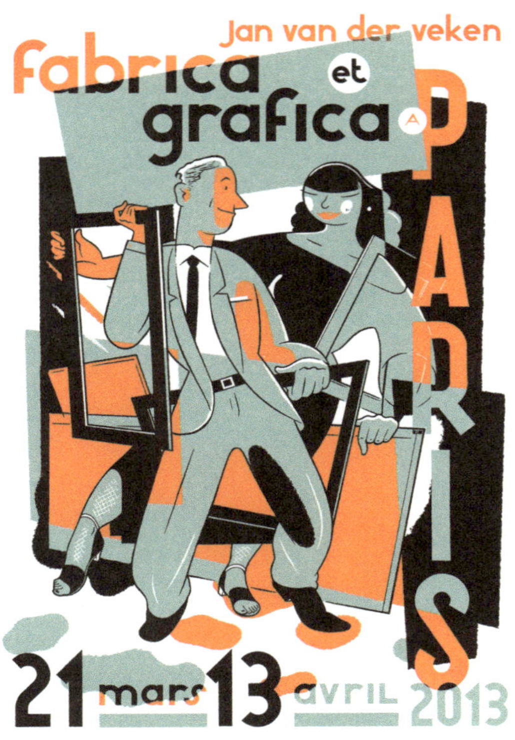

[02]

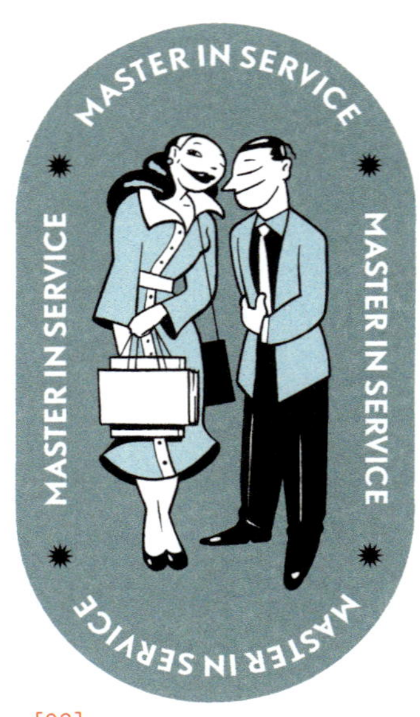

[03]

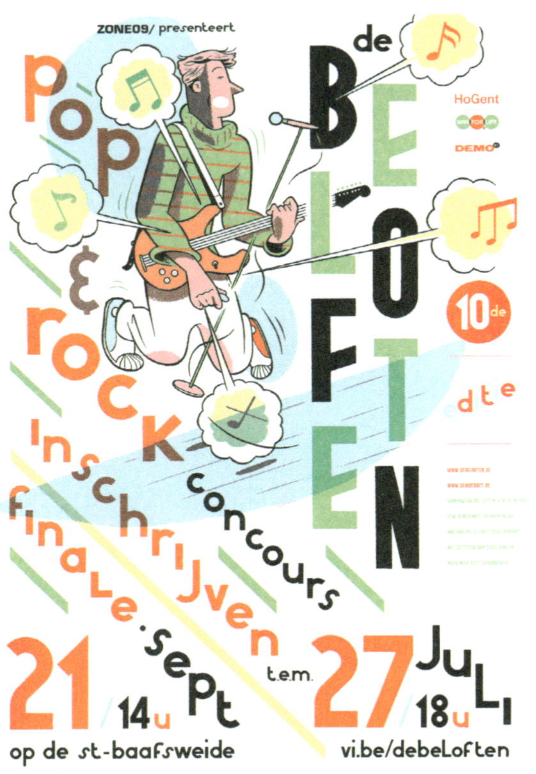

[04]

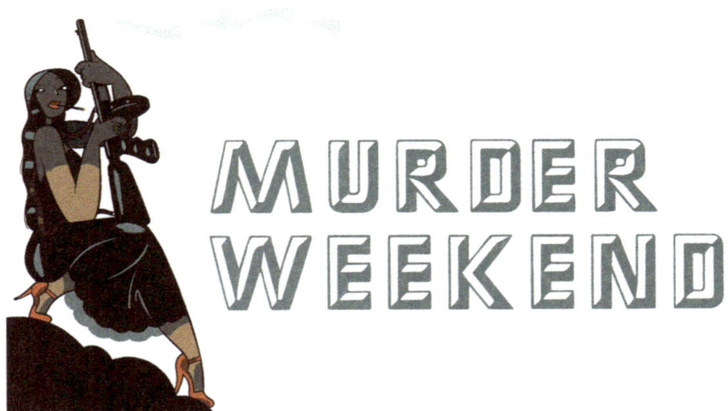

[05]

[01] **Literary Spring Poster**
      (Typography Herman Houbrechts)
      Boek.be
   ✳ 2010
____

[02] **Paris Expo Invitation**
      Personal Work
   ✳ 2013
____

[03] **Master in Service**
      Bart Persoons
   ✳ 2010
____

[04] **De Beloften Rock Poster**
      De Beloften
   ✳ 2013
____

[05] **Murder Weekend**
      Personal Work
   ✳ 2011

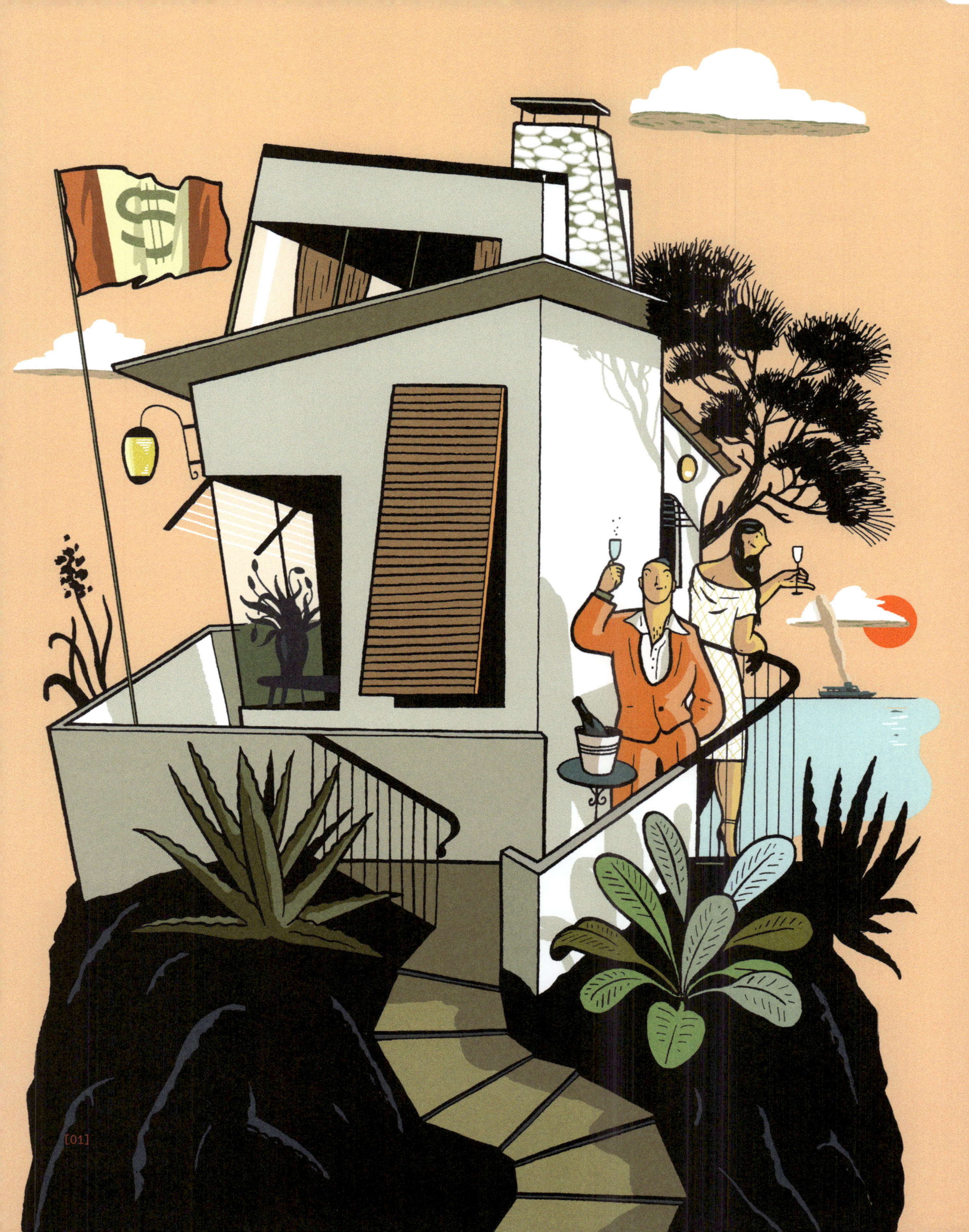

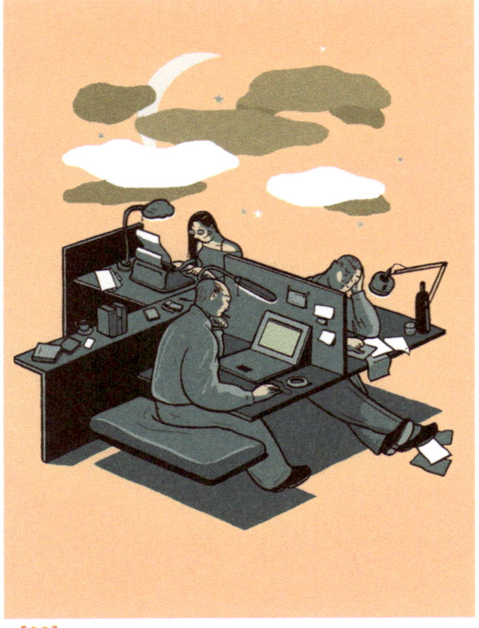

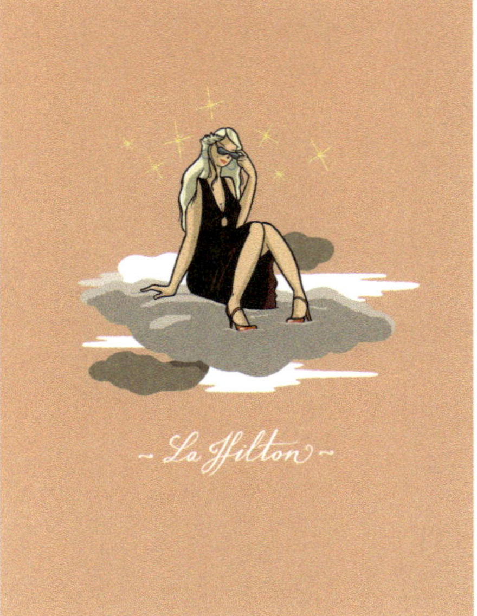

[02]

[03]

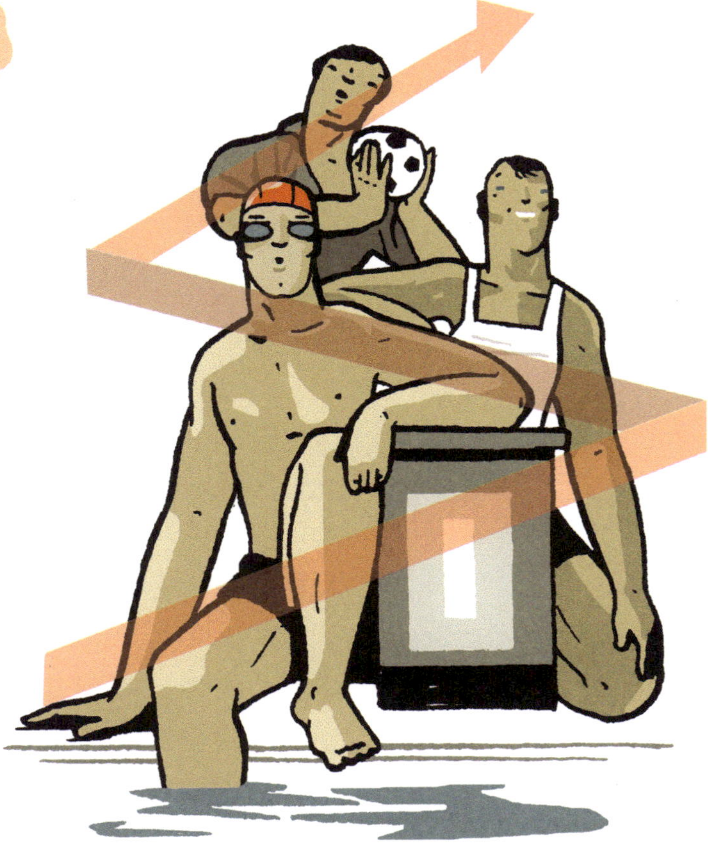

[04]

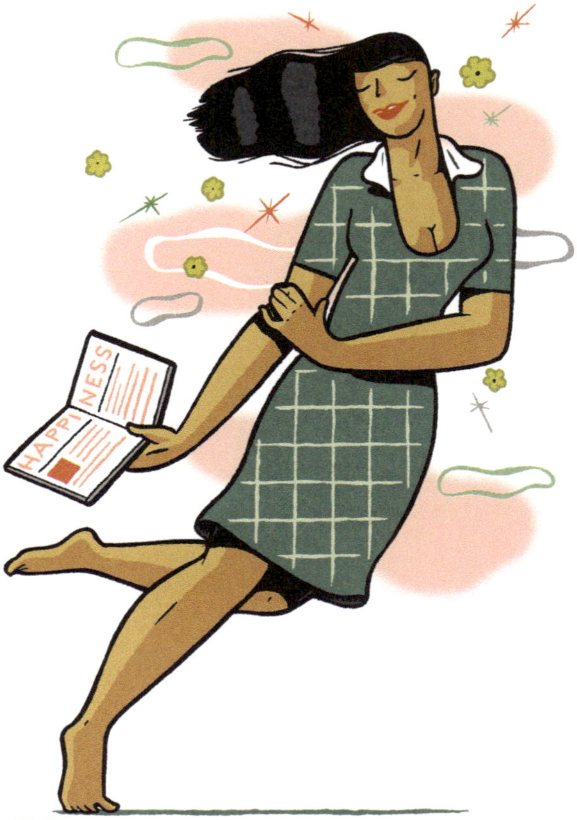

[05]

Standaard Boekhandel
*   2012

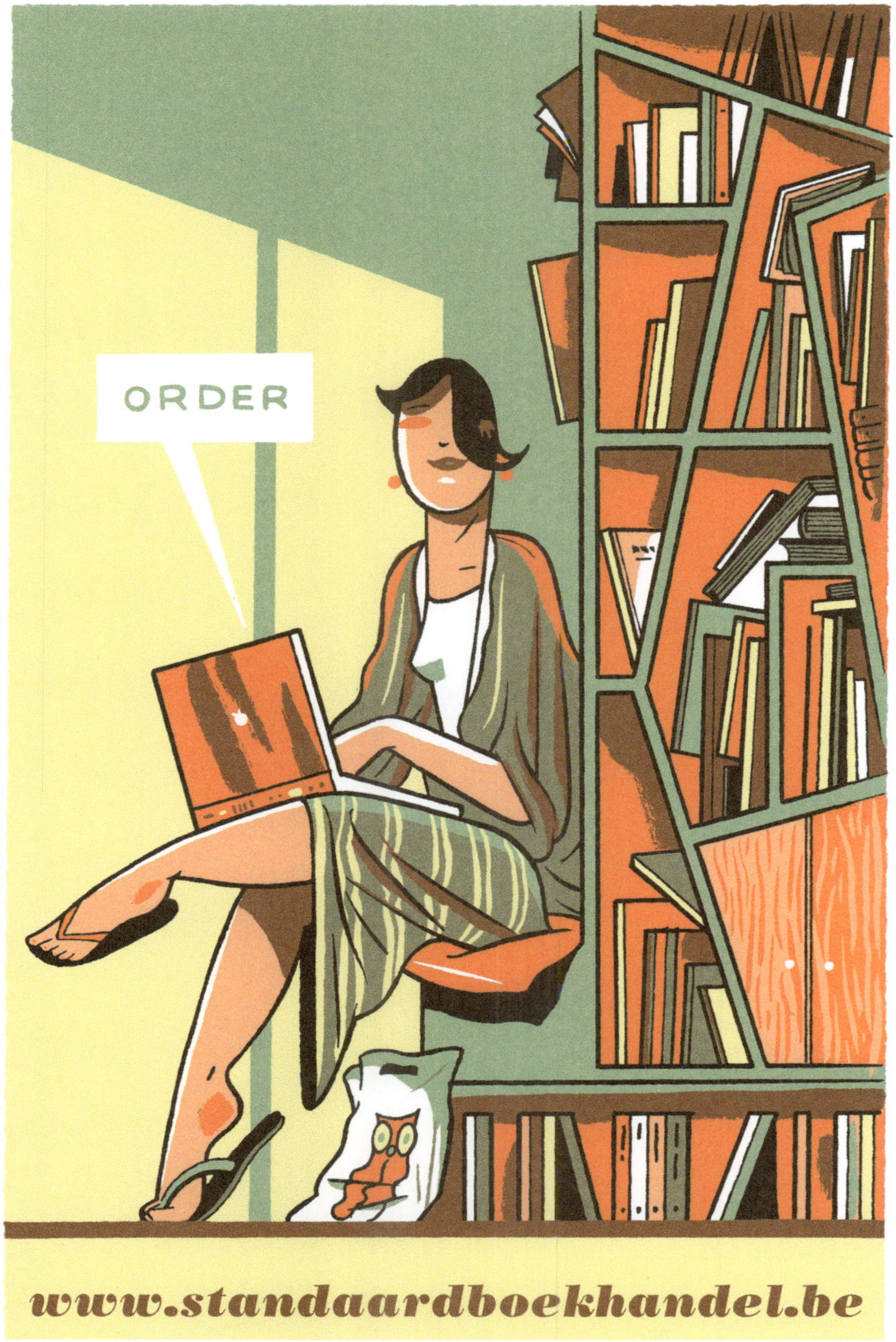

---

[02]

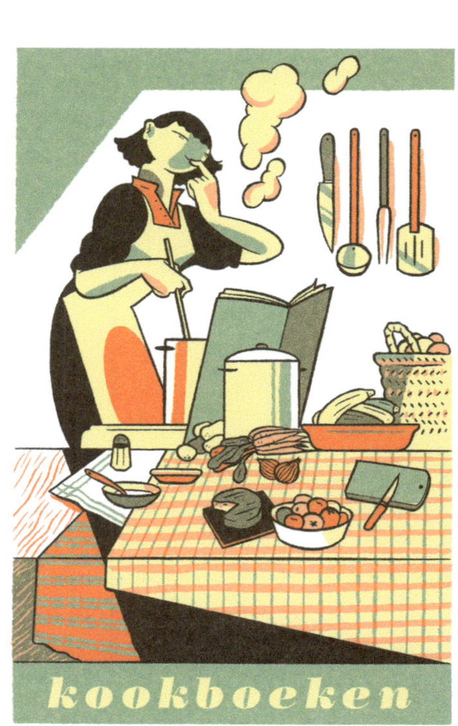

[01]

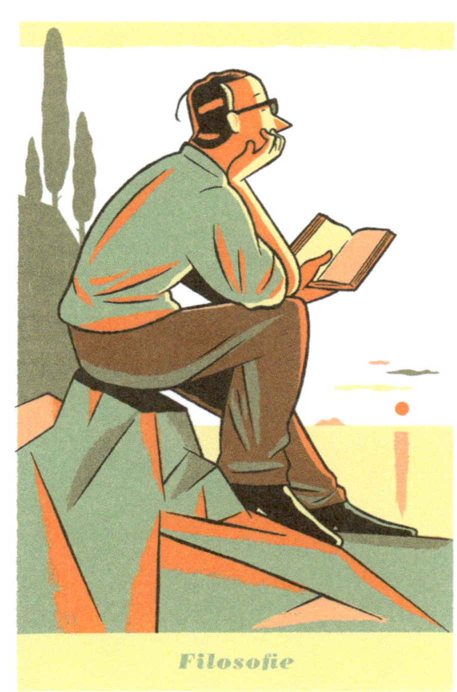

Filosofie

[03]

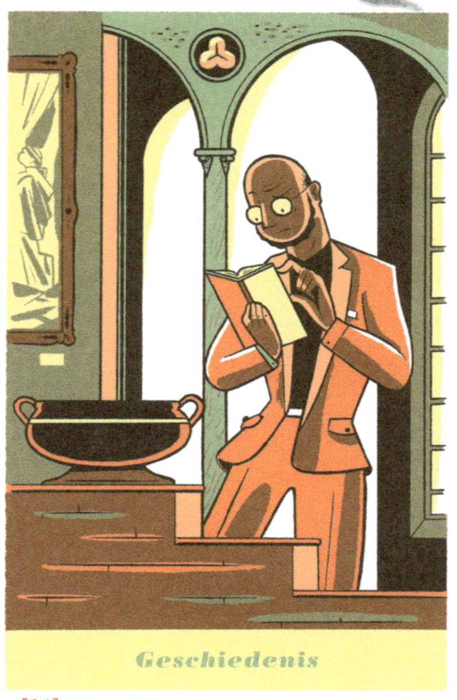

Geschiedenis

[04]

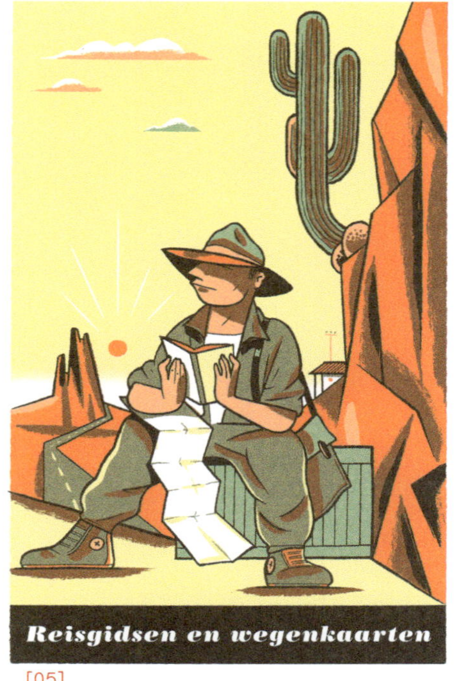

Reisgidsen en wegenkaarten

[05]

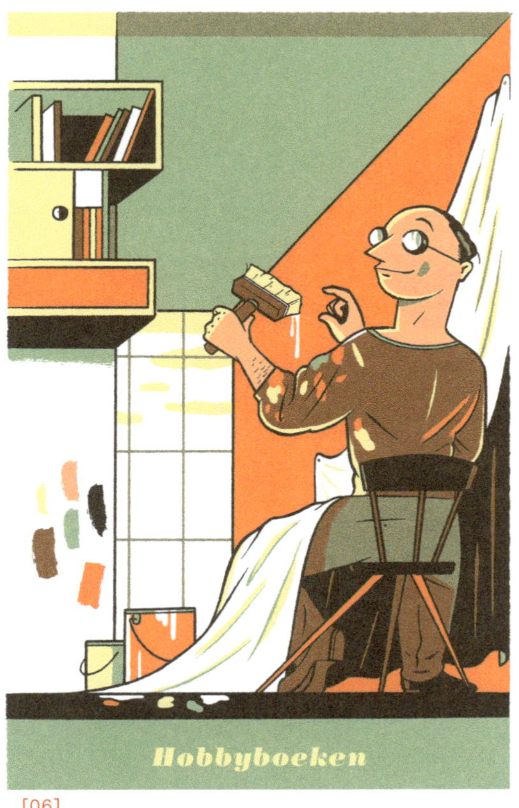

Hobbyboeken

[06]

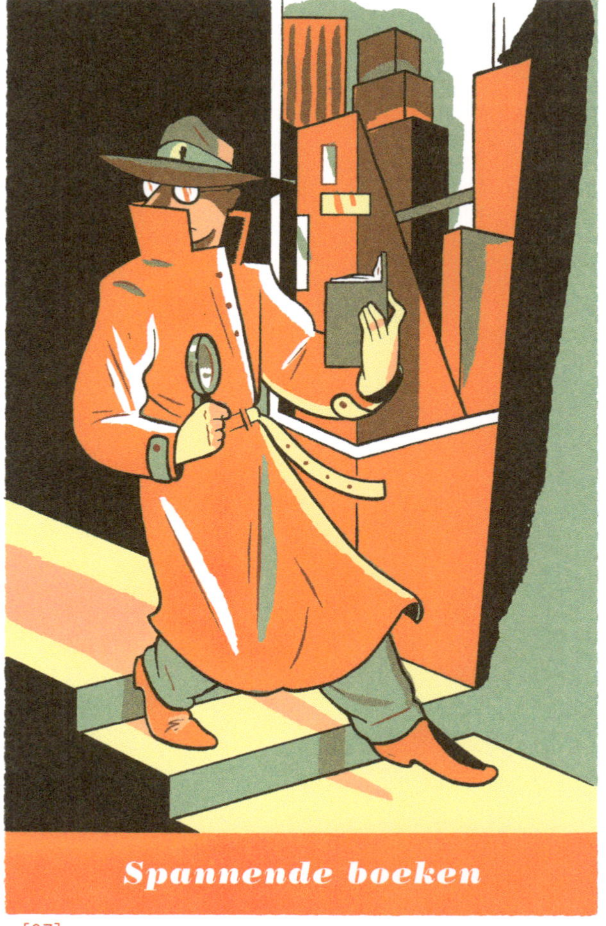

Spannende boeken

[07]

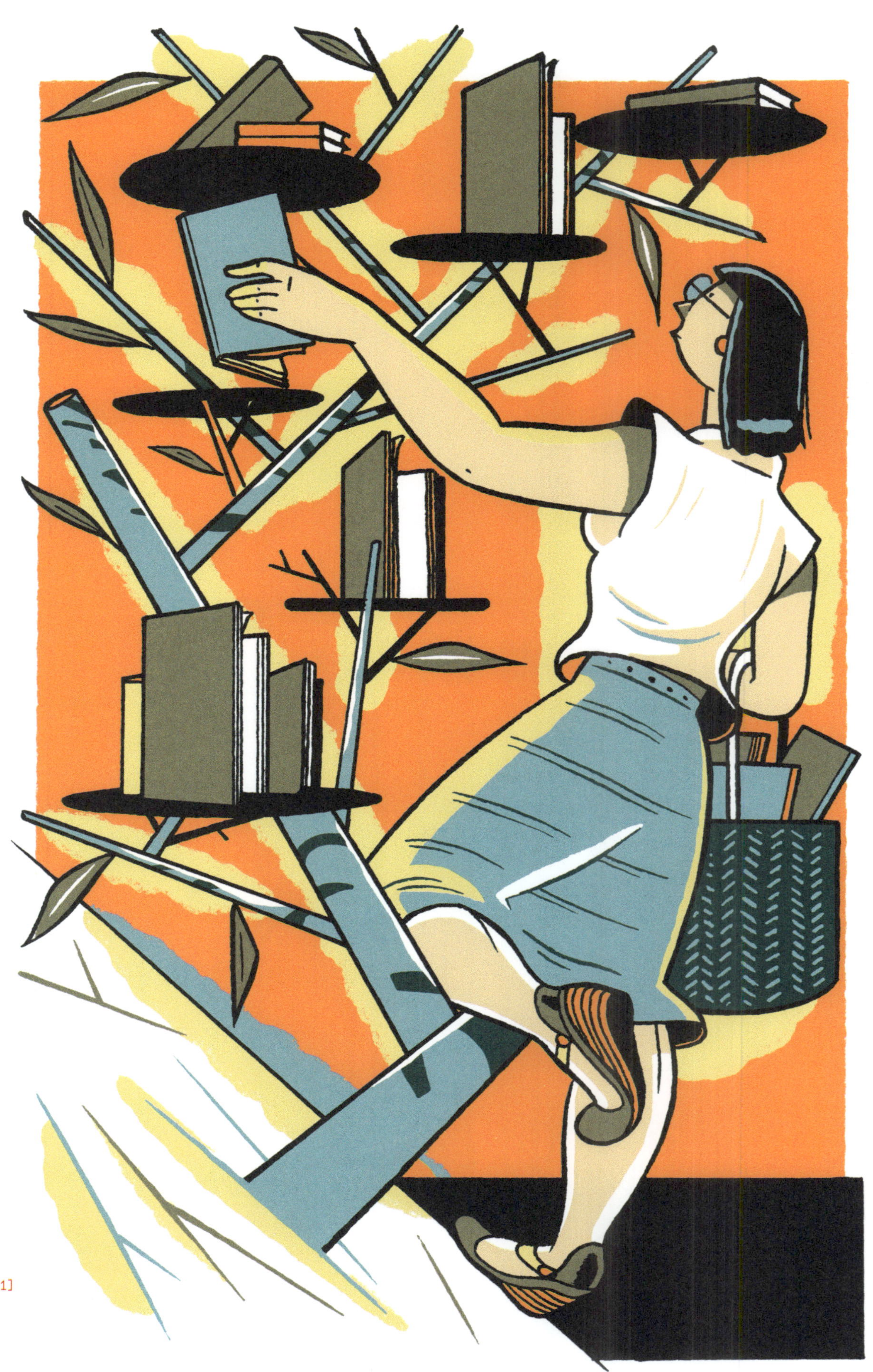

[01]

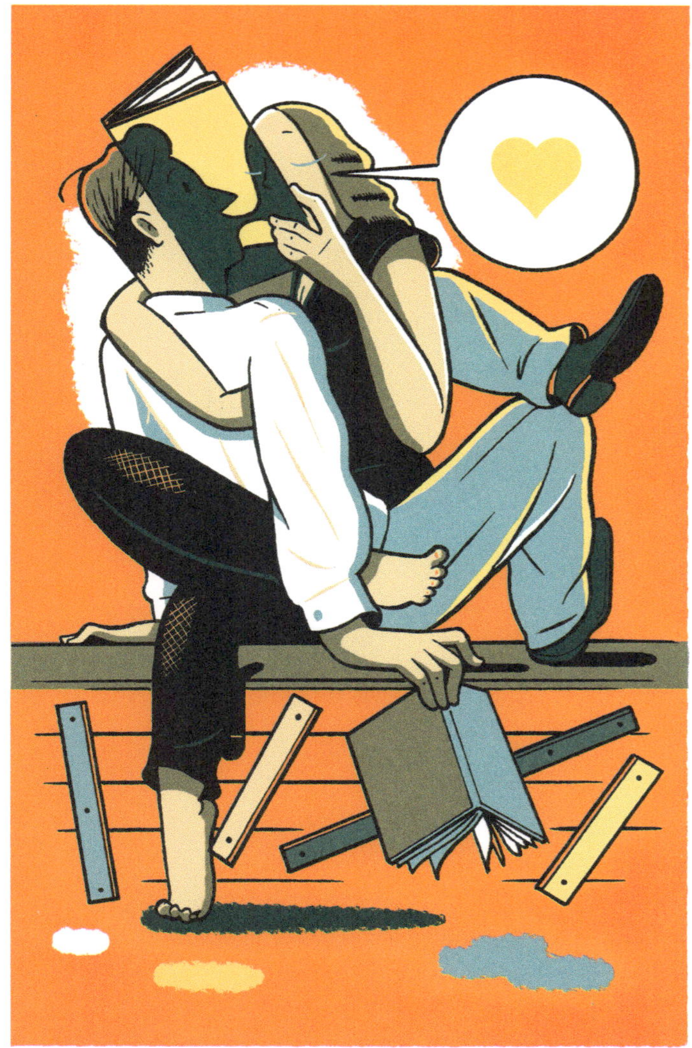

[02]

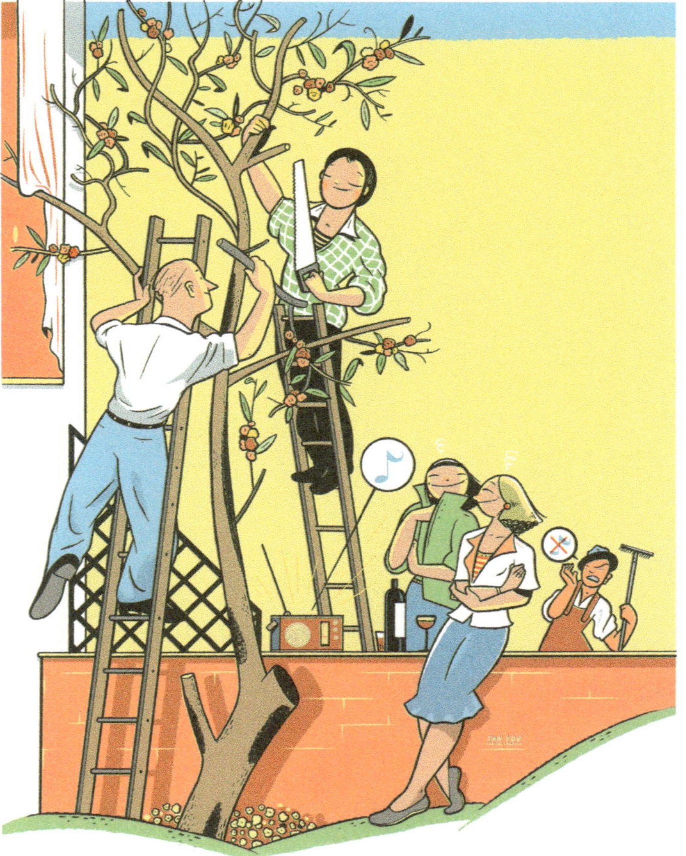

[03]

[04]

[01] **Book Harvest**

[02] **Valentine**

[03] **Covergirl**
✳   2012

       Standaard Boekhandel
✳   2013

———————

[04] **Meet your Neighbors**
       Humo Magazine
✳   2012

81

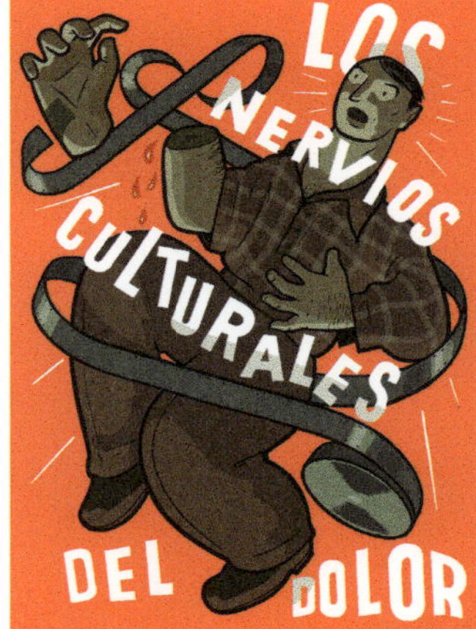

[01]

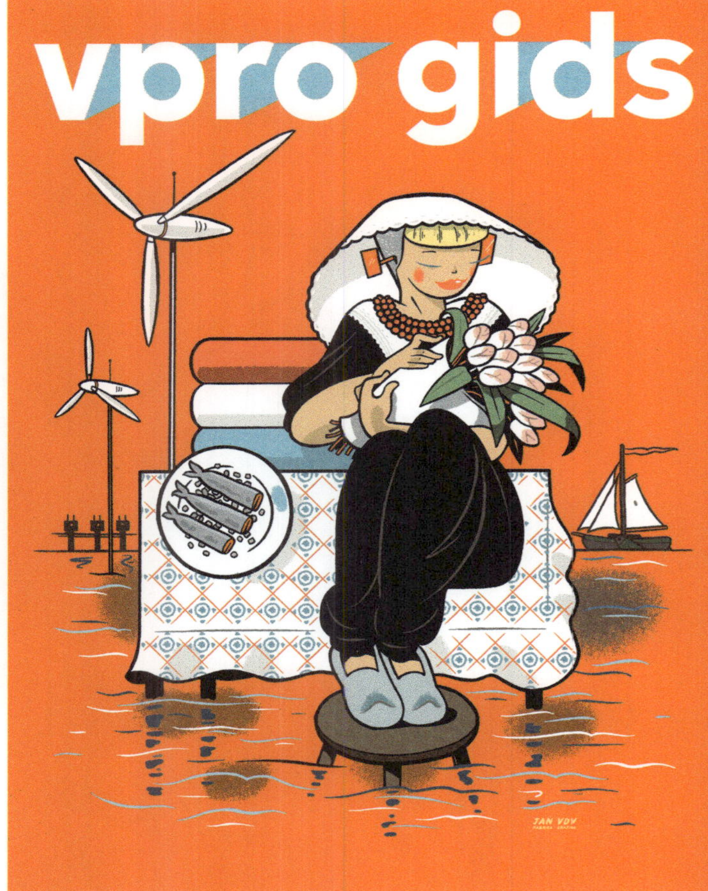

[02]

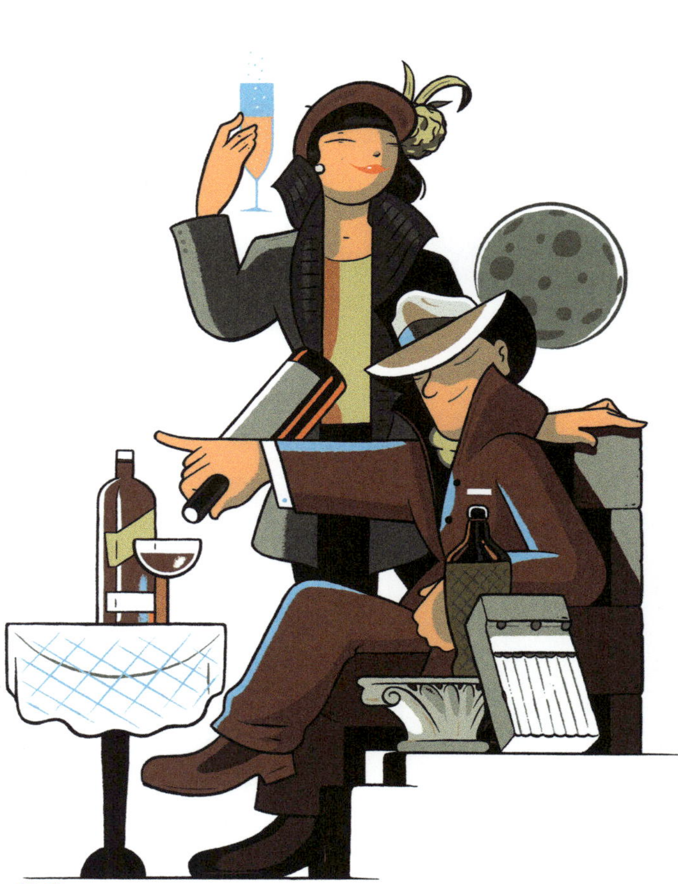
[03]

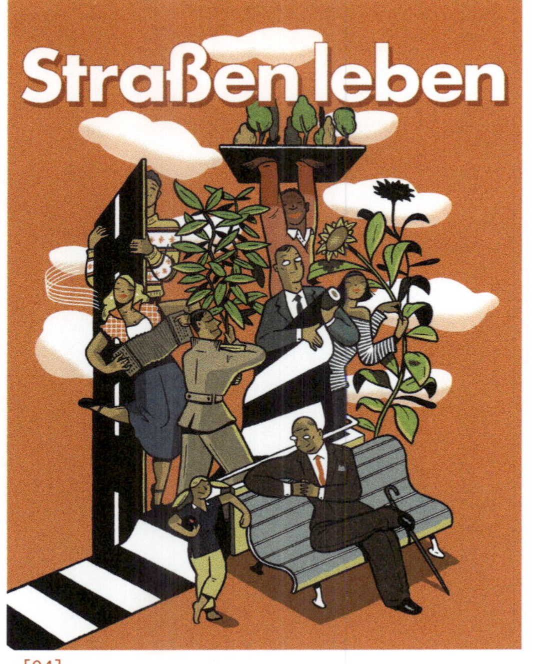

[04]

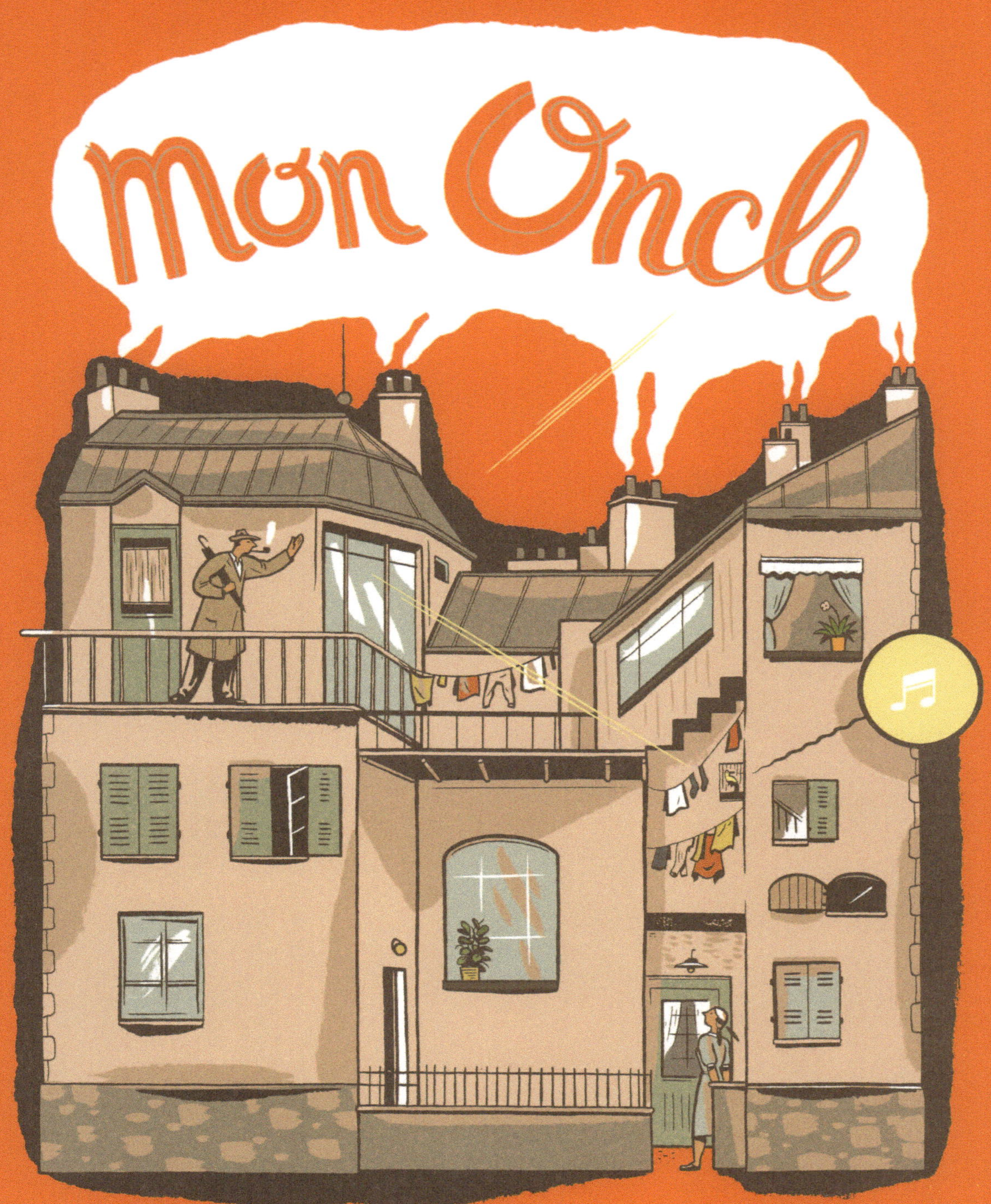

Mon Oncle
JACQUES
TATI
GAUMONT DISTRIBUTEURS PRESENTENT
UNE PRODUCTION DE FABRICA GRAFICA

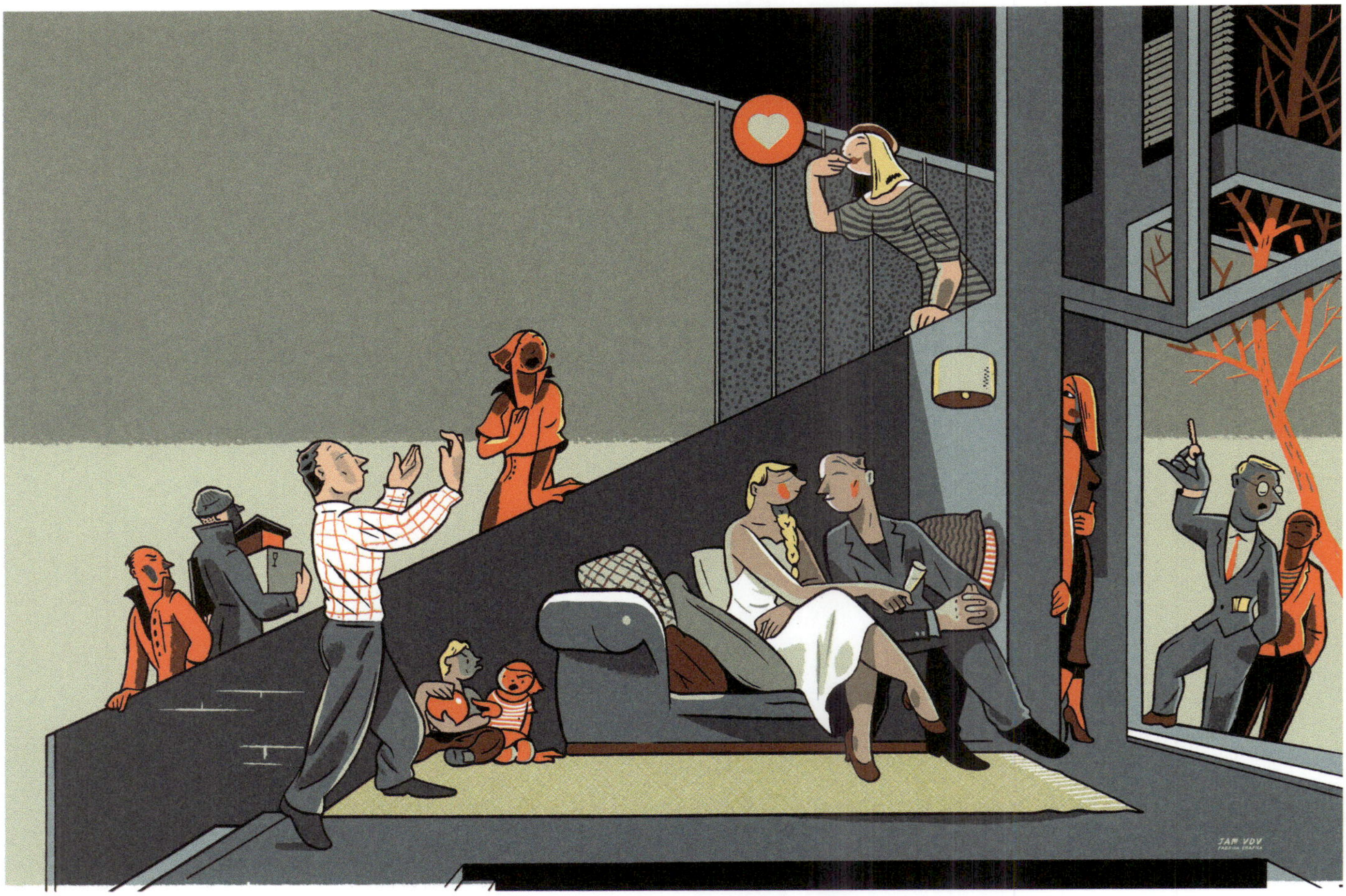

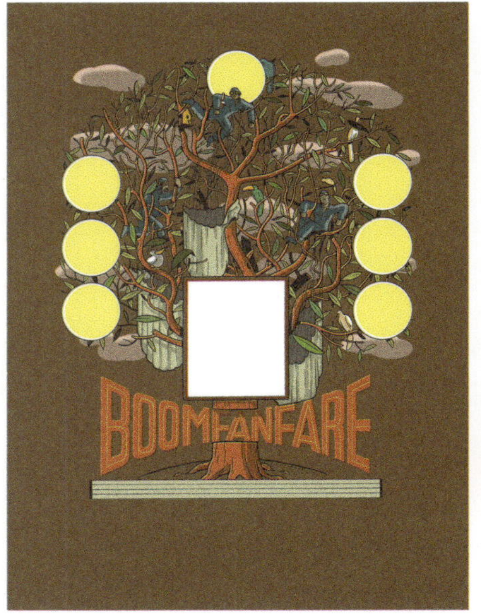

[02]

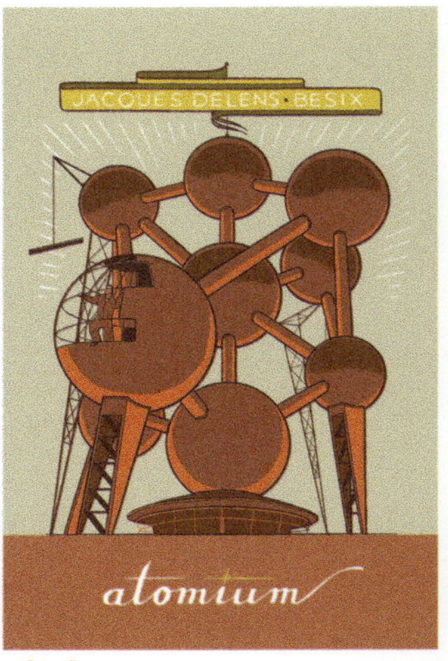

[03]

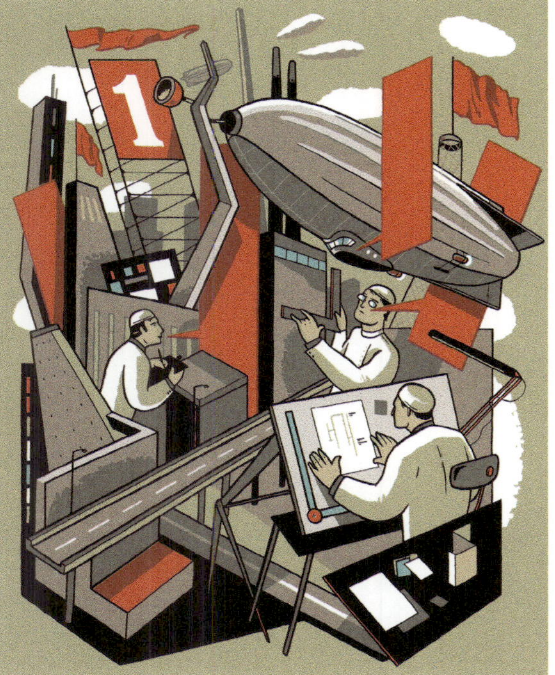

[04]

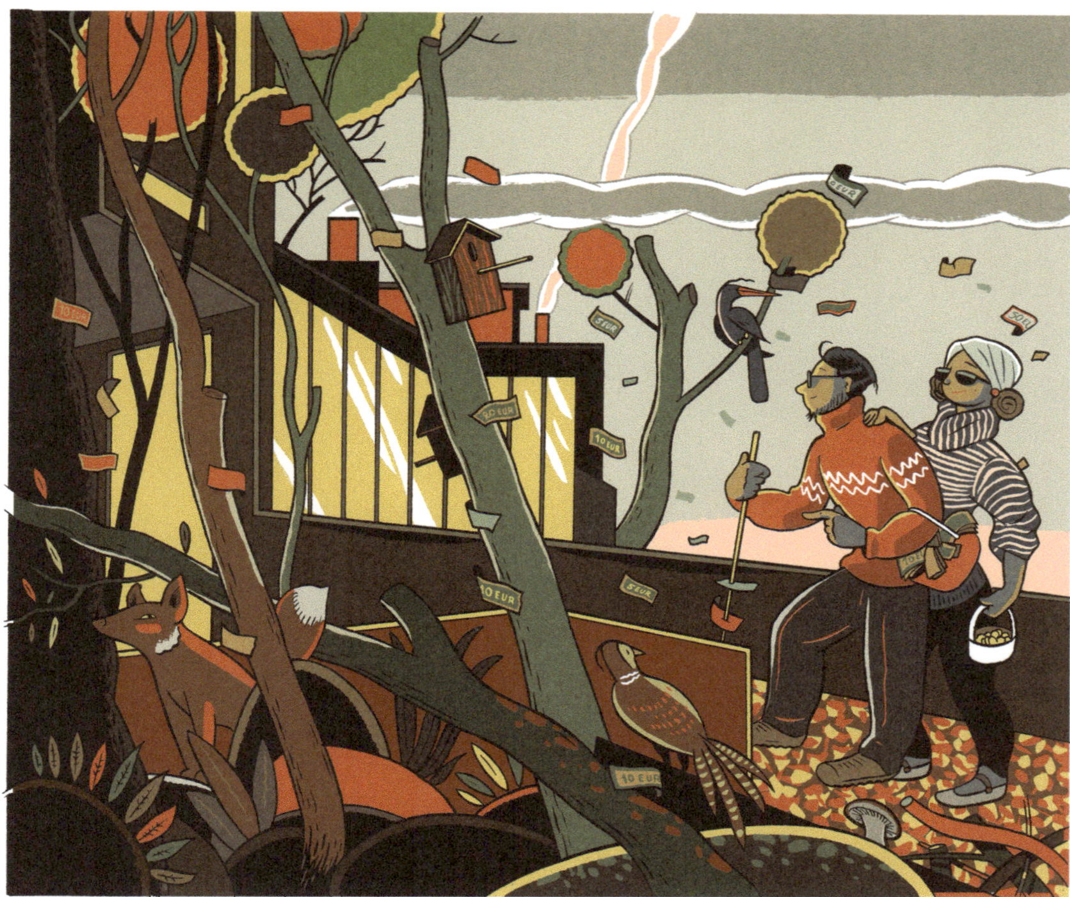

[05]

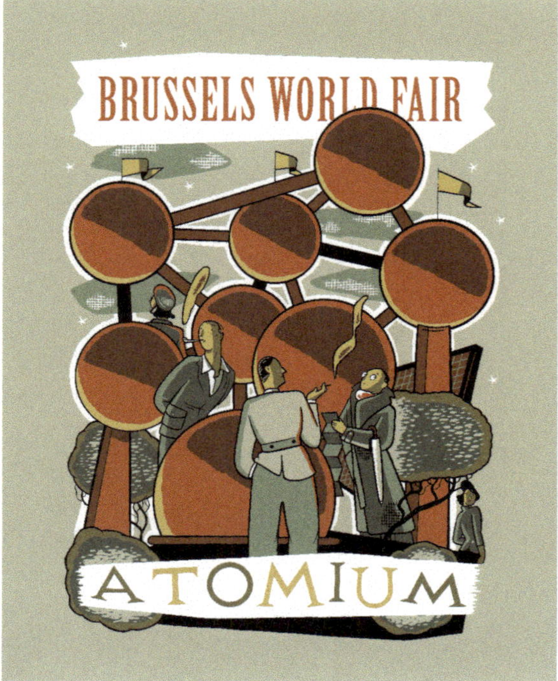

[06]

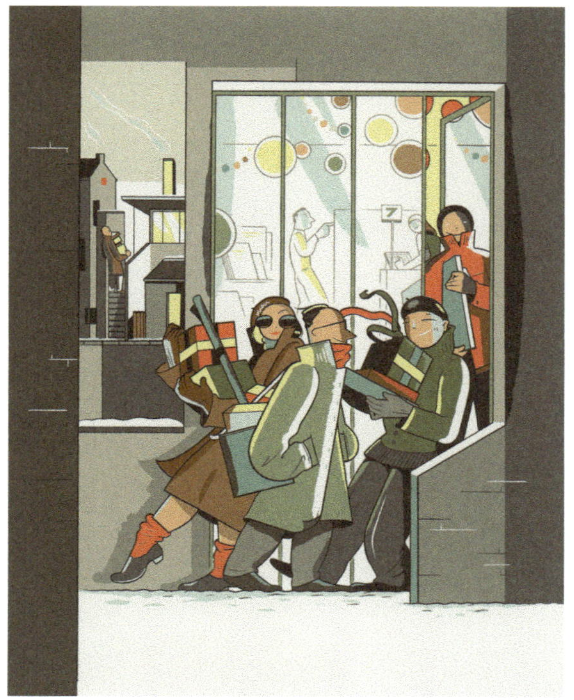

[07]

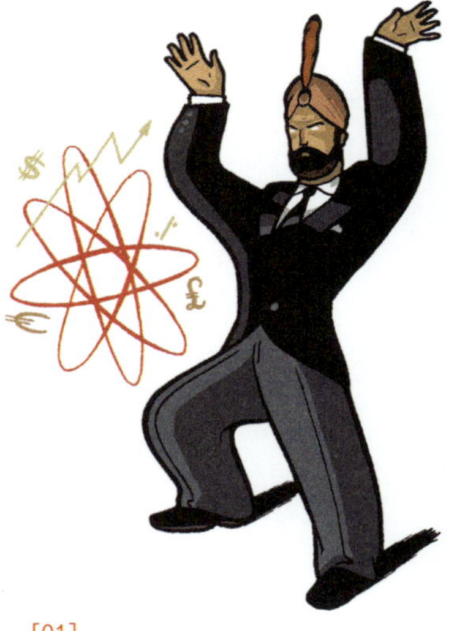

[01]

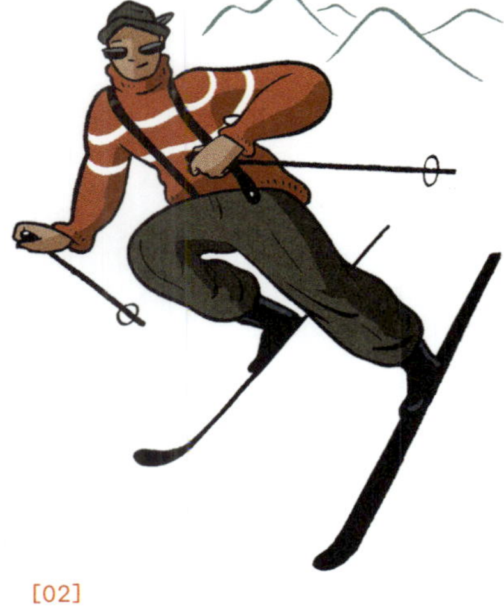

[02]

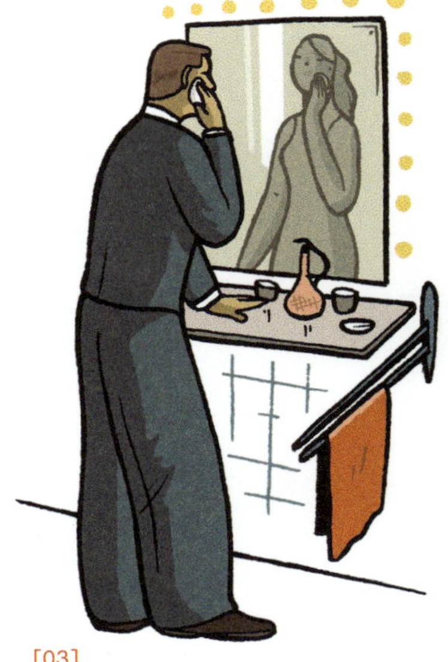

[03]

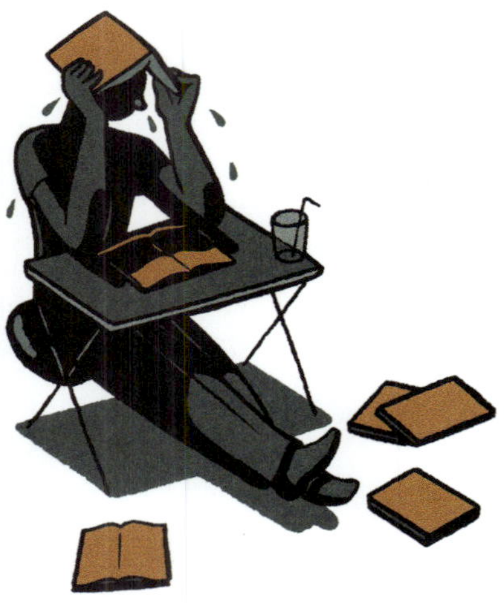

[04]

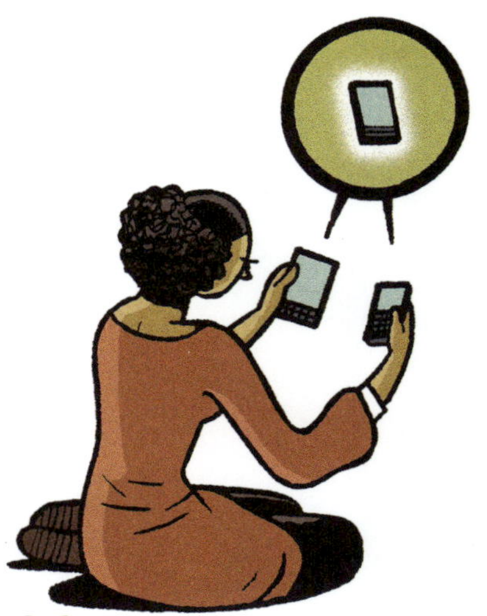

[05]

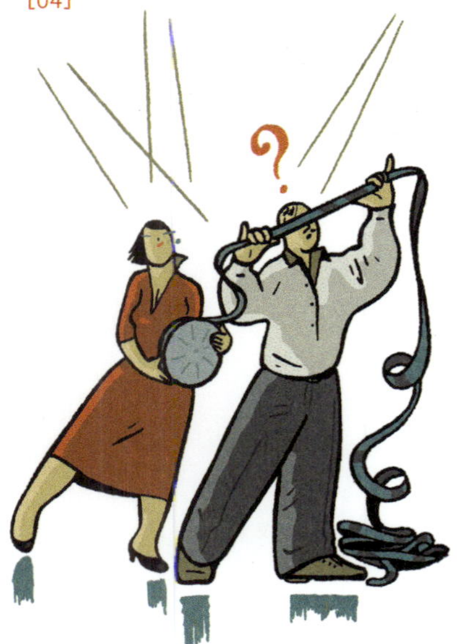

[06]

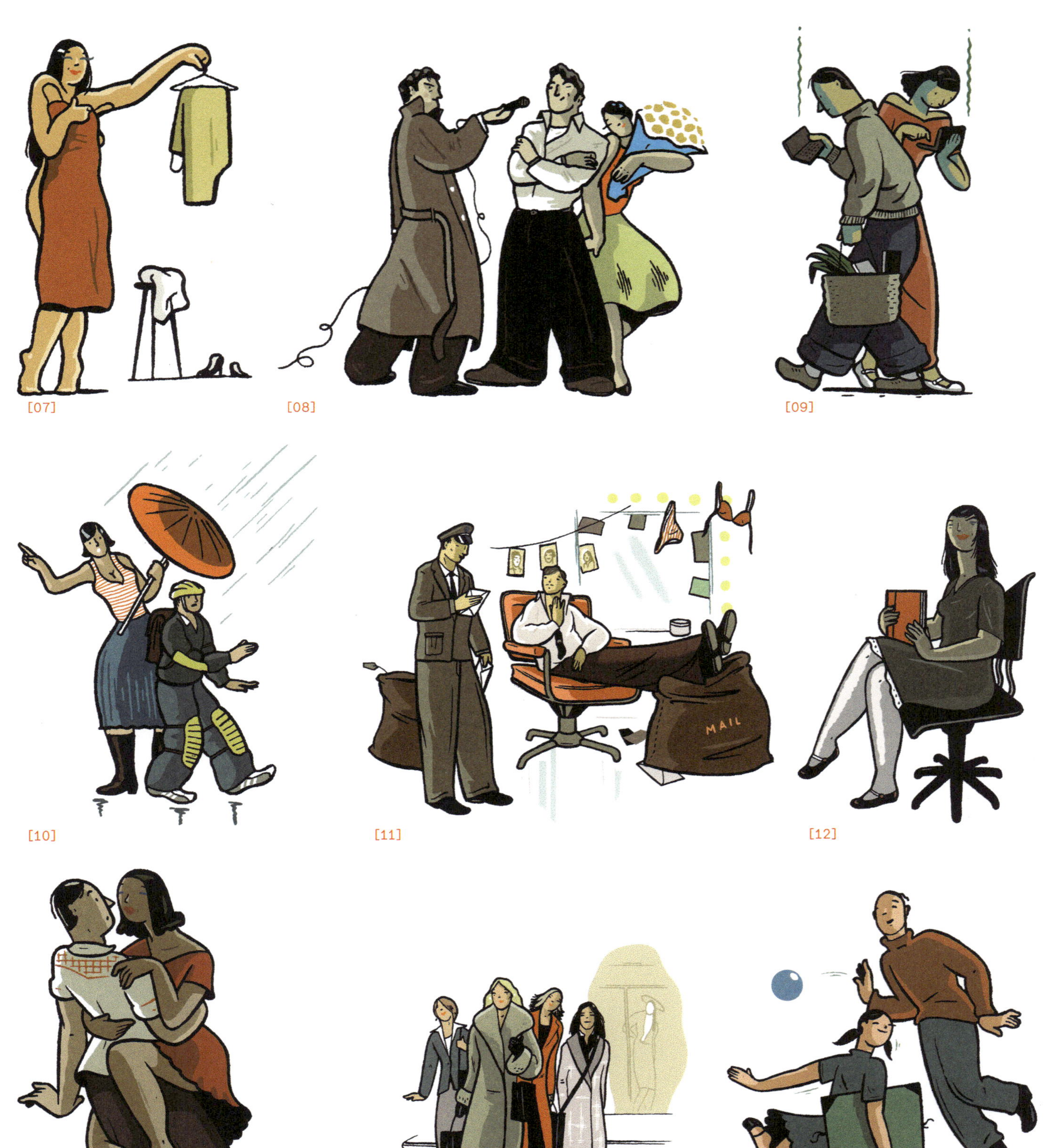
[07]
[08]
[09]
[10]
[11]
MAIL
[12]
[13]
[14]
[15]

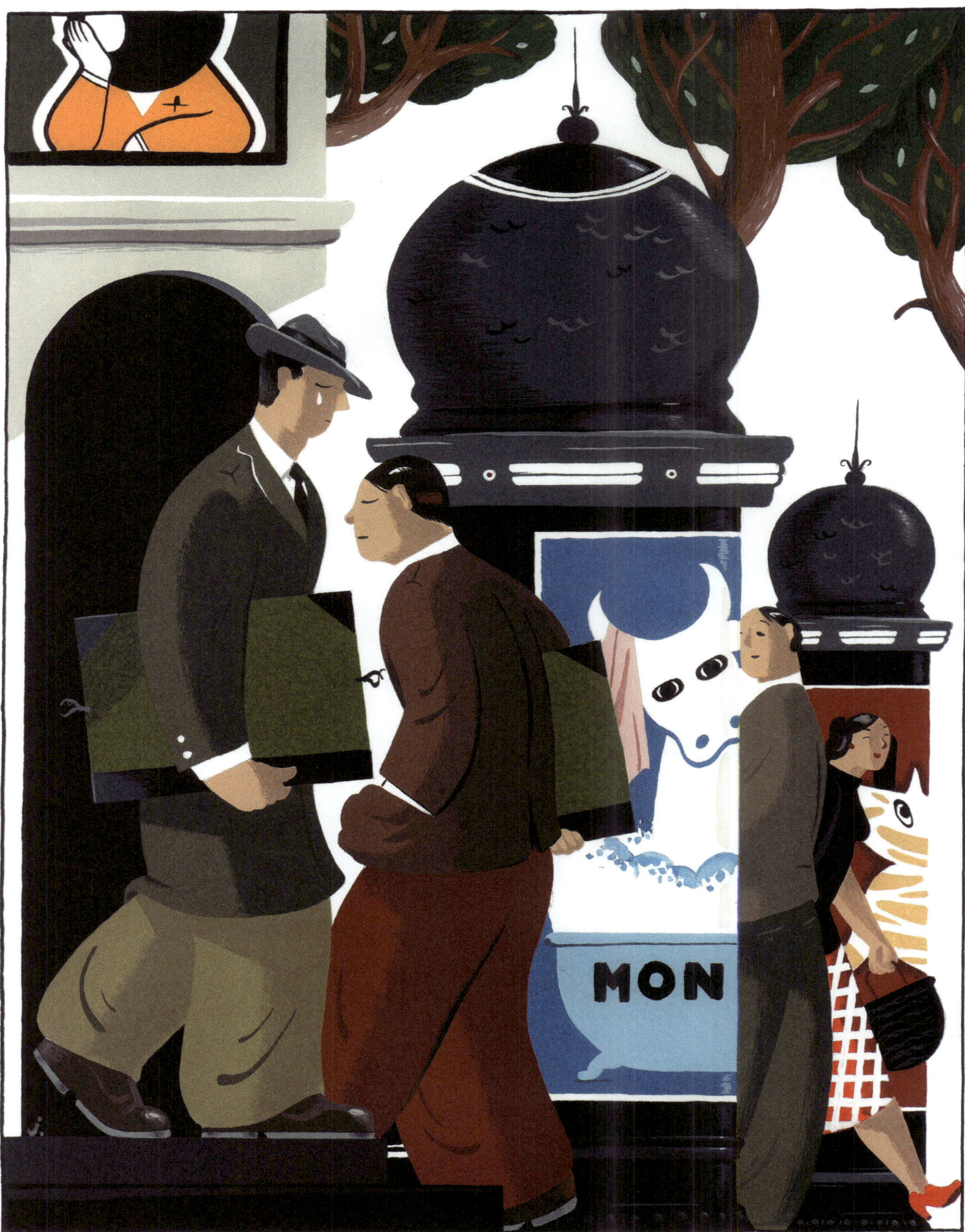

[01]

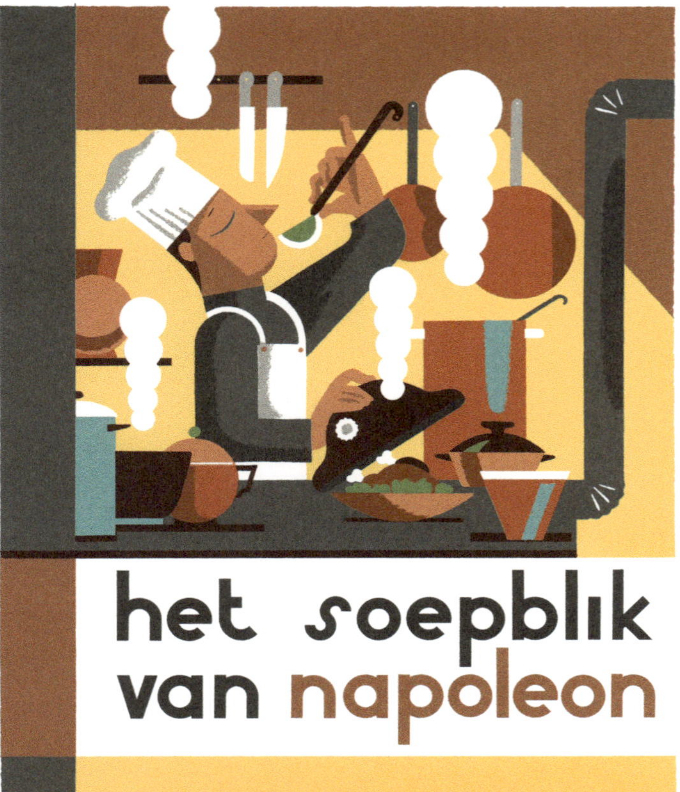

[02]

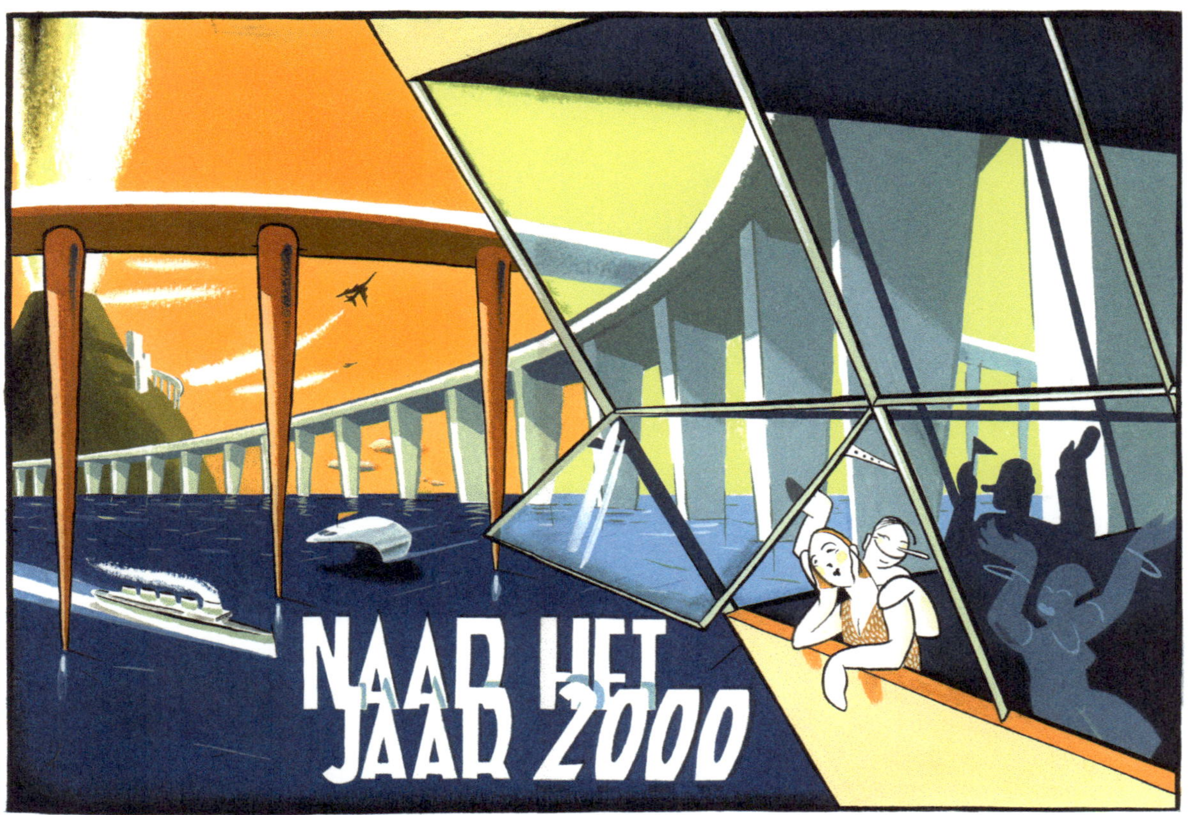

[03]

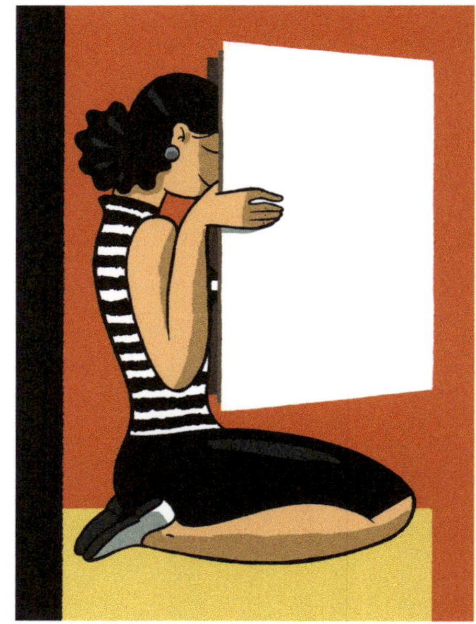

[01]

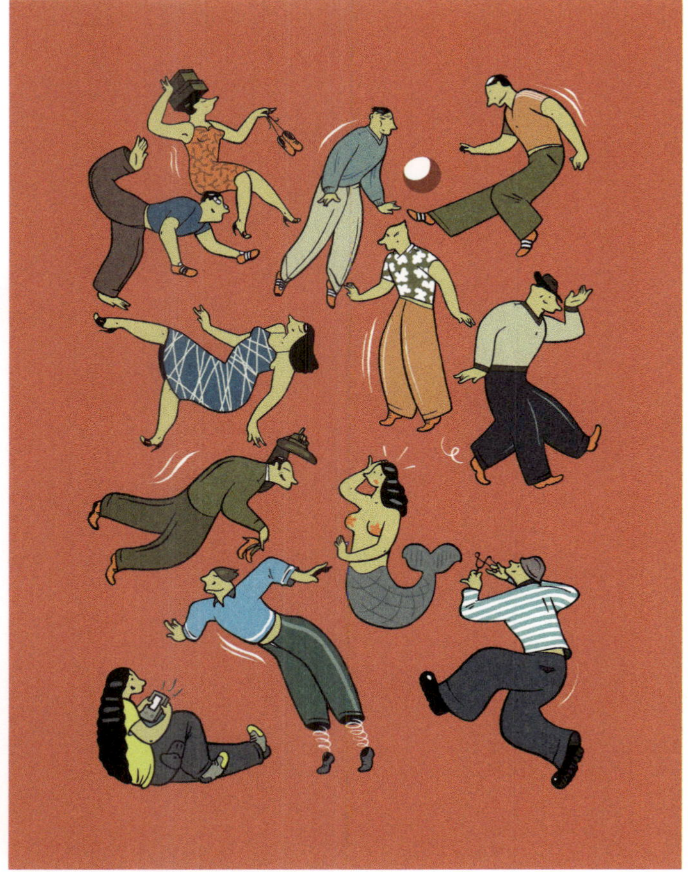

[02]

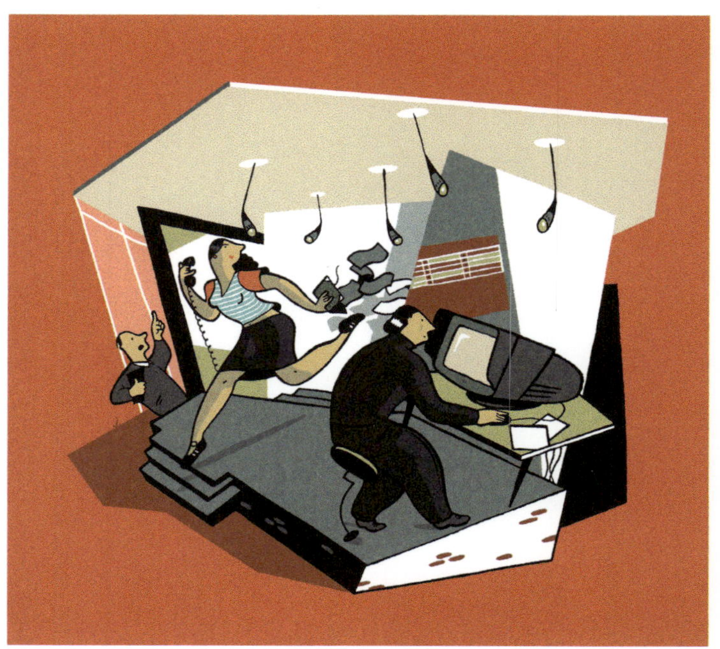

[03]

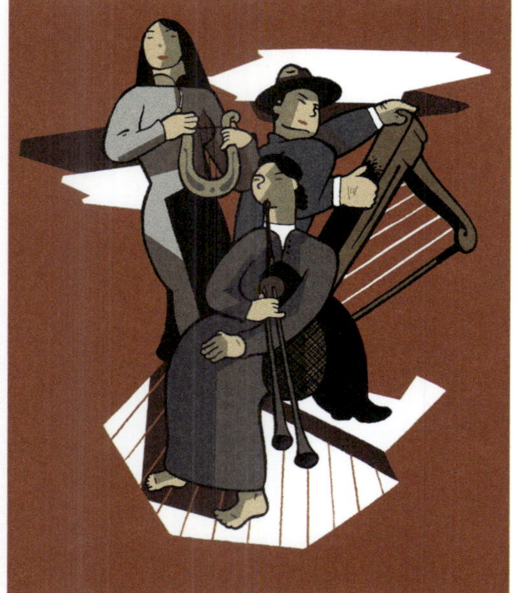

[04]

[05]

HOOPTYRIDES

[06]

NIHIL OPSTAT, IMPRIMATUR
goed gedrukt, is half gewonnen
goff

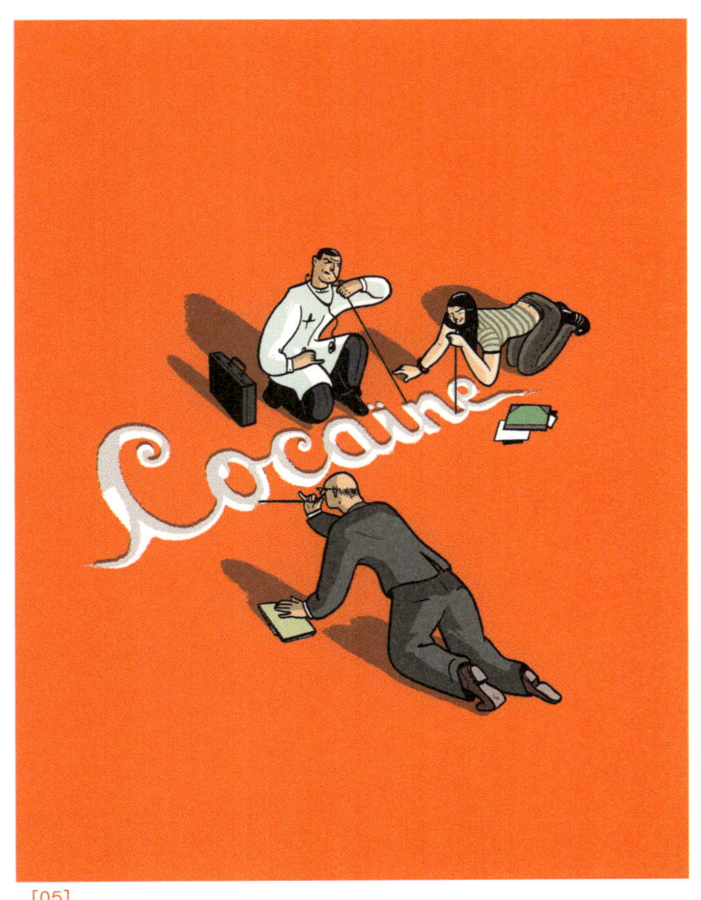

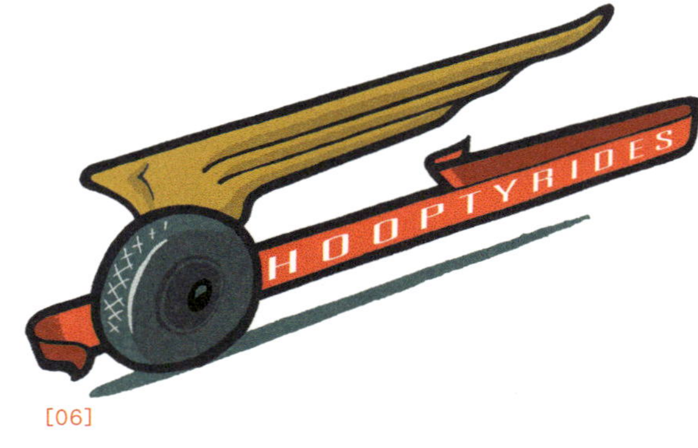

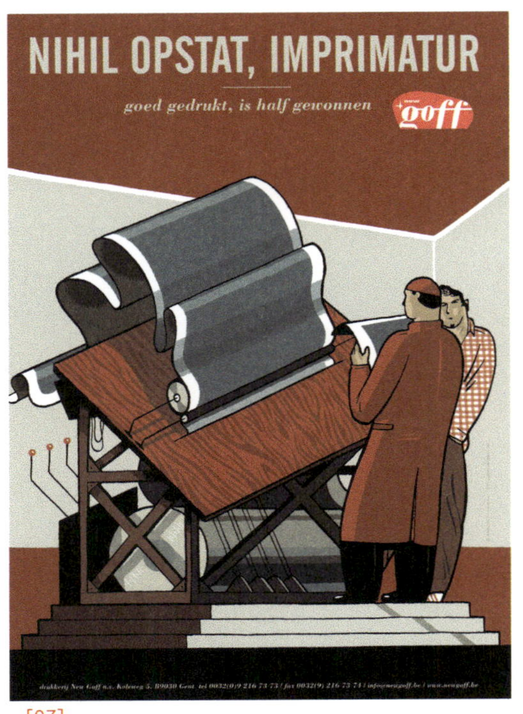

[07]

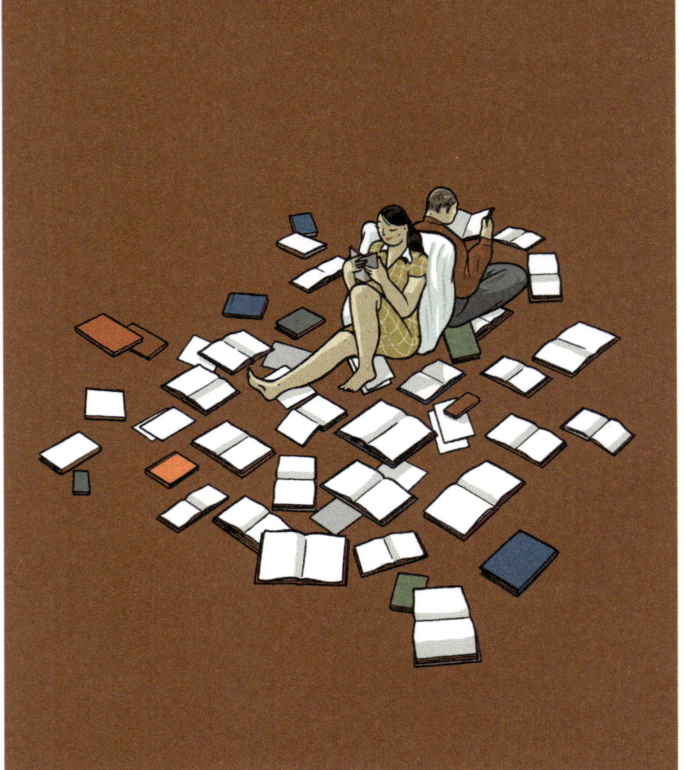

[08]

[01] **Circus Acts**
Circuscentrum
* 2009

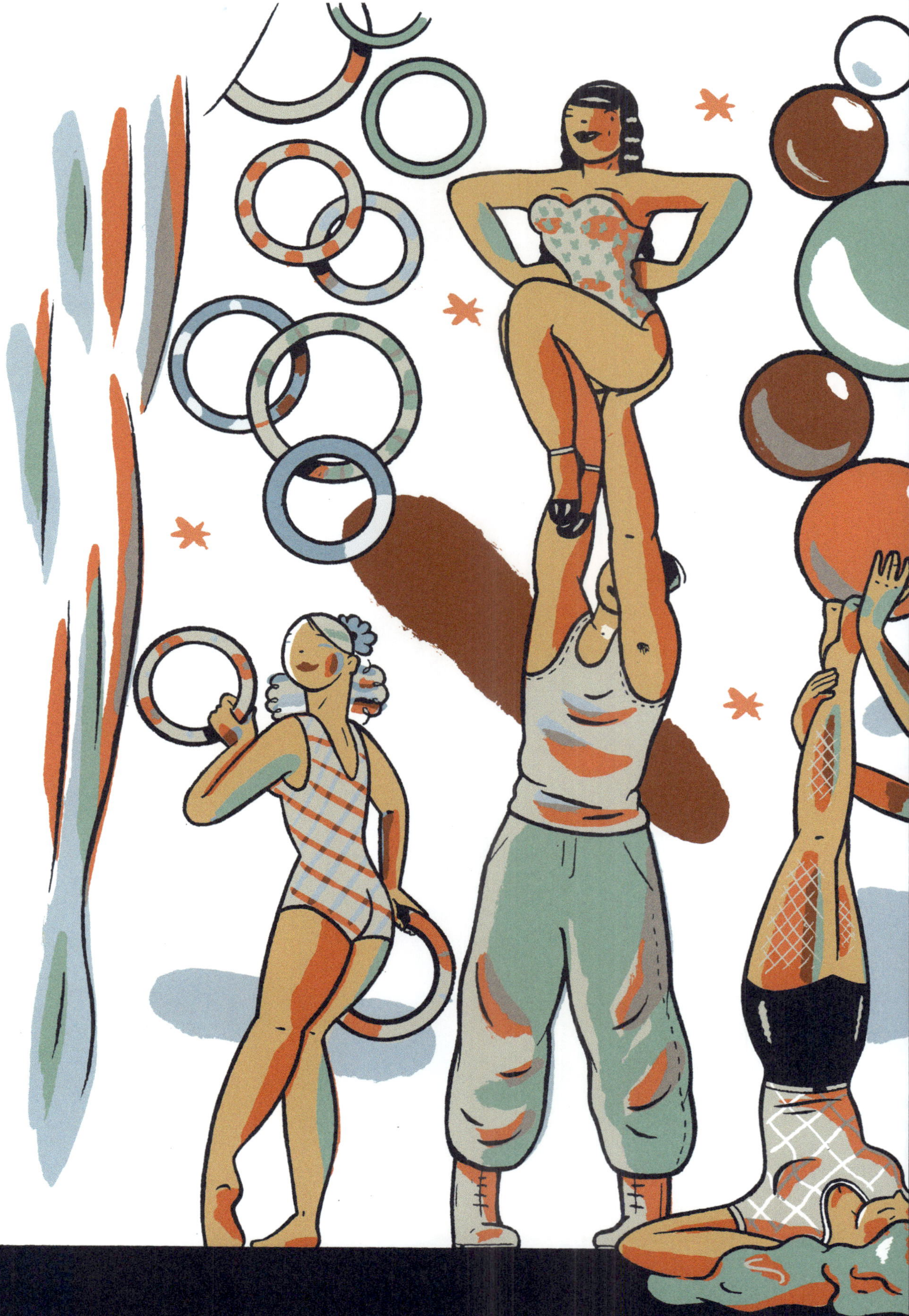

[01]

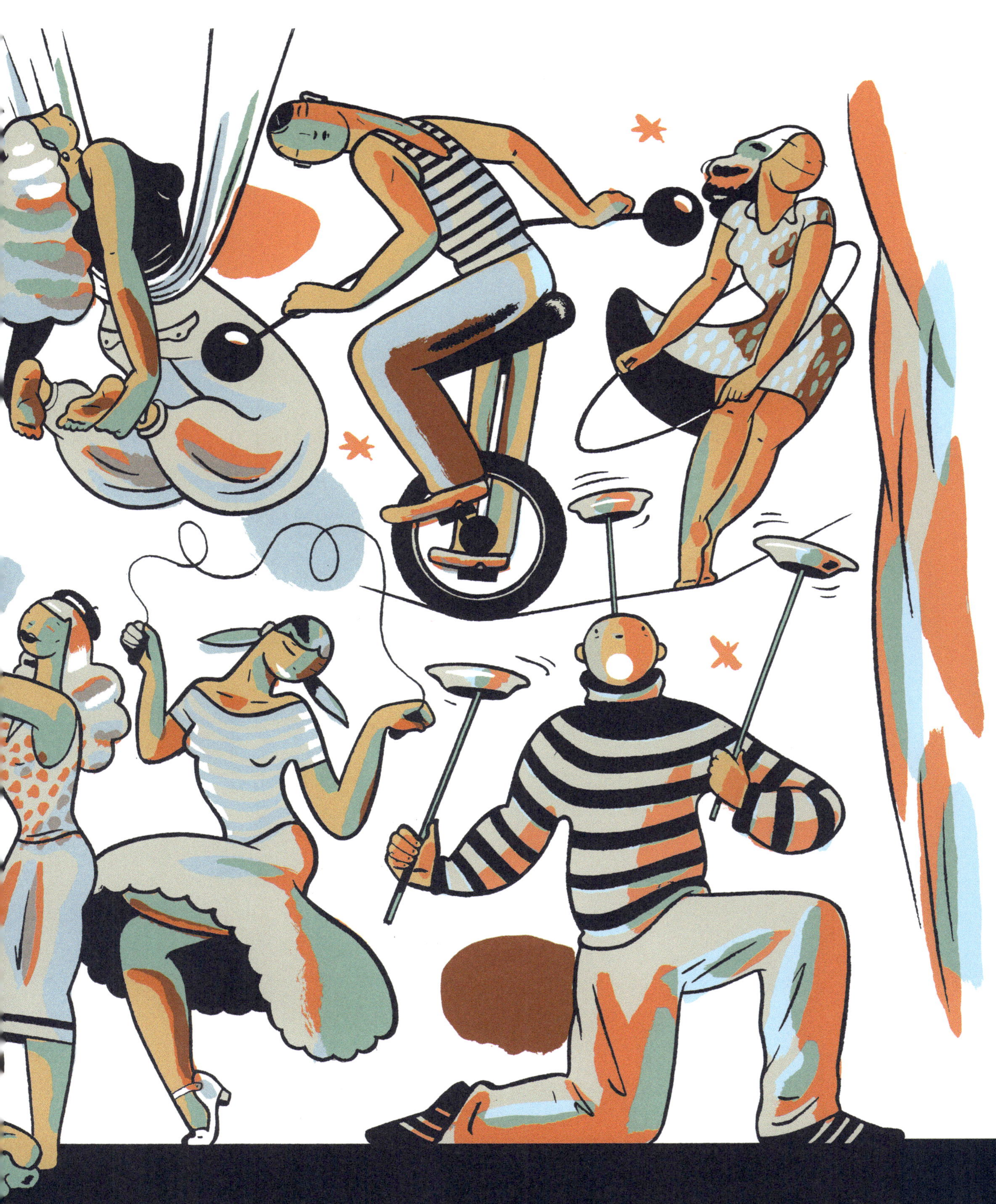

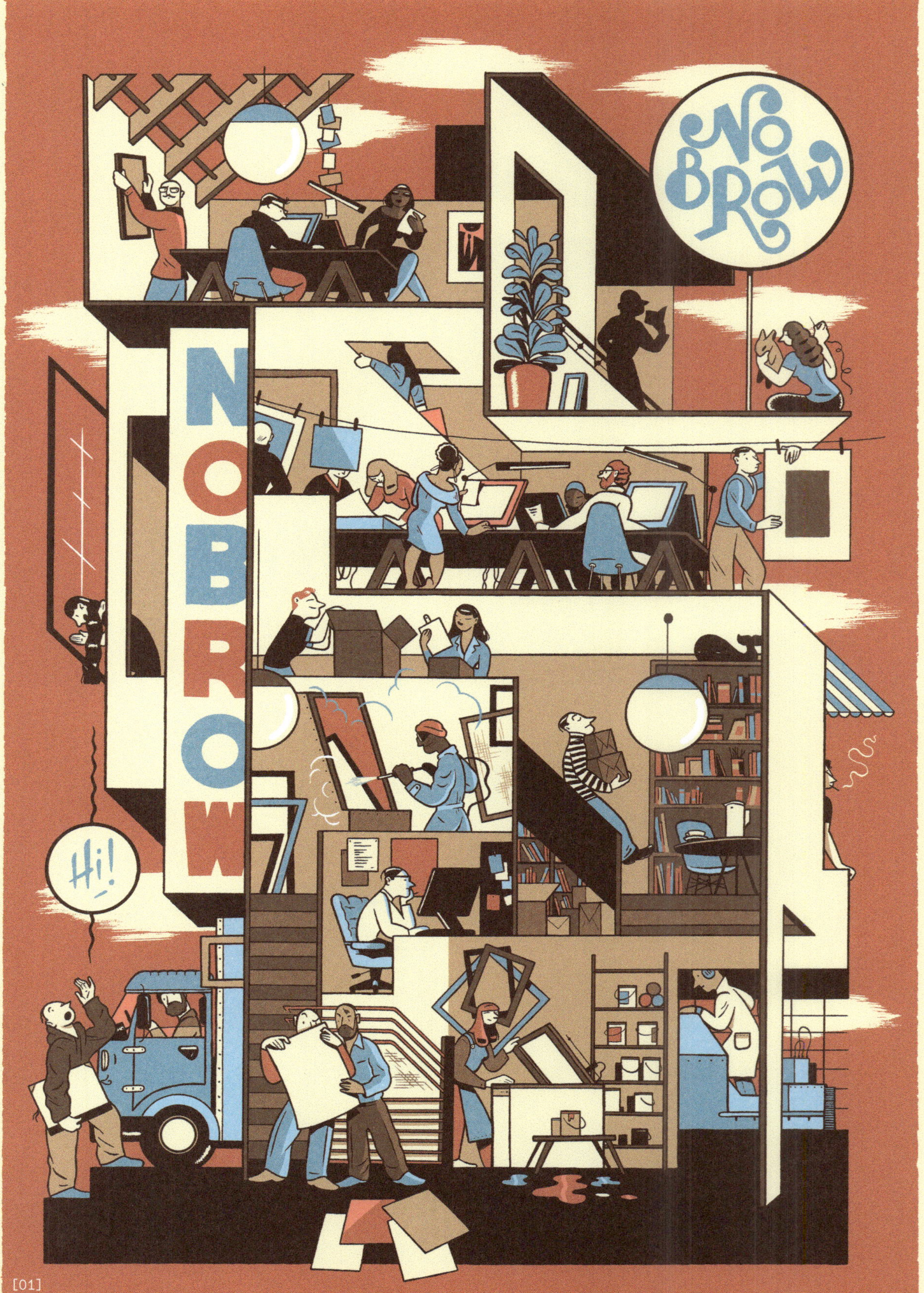

NO BROW
NOBROW
Hi!

SAMPLER
Drawn & Quarterly
SPRING 2003

[02]

MEULE
SLEE
KOERSE
10 DEC
gent
Print&co

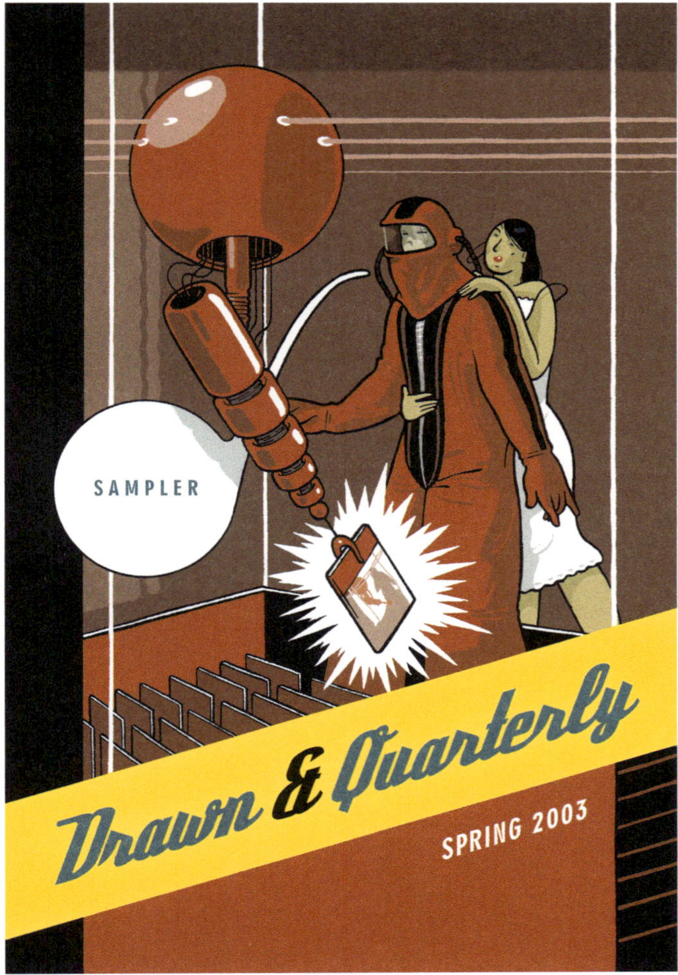

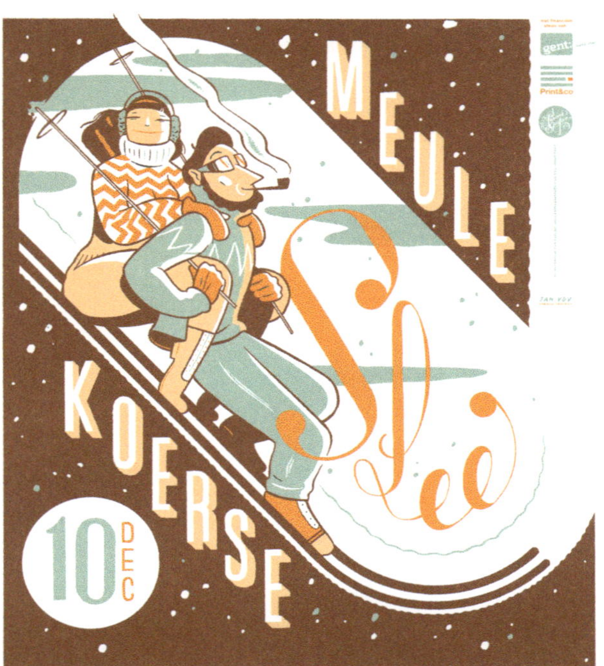

[03]

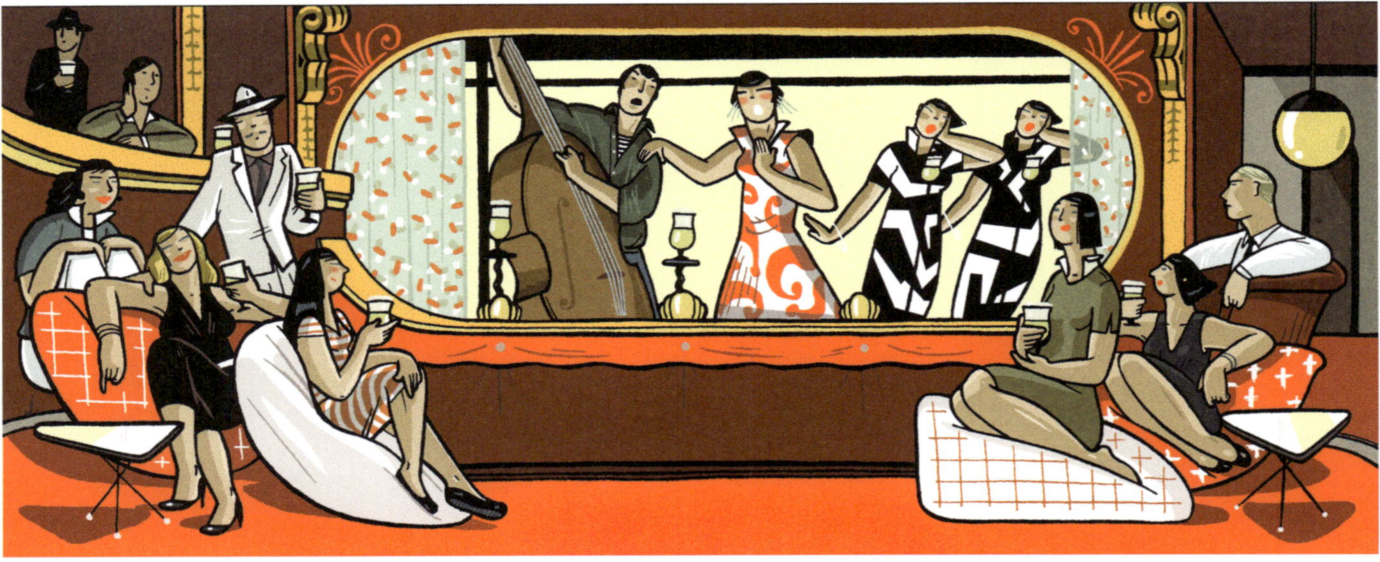

[04]

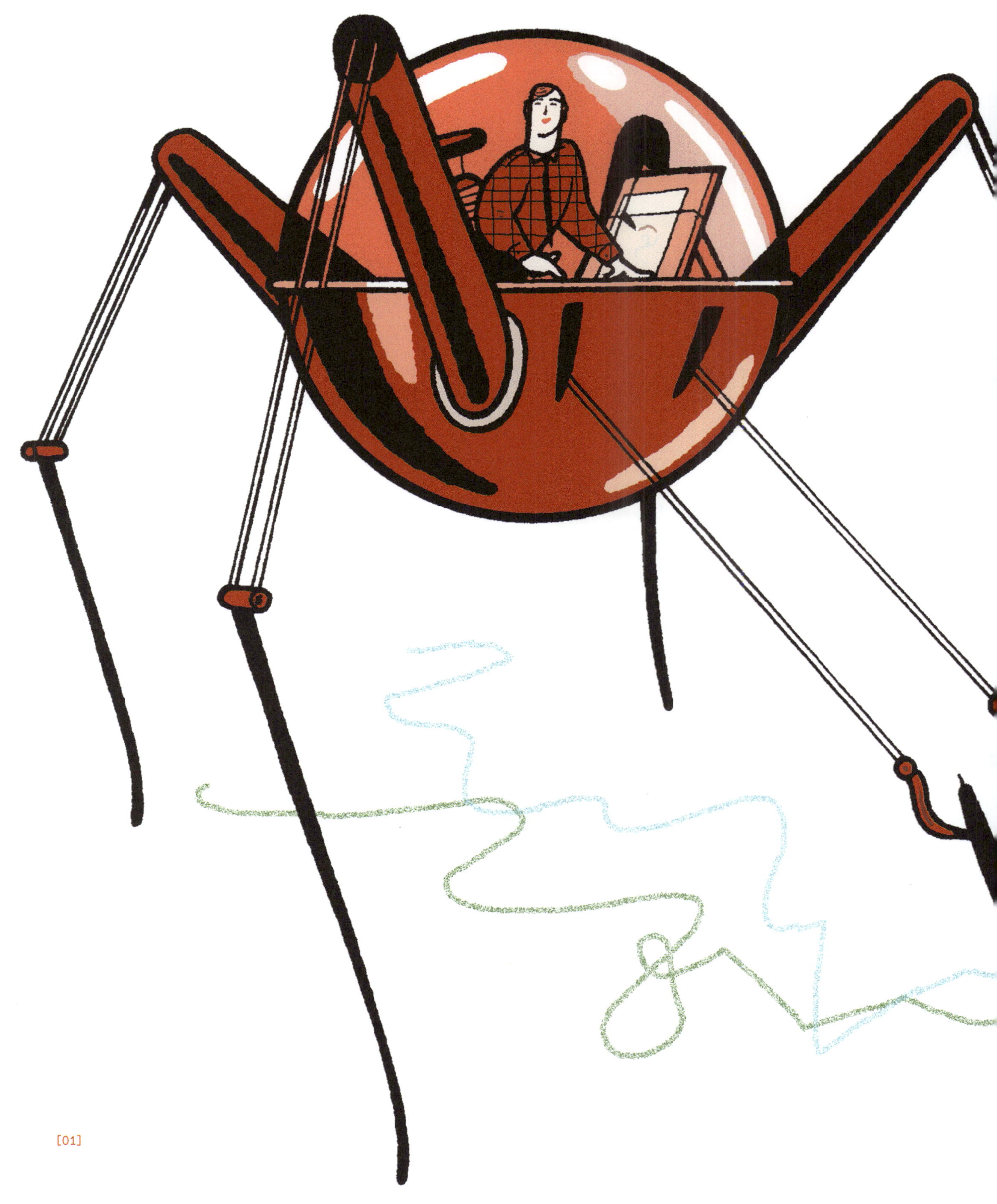

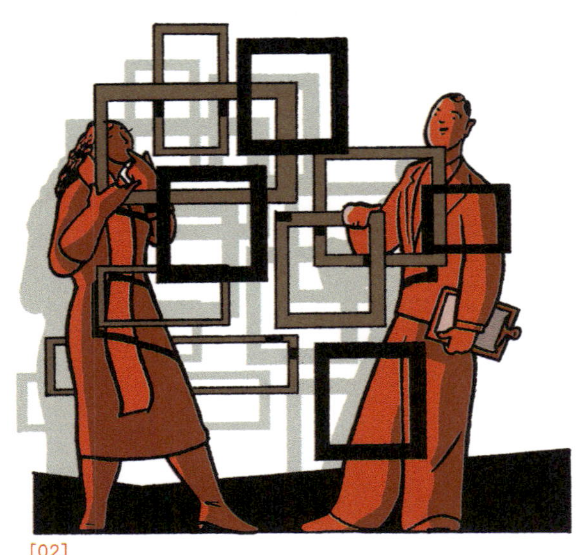
[02]

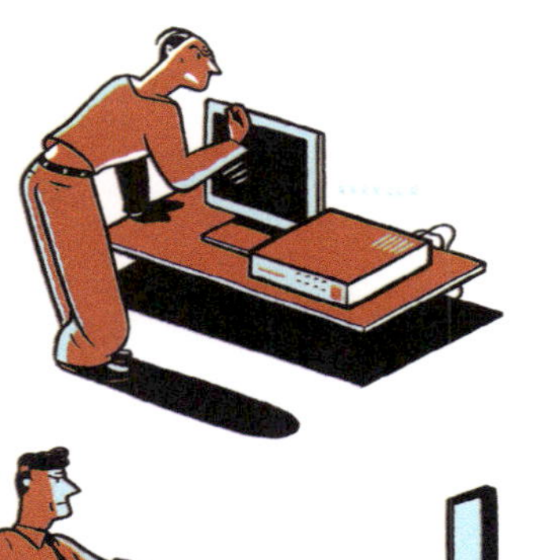
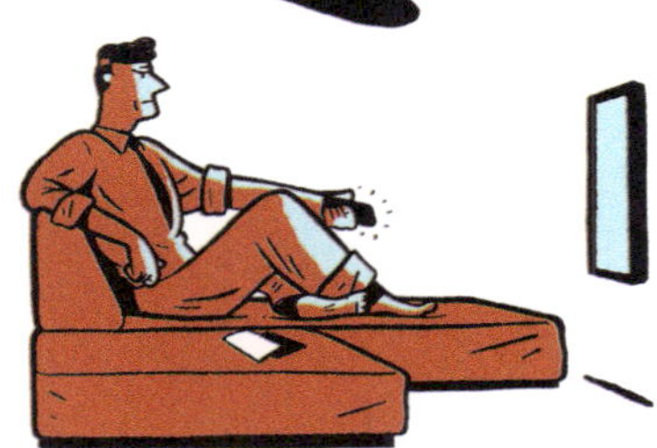
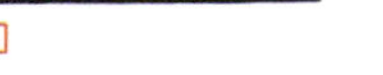

[03]

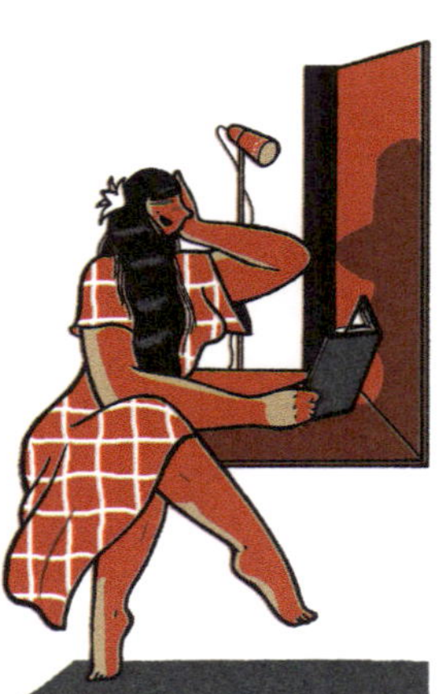

[04]

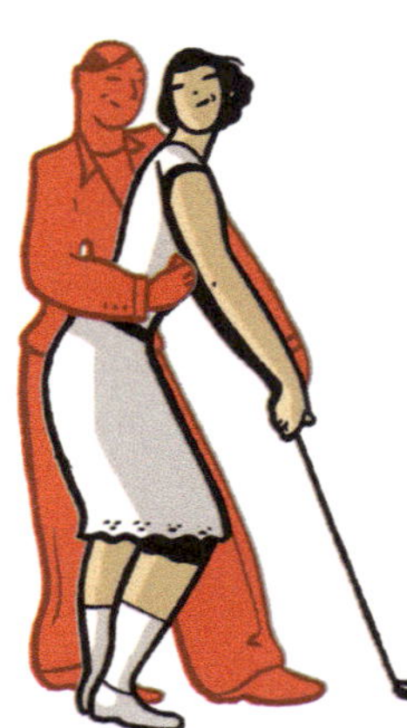

[05]

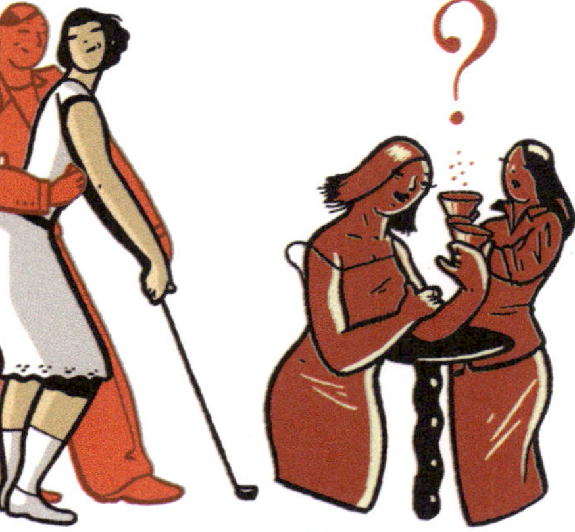

[06]

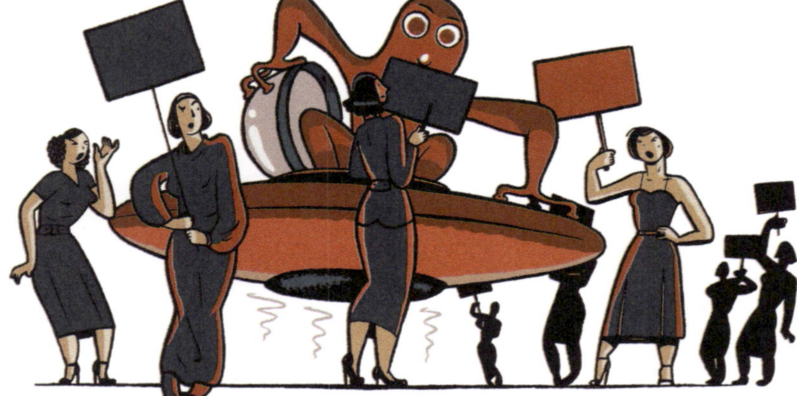

[07]

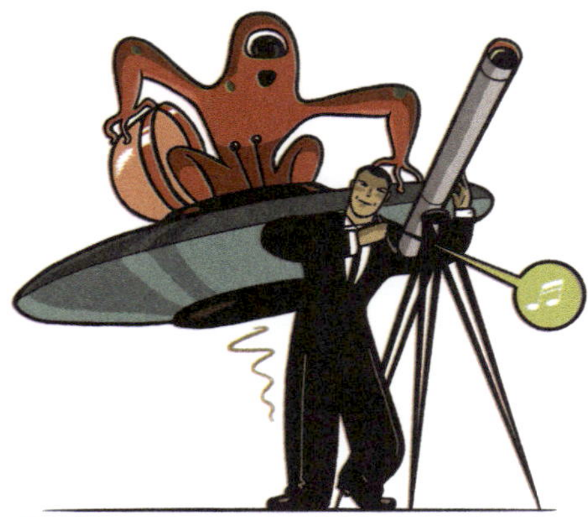

[08]

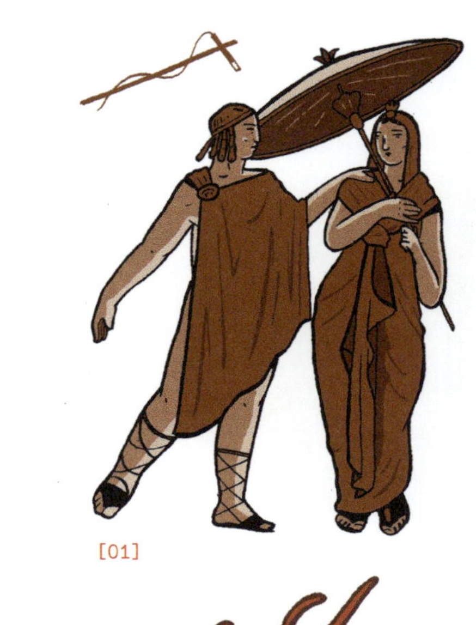

[01]

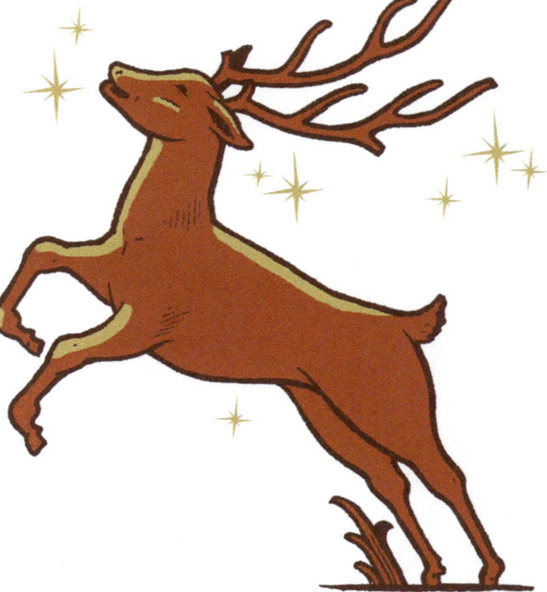

[02]

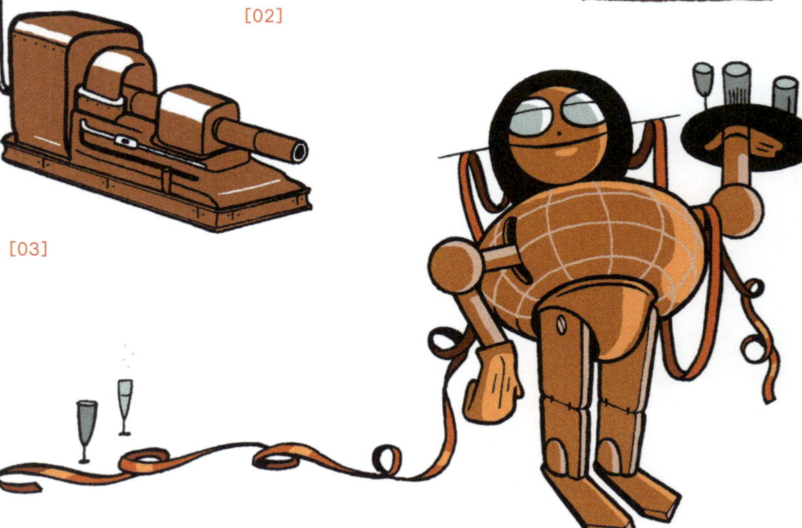

[03]

[04]

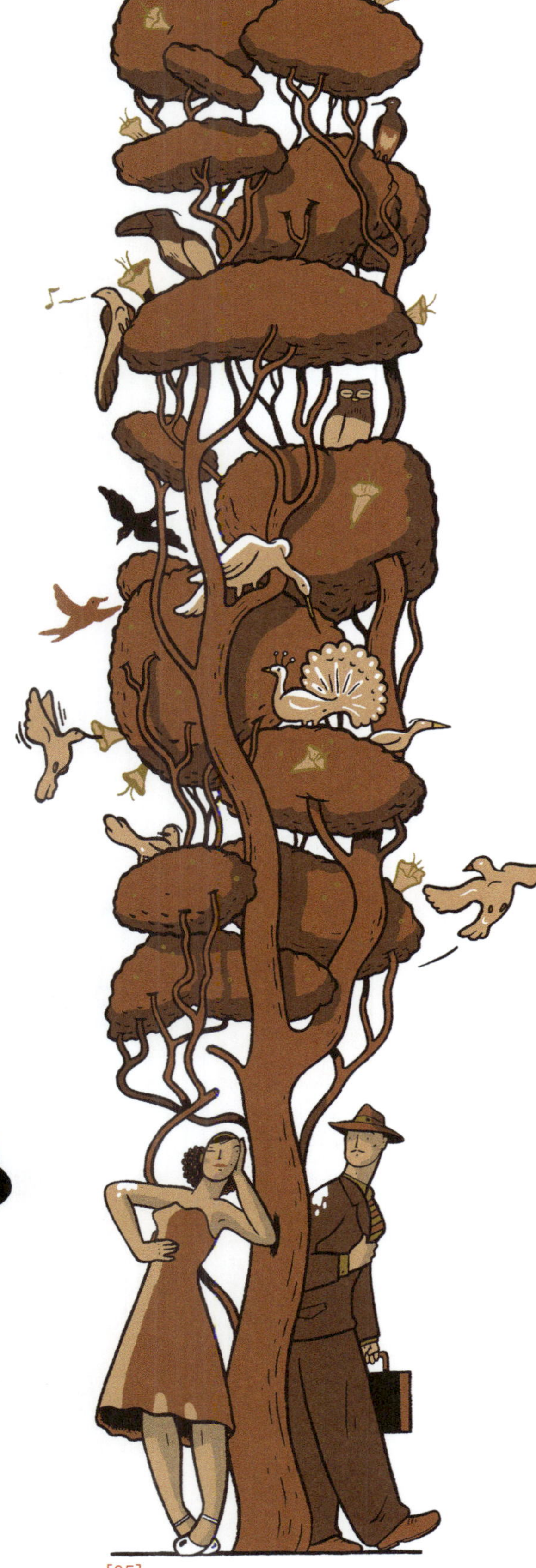

[05]

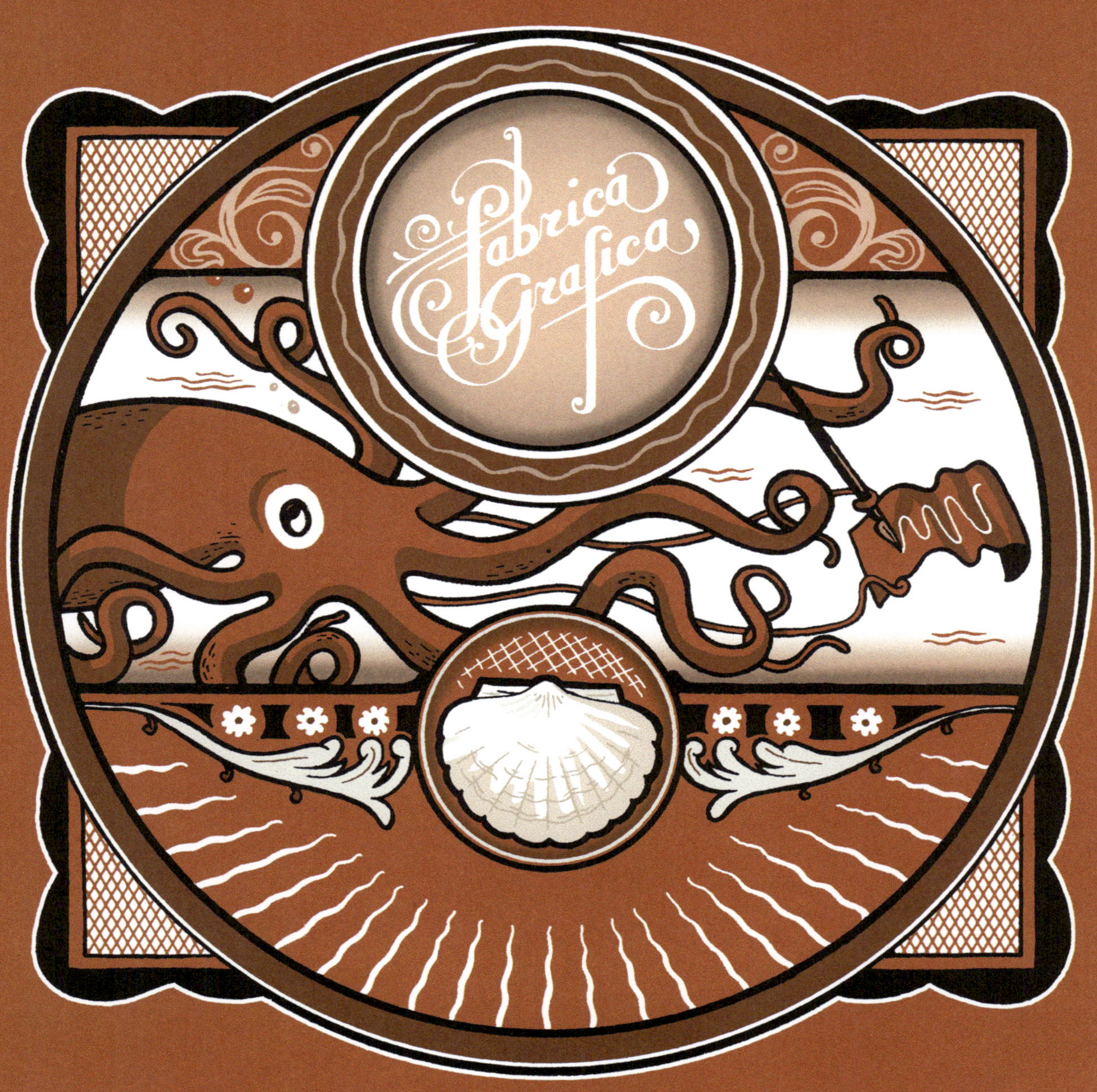
Fabrica Grafica

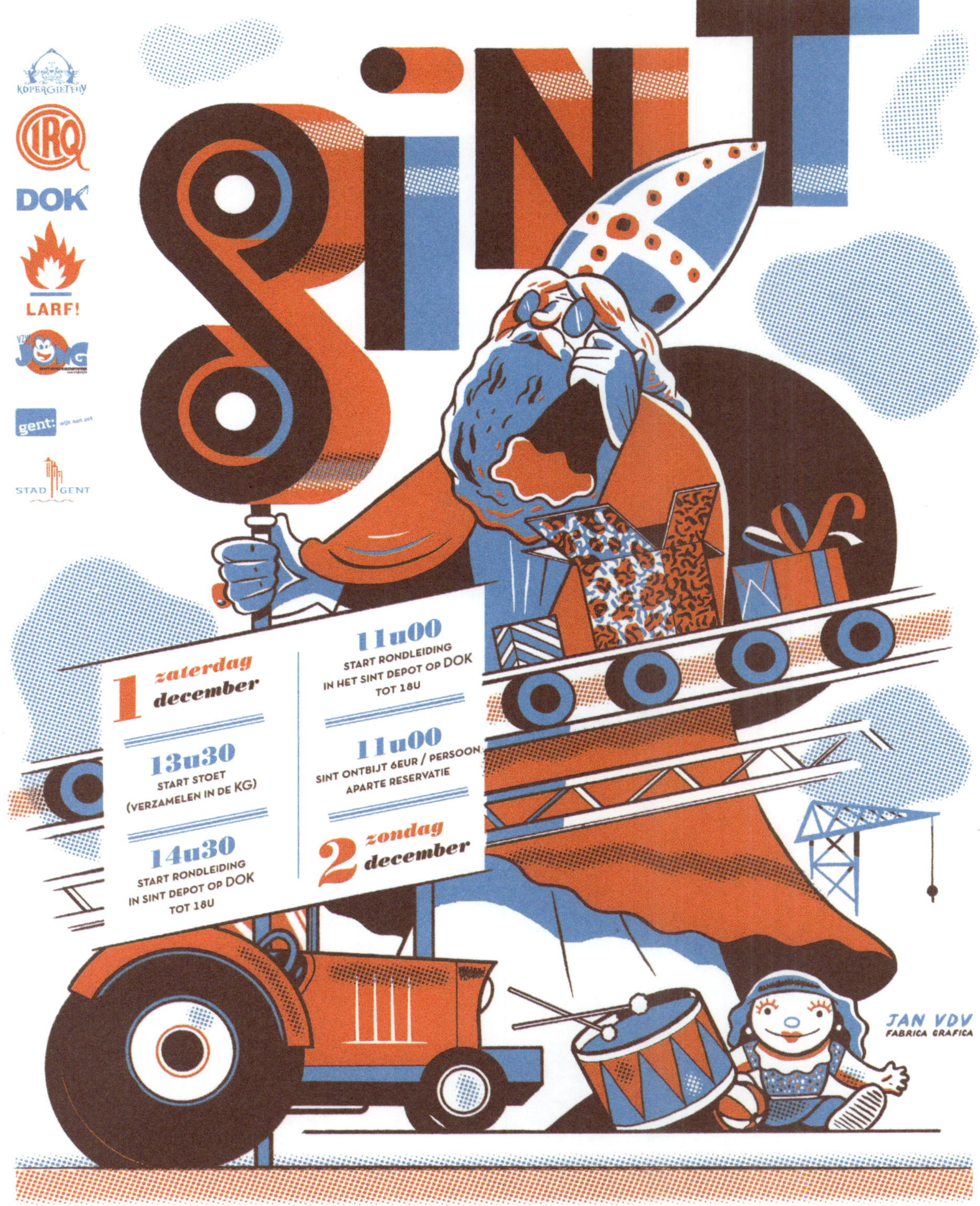

DE FABRIEK VAN DE
SINT
KOPERGIETERY
CIRQ
DOK
LARF!
JONG
gent:
STAD GENT
1 zaterdag december
13u30
START STOET
(VERZAMELEN IN DE KG)
14u30
START RONDLEIDING
IN SINT DEPOT OP DOK
TOT 18U
11u00
START RONDLEIDING
IN HET SINT DEPOT OP DOK
TOT 18U
11u00
SINT ONTBIJT 6EUR / PERSOON
APARTE RESERVATIE
2 zondag december
JAN VDV
FABRICA GRAFICA
RESERVATIES VIA KOPERGIETERY / 09 233 70 00 / INFO@KOPERGIETERY.BE OF VIA CIRQ / SINT@CIRQ.BE
DOK Gent bevindt zich in de Koopvaardijlaan (zijlaan Afrikalaan). zie ook www.dokgent.be

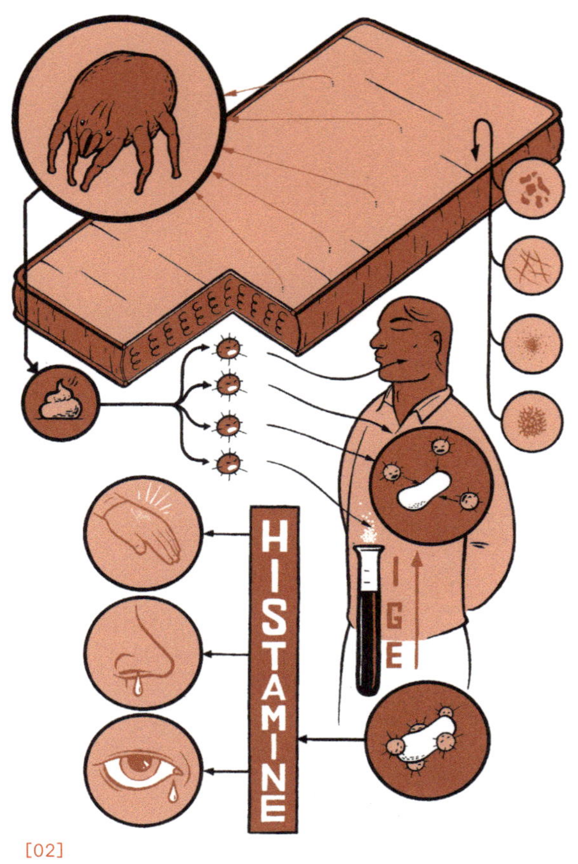

[02]

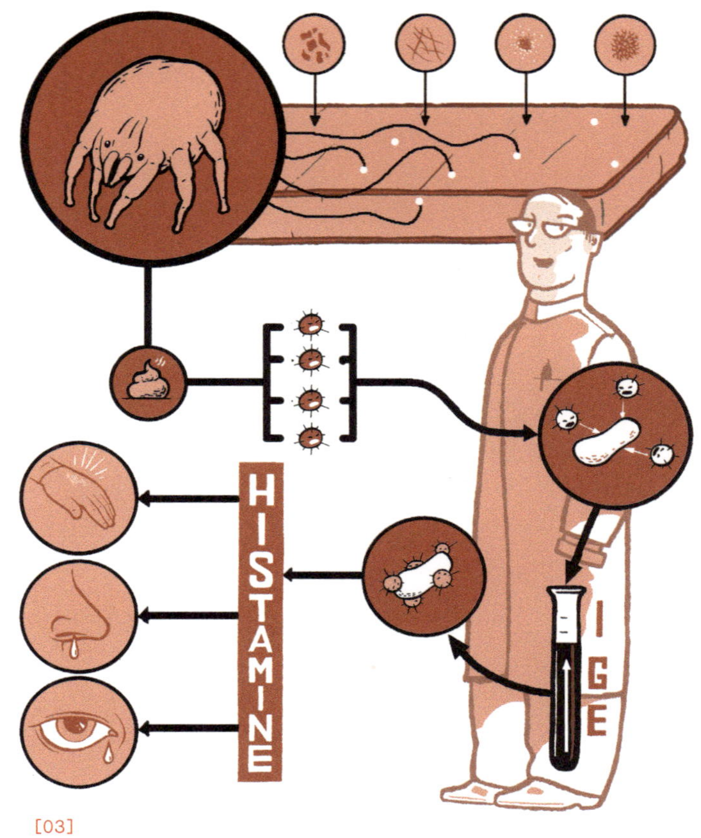

[03]

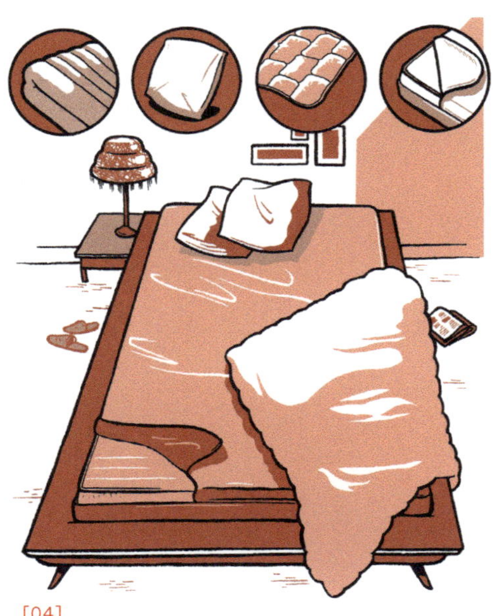

[04]

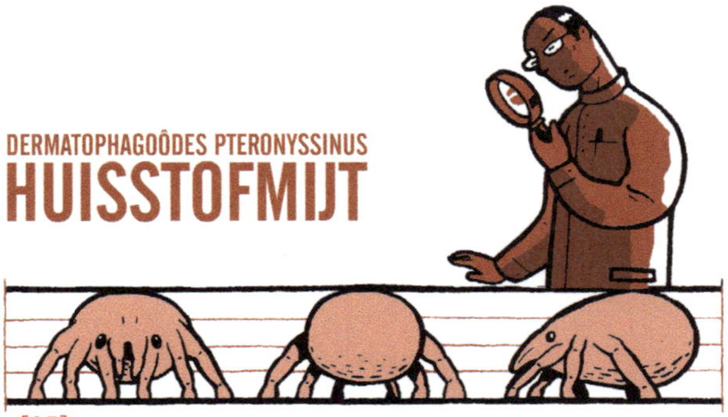

[05]

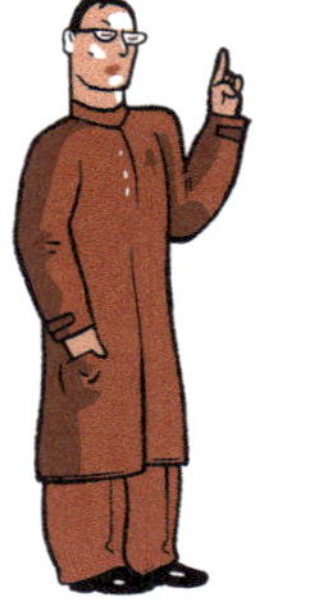

[06]

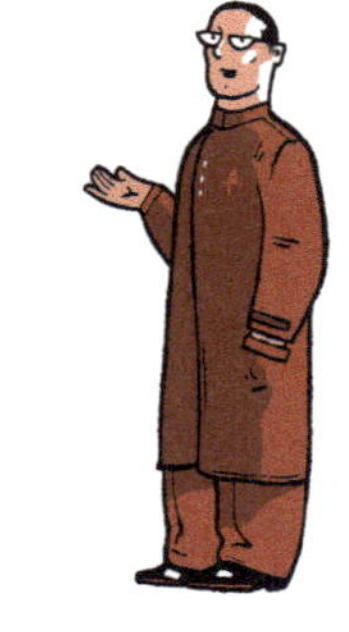

[07]

[01] **Sint Poster**
      Cirq
*   2012

[02] to [07] **Alergic Reactions
      Explained**
      Kwadrant Studio
*   2008

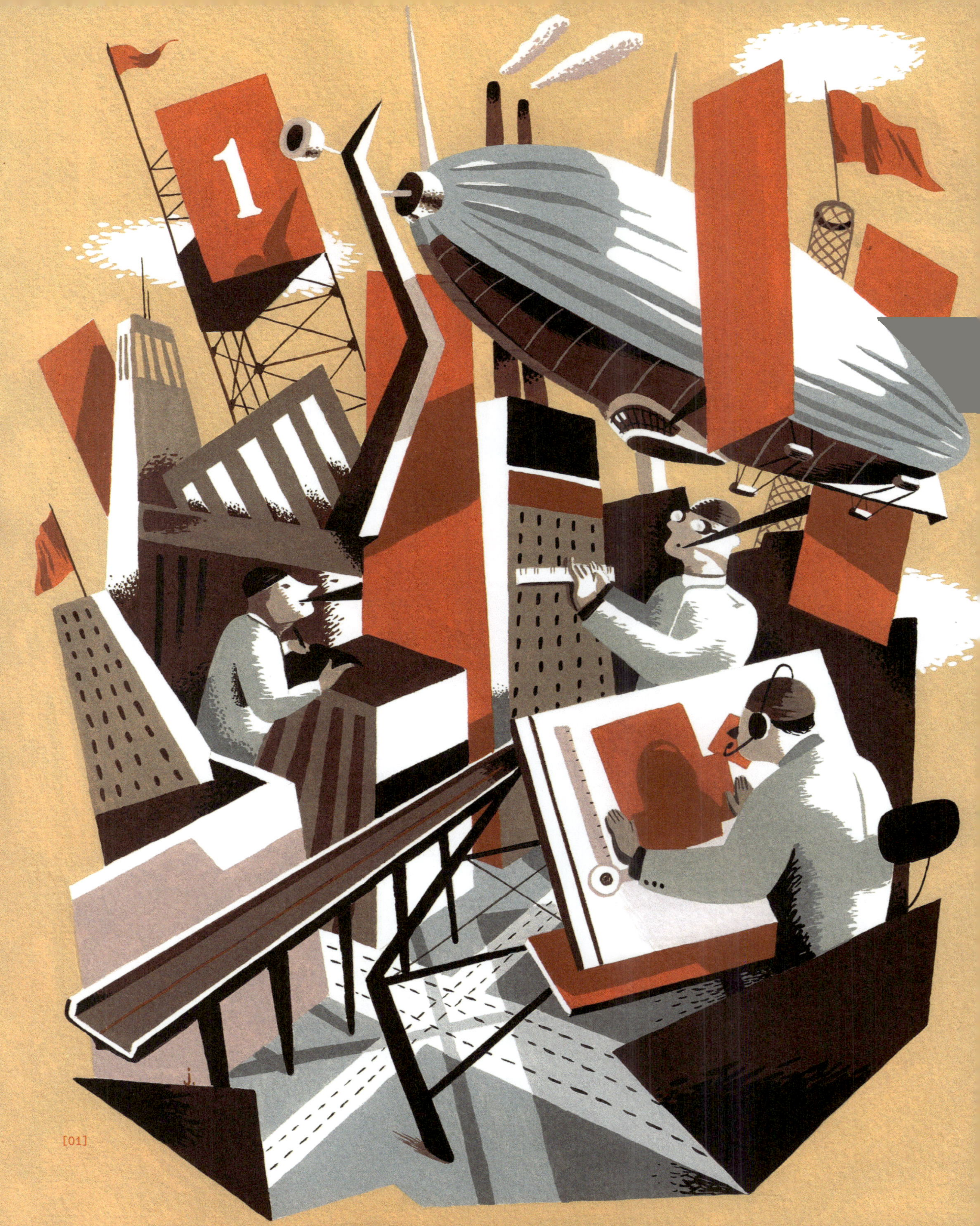
1

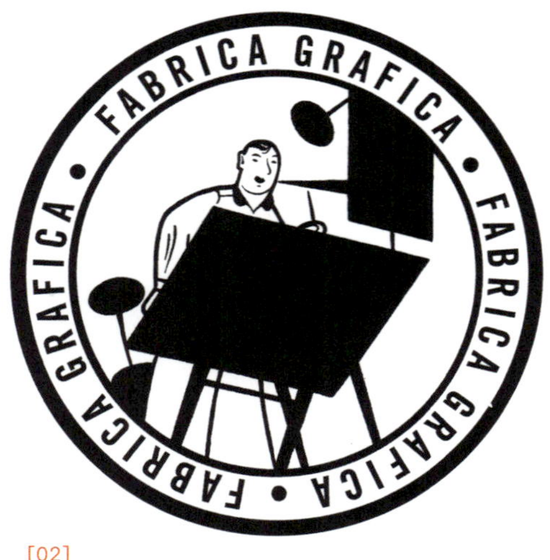

[02]

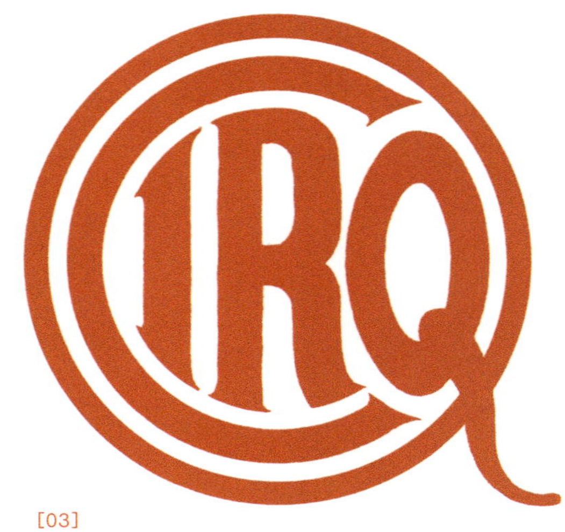

[03]

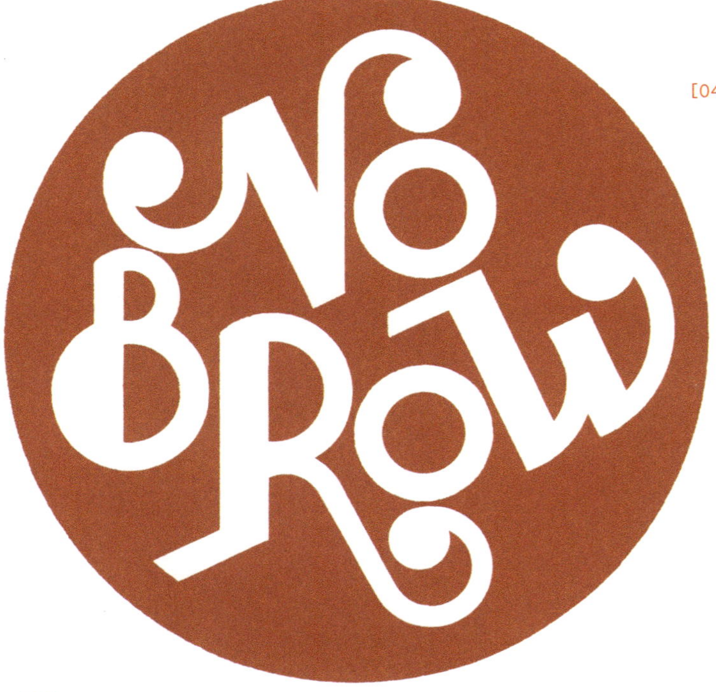

[05]

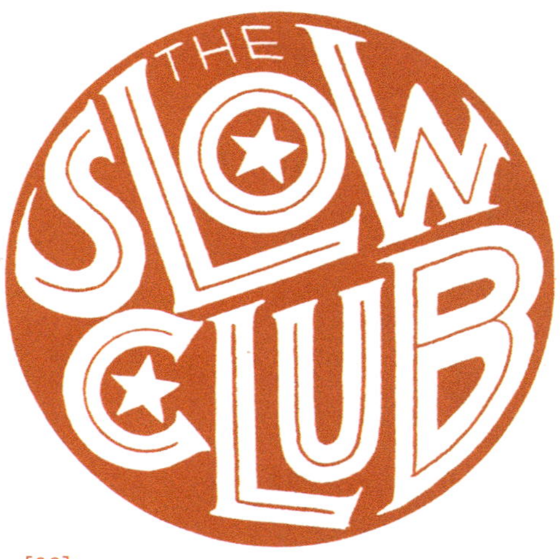

[06]

[04]

[01] **The City (gouache)**
Personal Work
2003

[02] **Logo Design Fabrica Grafica**
Personal Work
2003

[03] **Cirq Logo**
Cirq
2006

[04] to [05] **Logo Design NoBrow**
NoBrow
2011

[06] **Logo Design Slow Club**
Slow Club
2006

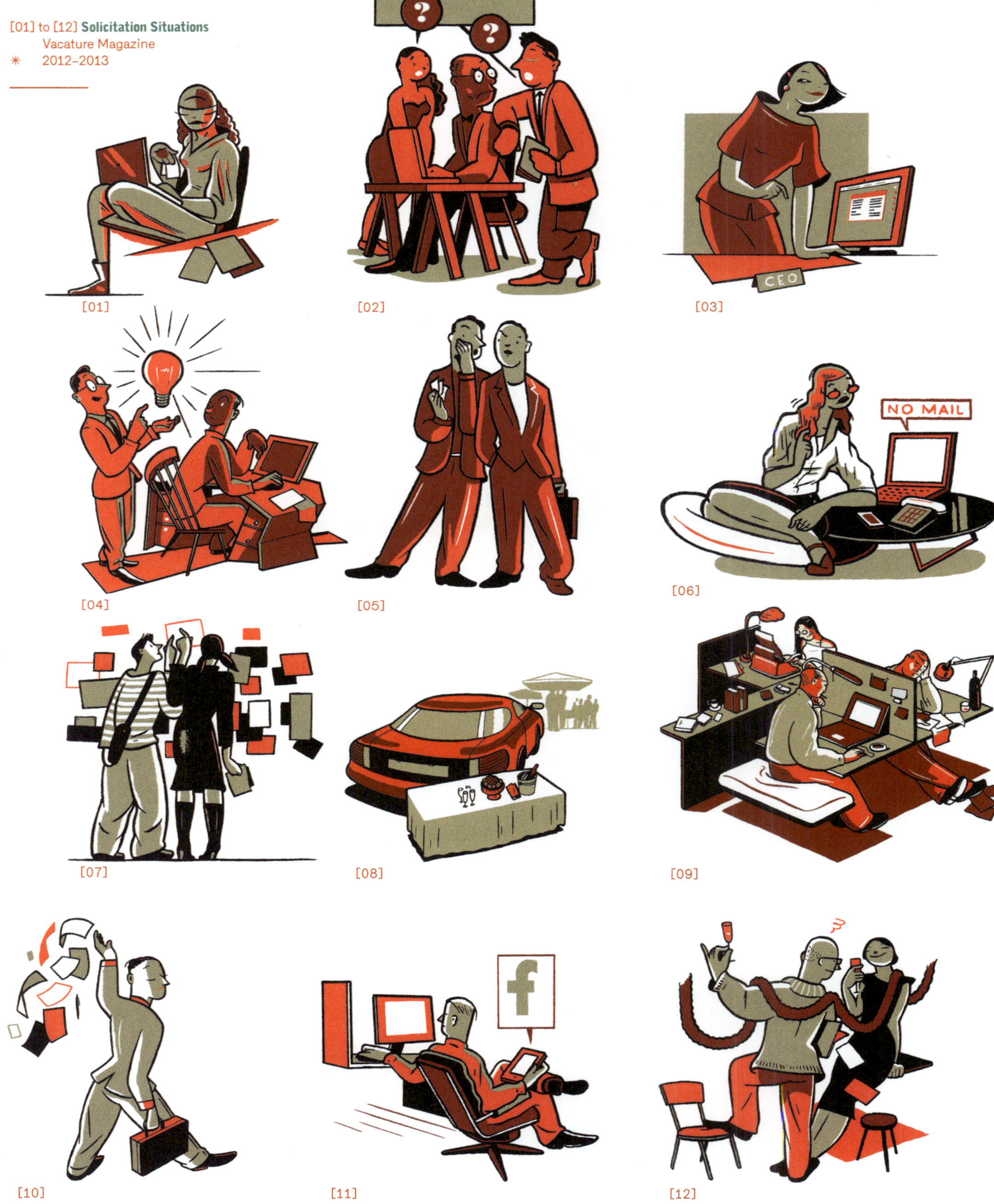

[01] to [12] Solicitation Situations
Vacature Magazine
2012–2013
[01]
[02]
[03]
CEO
[04]
[05]
[06]
NO MAIL
[07]
[08]
[09]
[10]
[11]
f
[12]

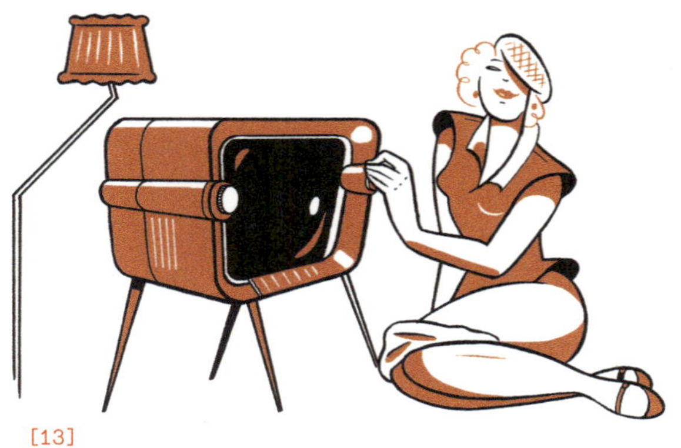

[13]

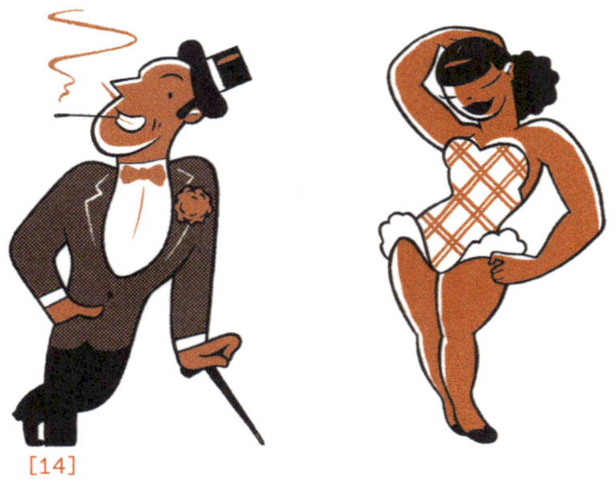

[14]

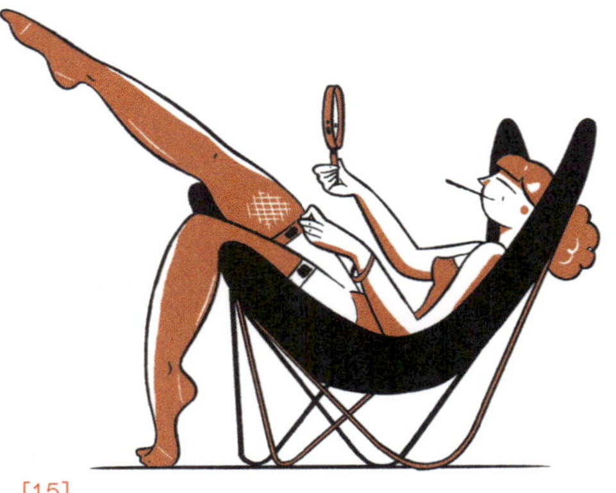

[15]

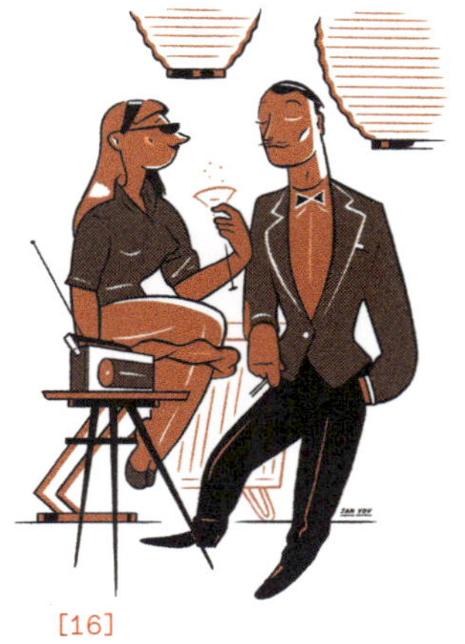

[16]

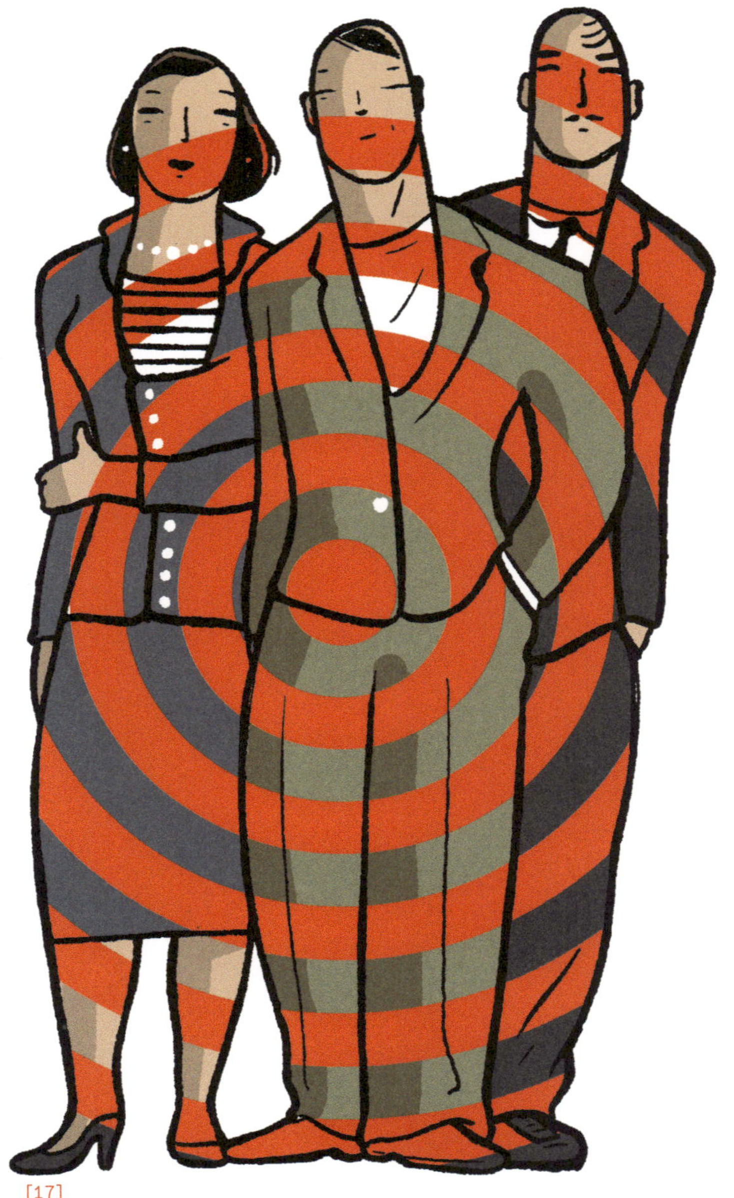

[17]

[13] **Retrovision**

[14] **Mascotte**

[15] **Mighty Legs**

[16] **At the Bar**
Radio Modern
✳ 2012

———

[17] **Bull's Eye**
Vara Magazine
✳ 2006

———

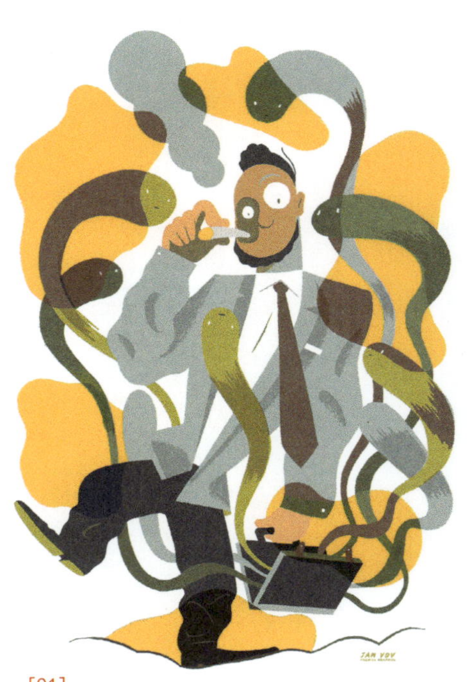

[01]

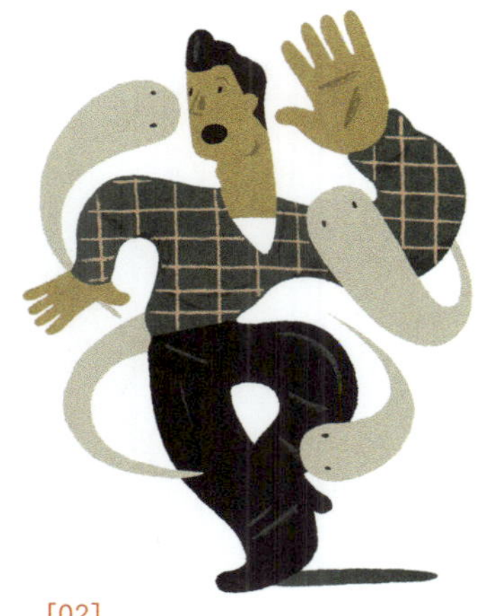

[02]

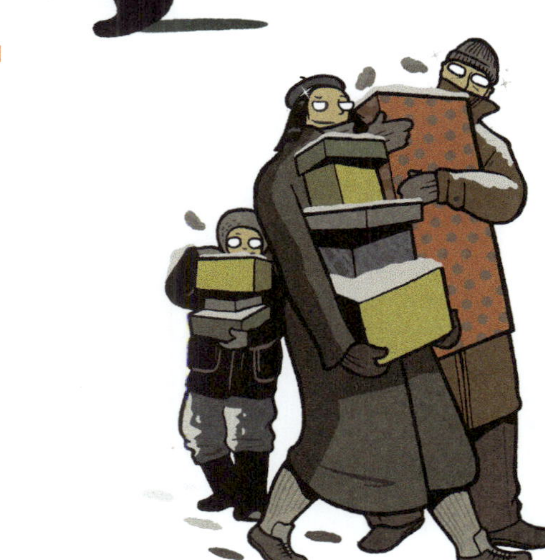

[03]

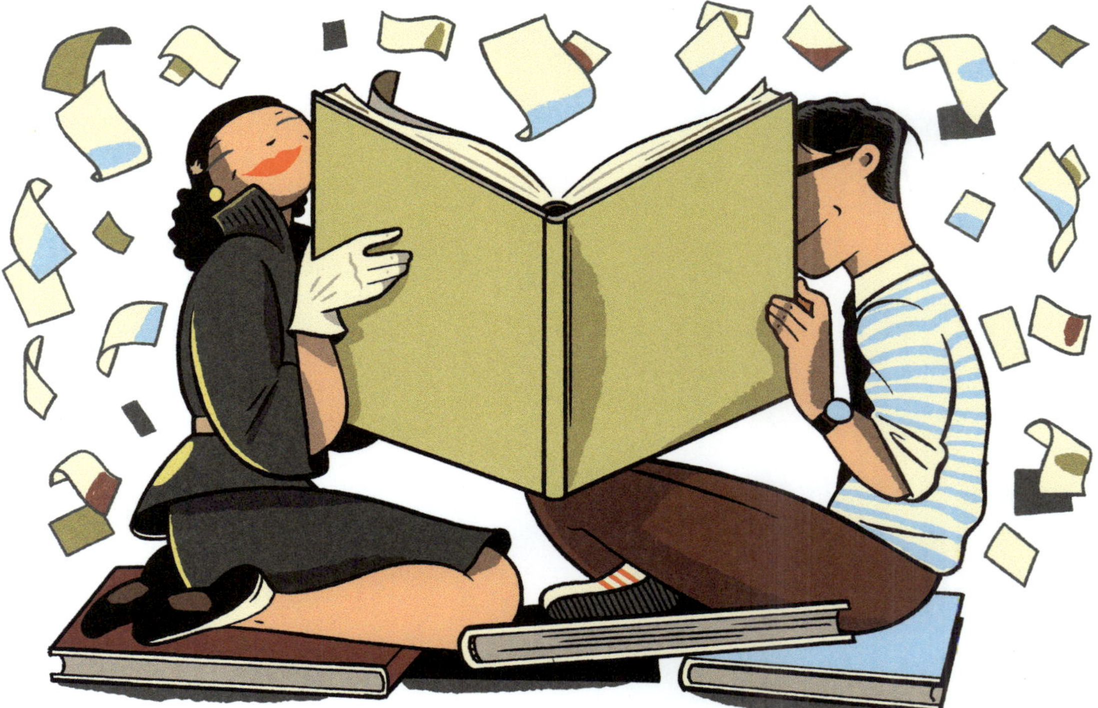

[04]

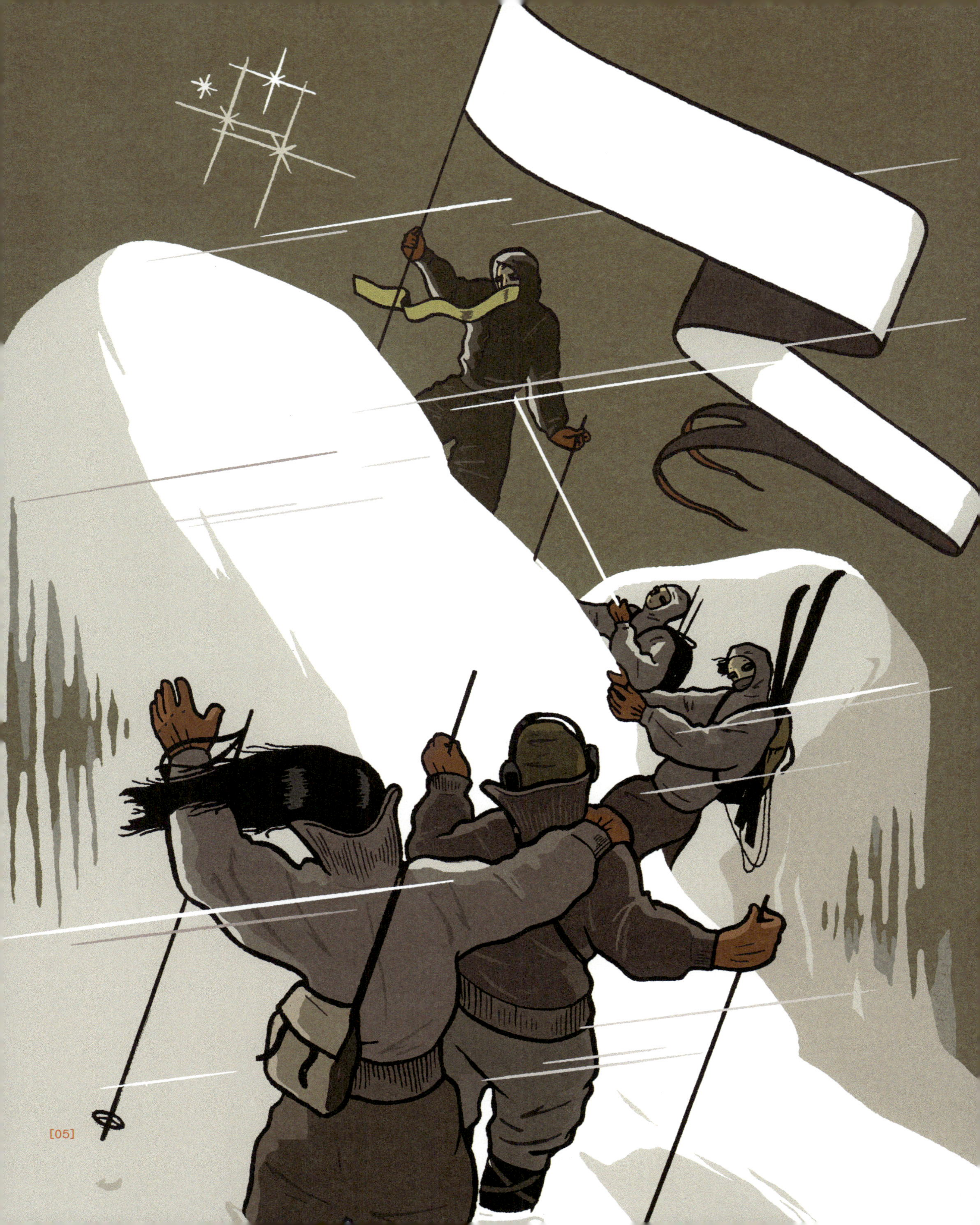

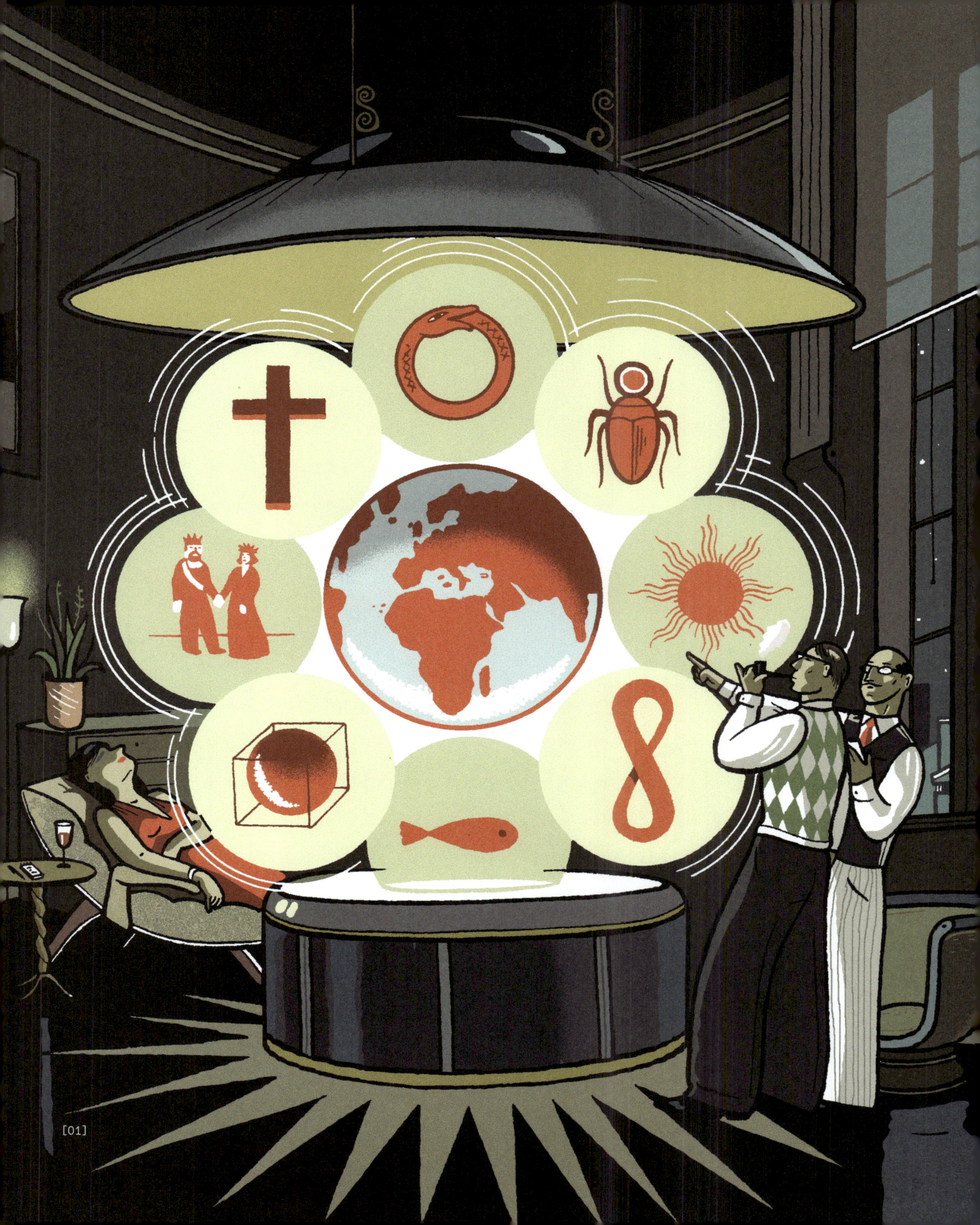

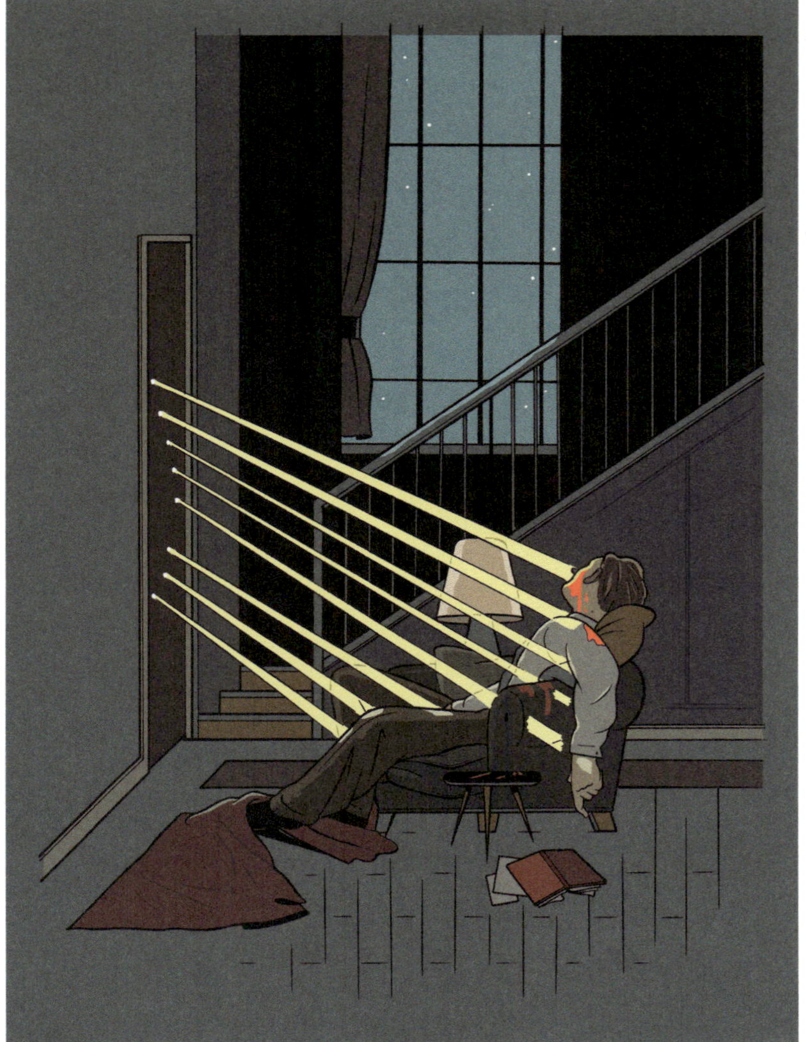

[02]

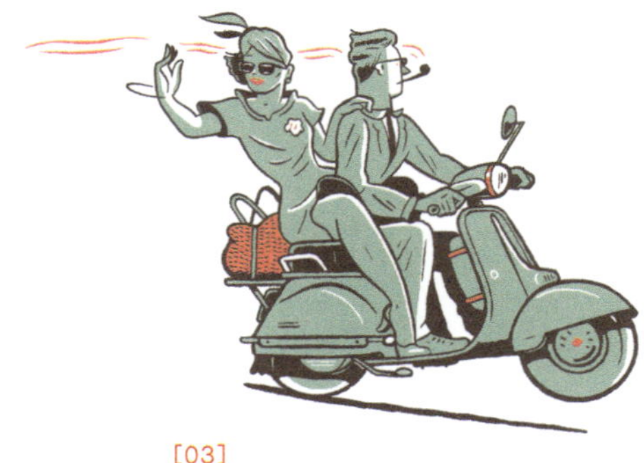

[03]

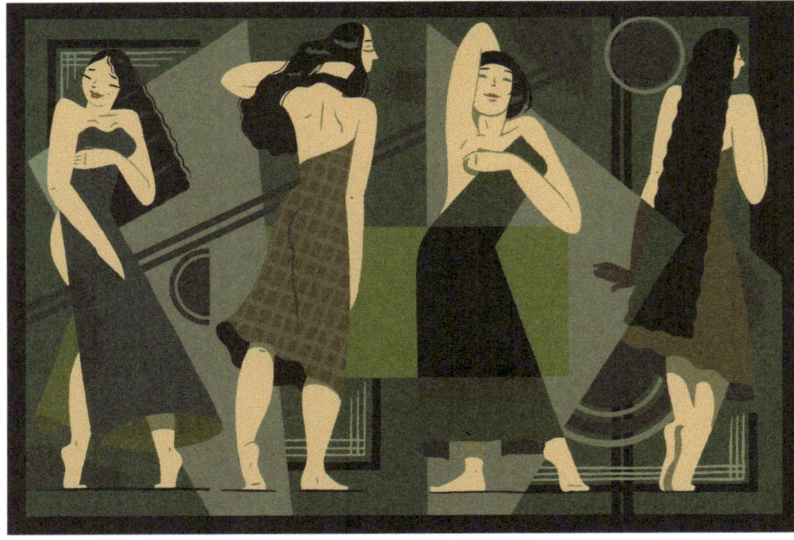

[04]

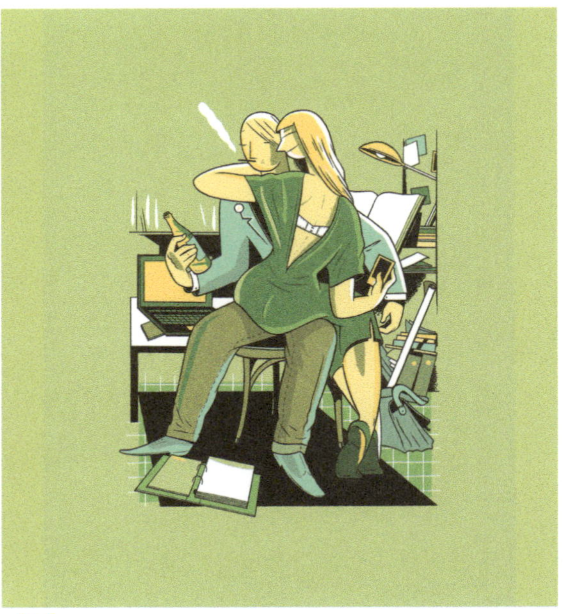

[05]

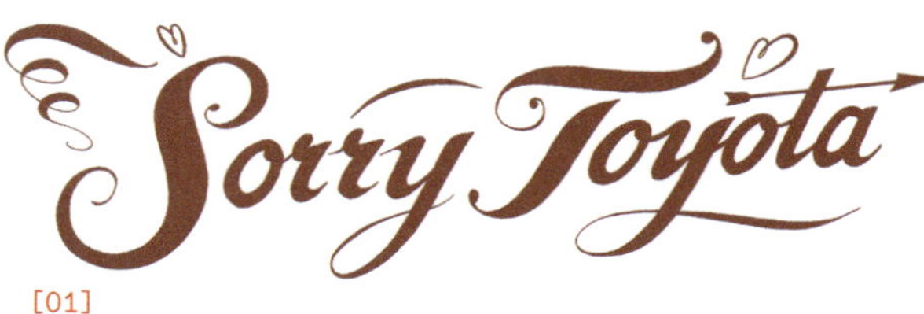

[01]

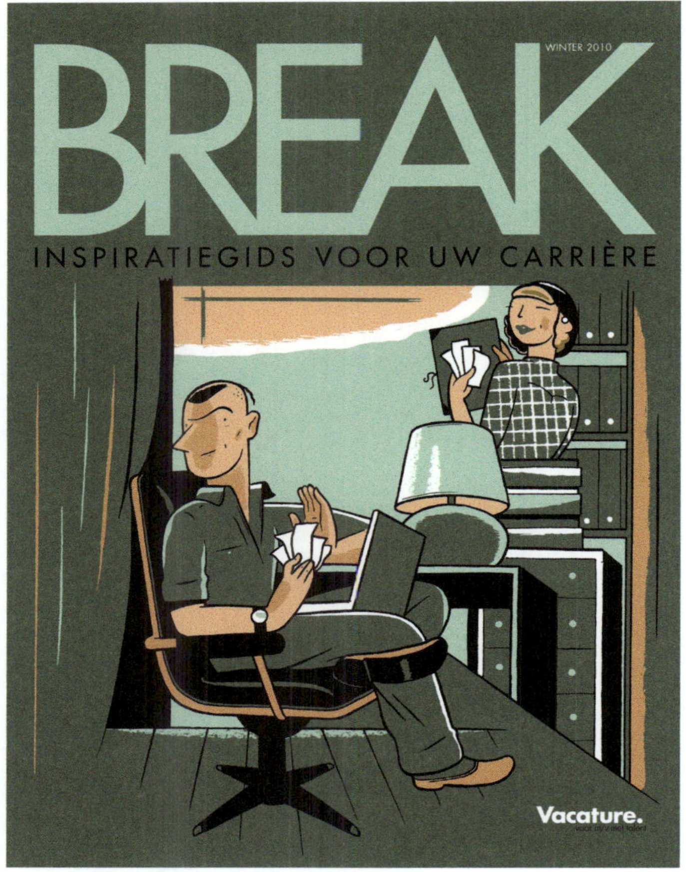

[02]

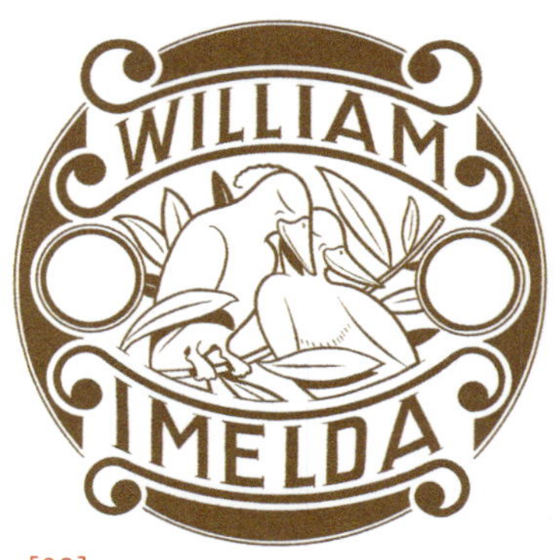

[03]

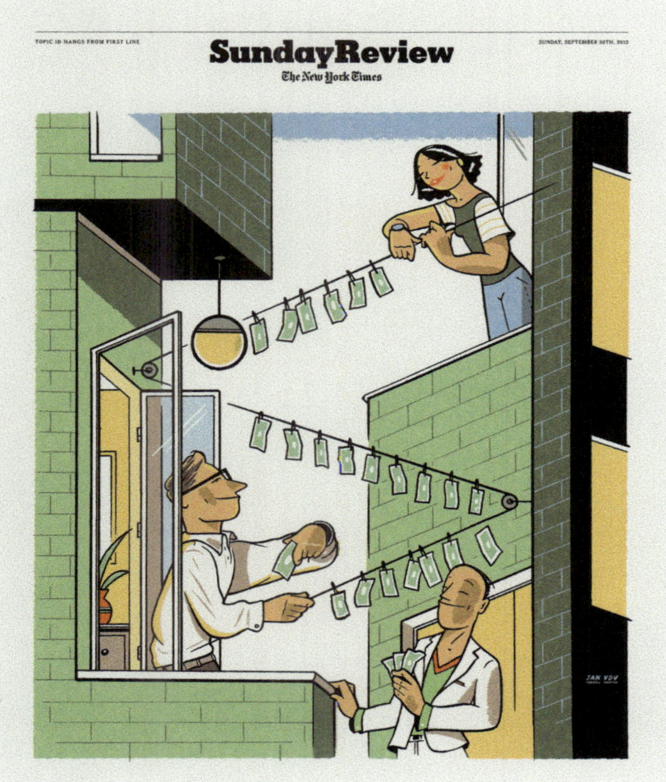

[04]

[01] **Various Hand Lettering**
Diverse Commissions
✳ 2006 – 2013

[02] **Salary Issue**
Break Magazine
✳ 2010

[03] **Wedding Logo**
William and Imelda
✳ 2007

[04] **Happy Taxes**
New York Times
✳ 2013

[05] **Bob Brozman Poster**
De Warande
✳ 2006

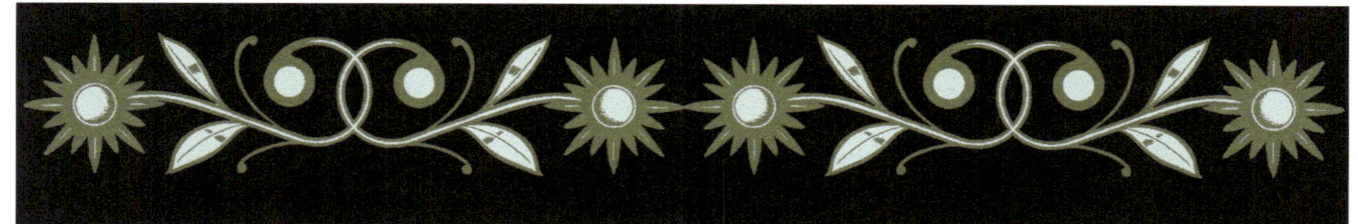

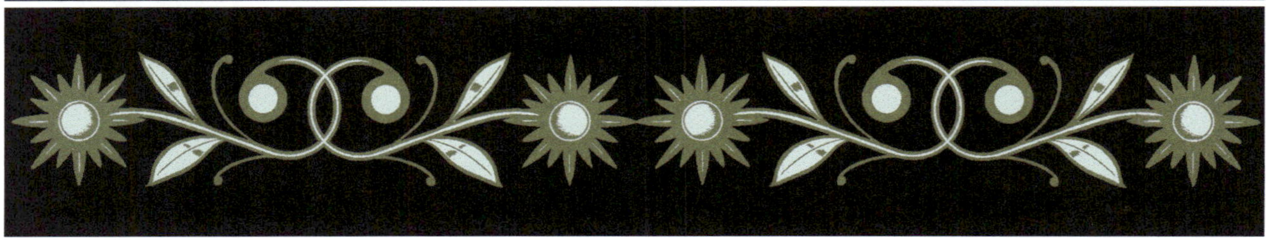

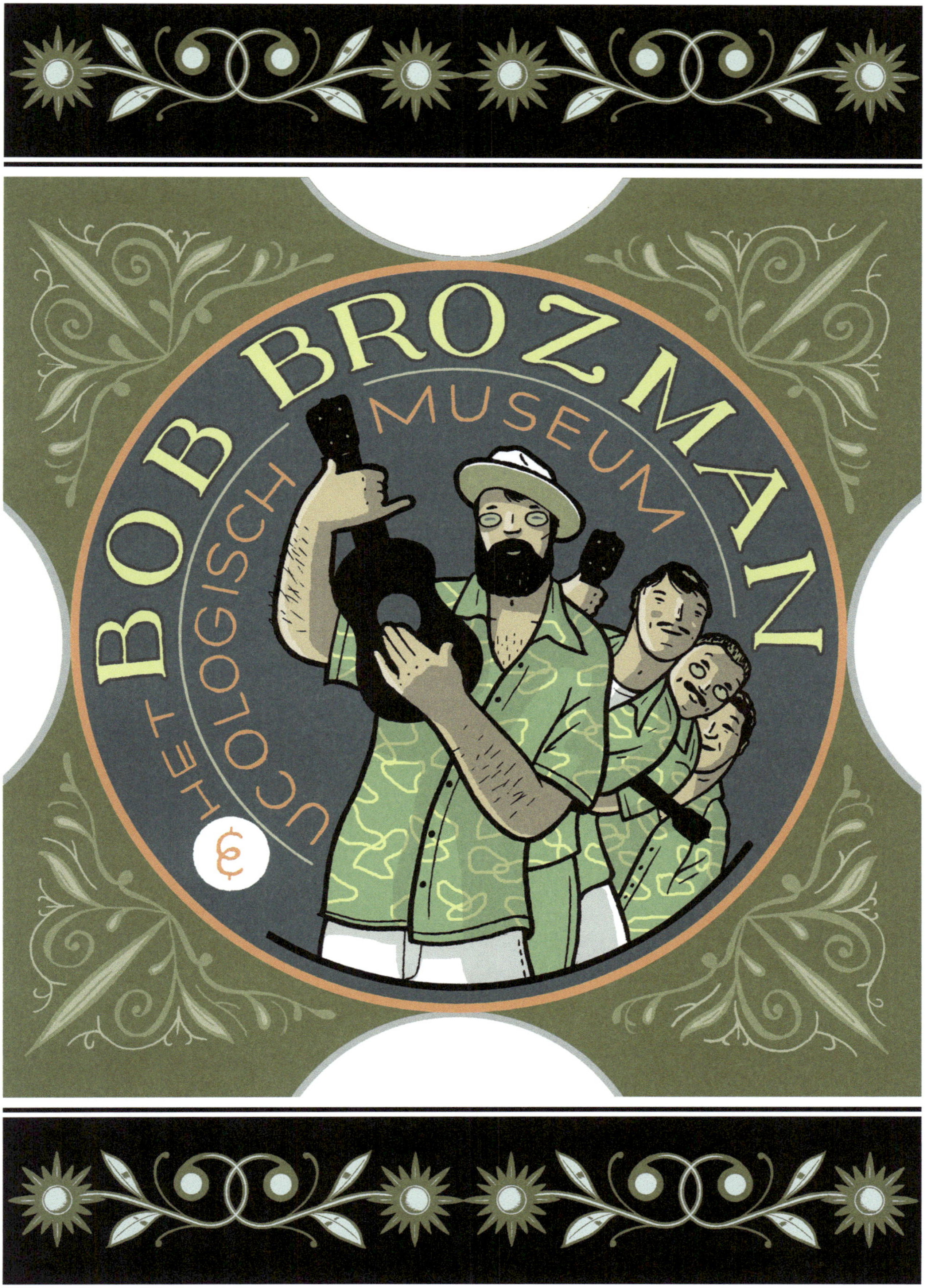

BOB BROZMAN
HET MUSEUM
COLOGISCH

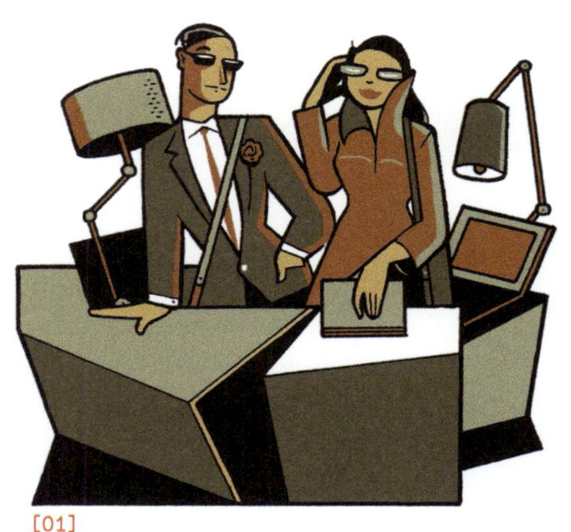

[01]

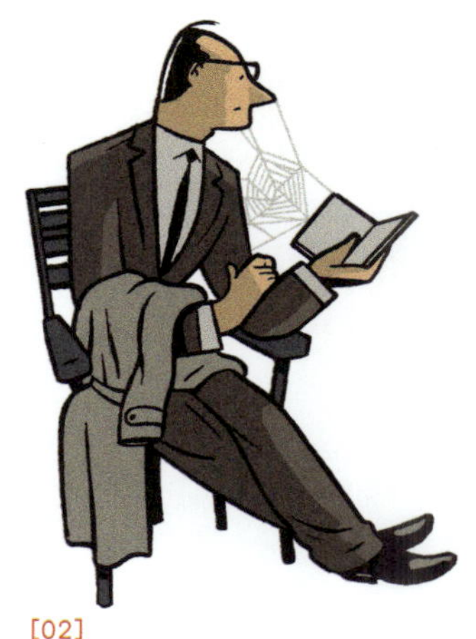

[02]

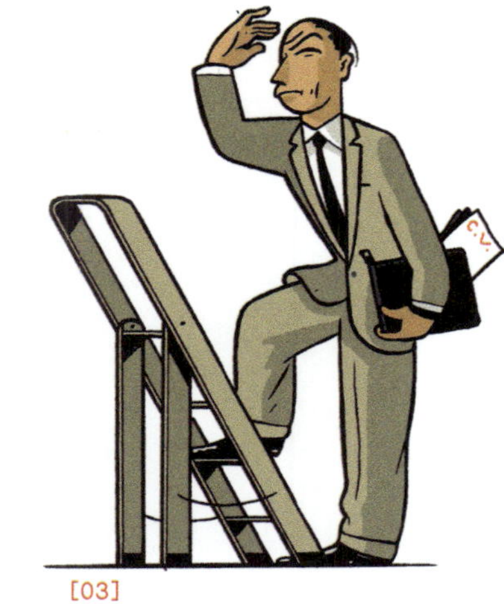

[03]

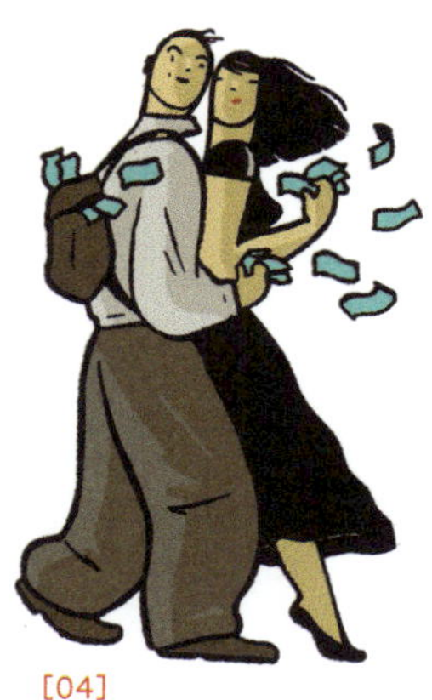

[04]

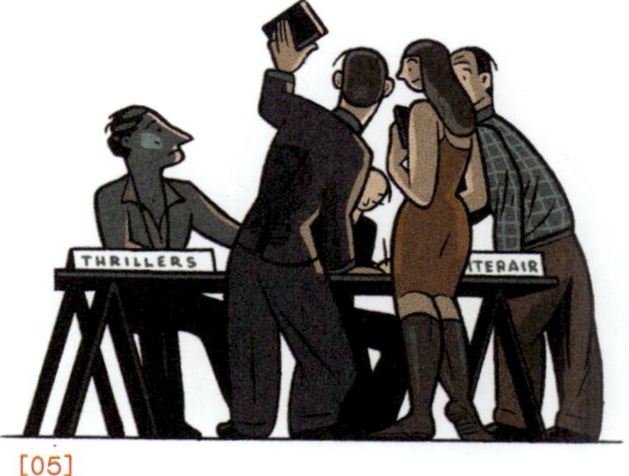

[05]

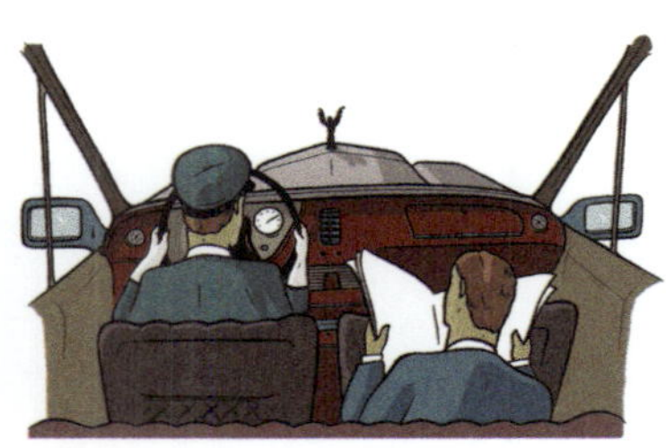

[06]

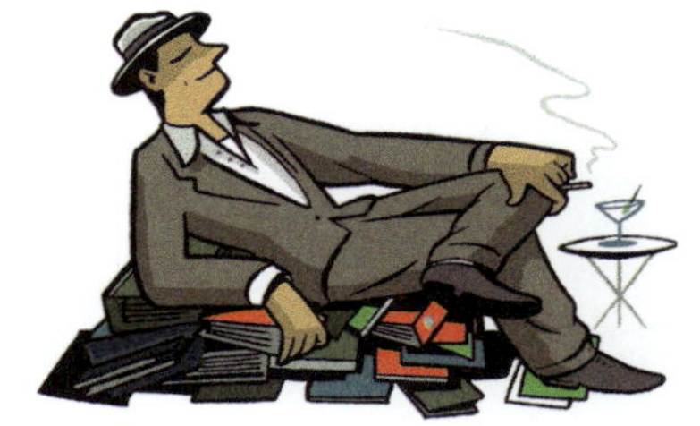

[07]

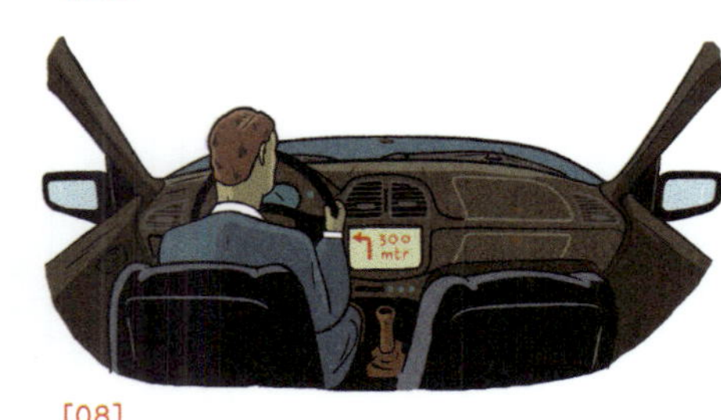

[08]

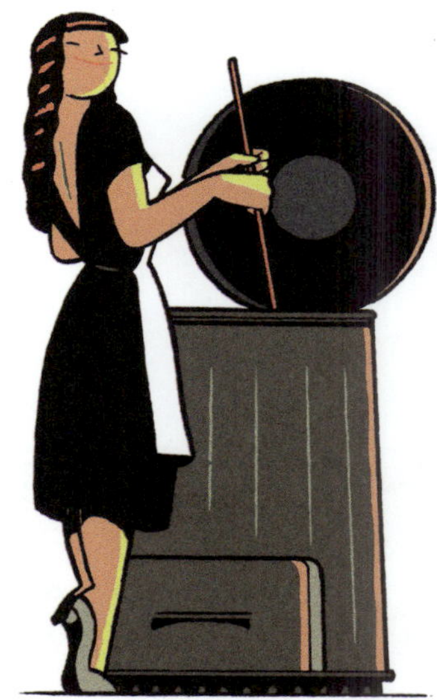

[09]

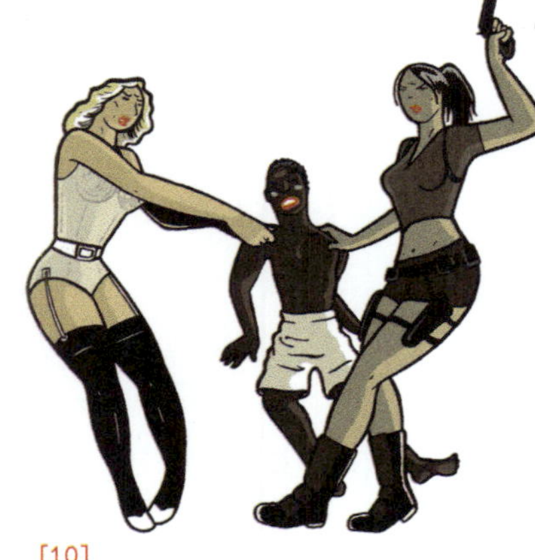

[10]

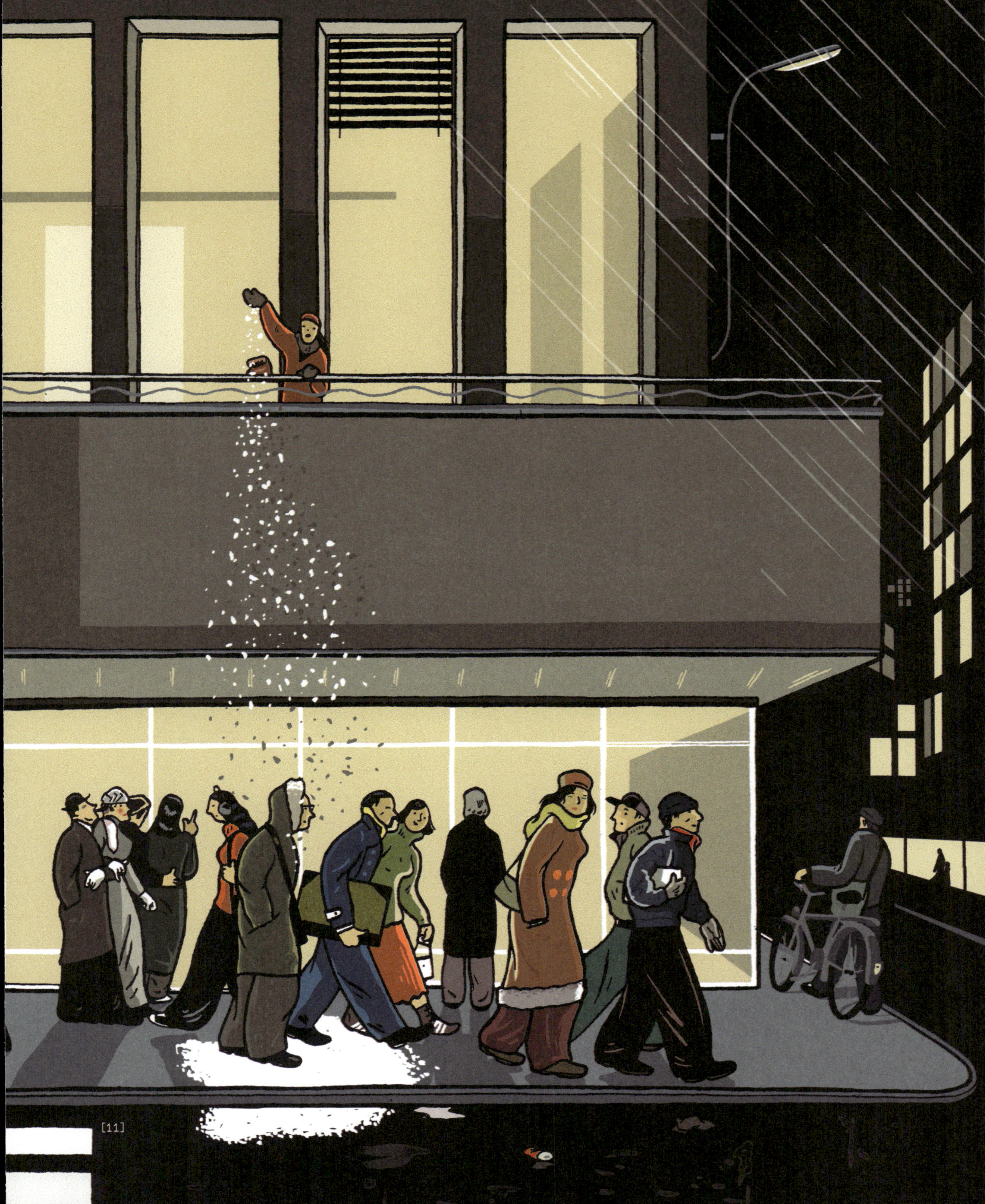

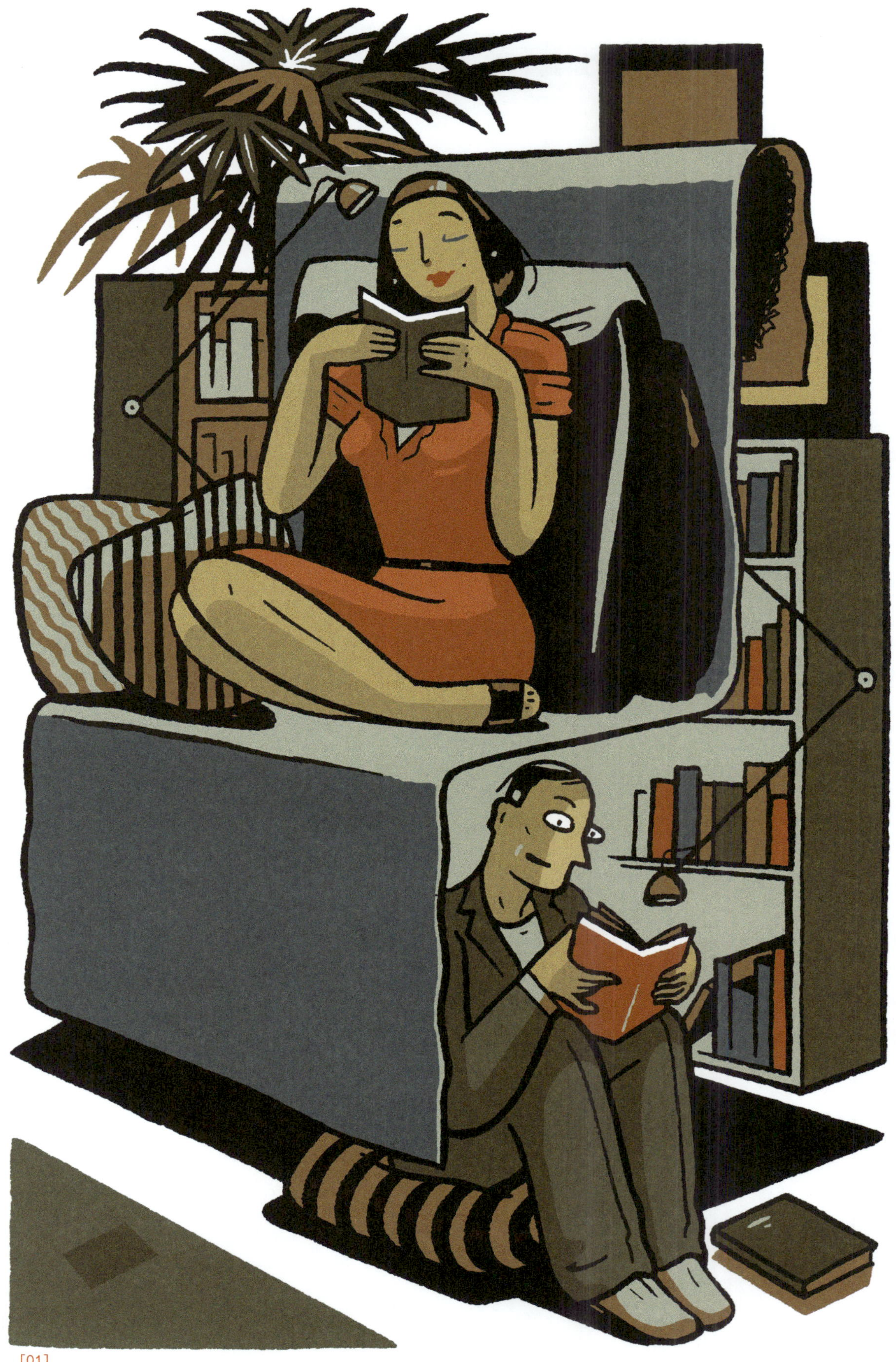

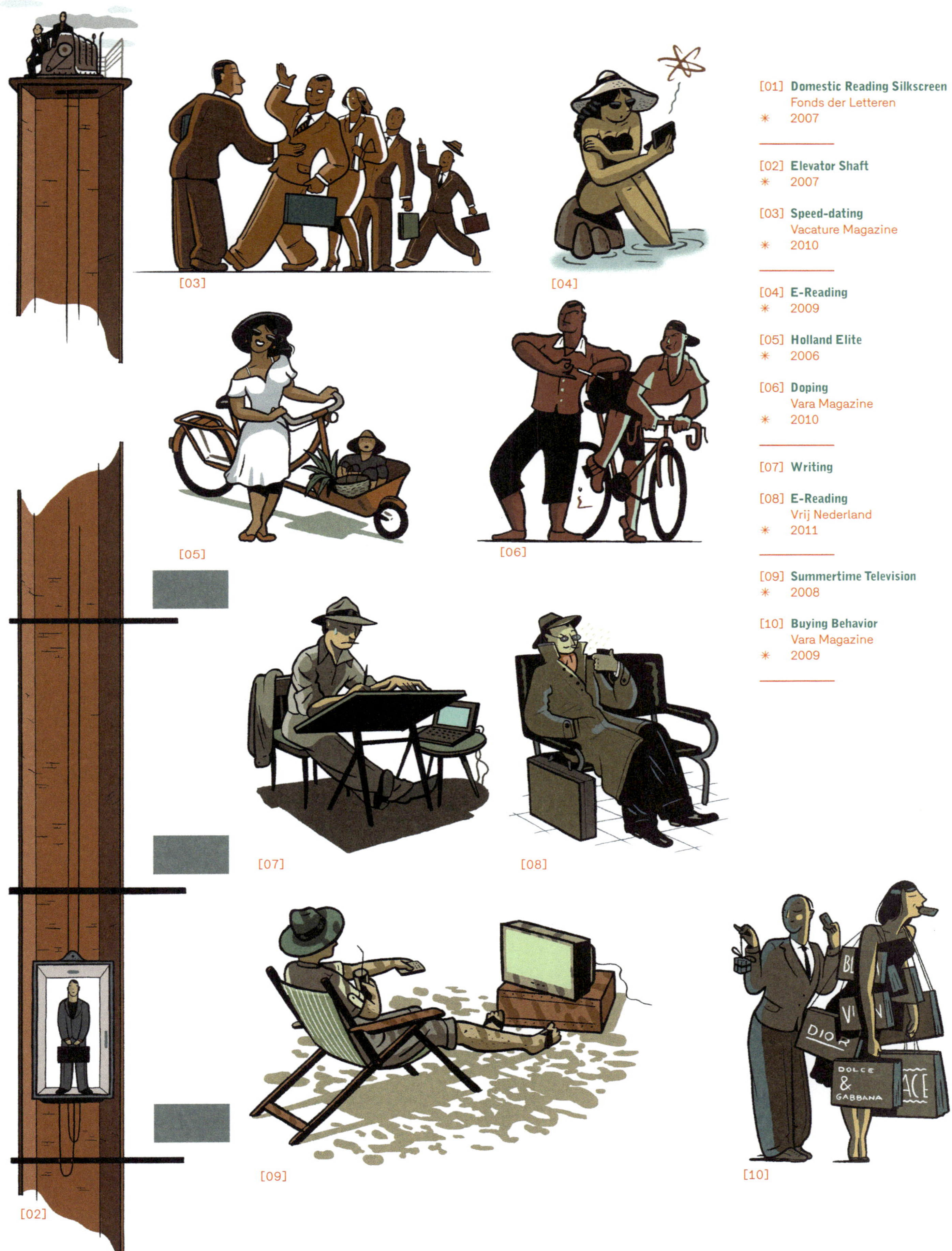

DIOR
DOLCE & GABBANA

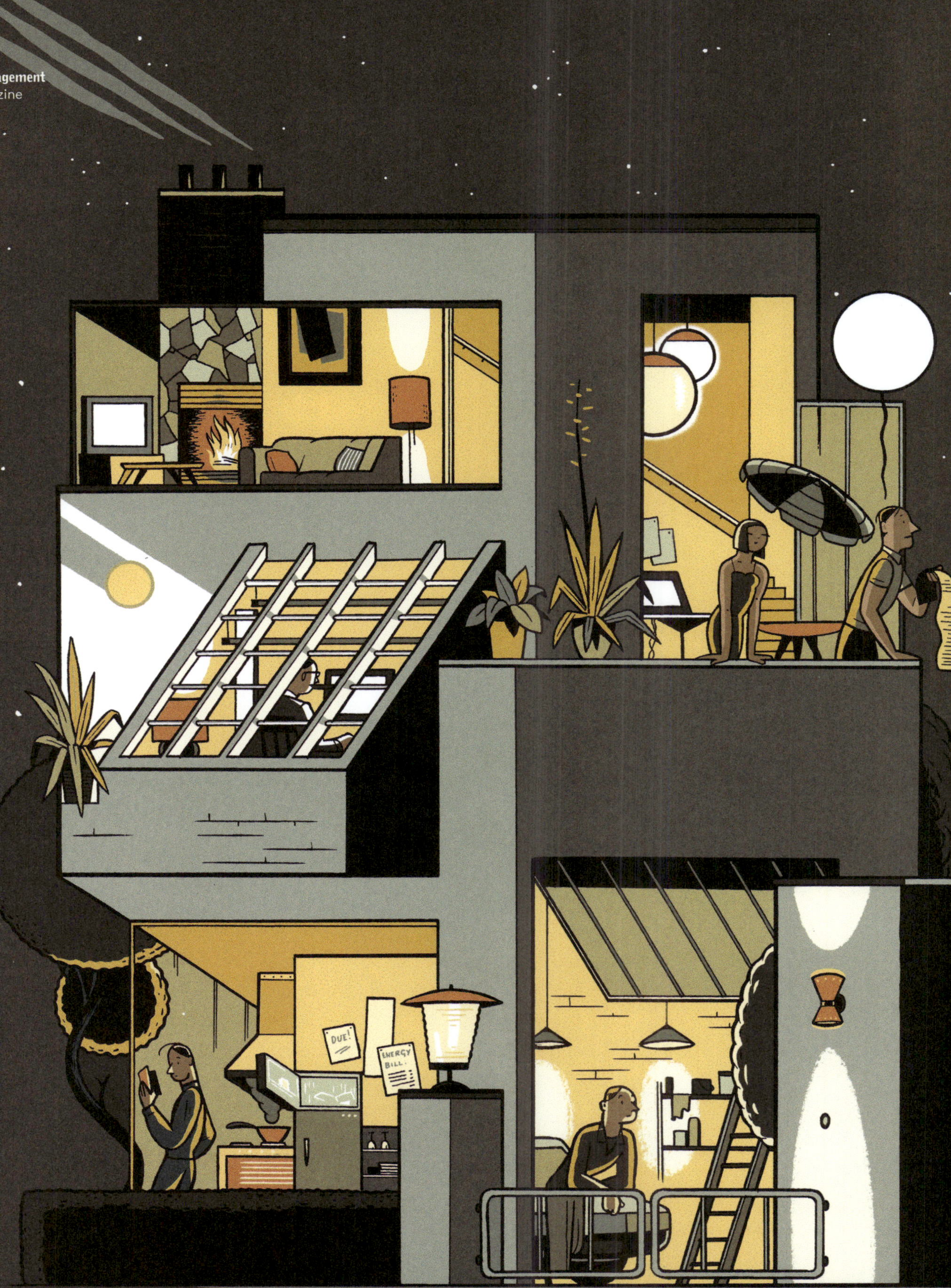
DUE!
ENERGY
BILL.

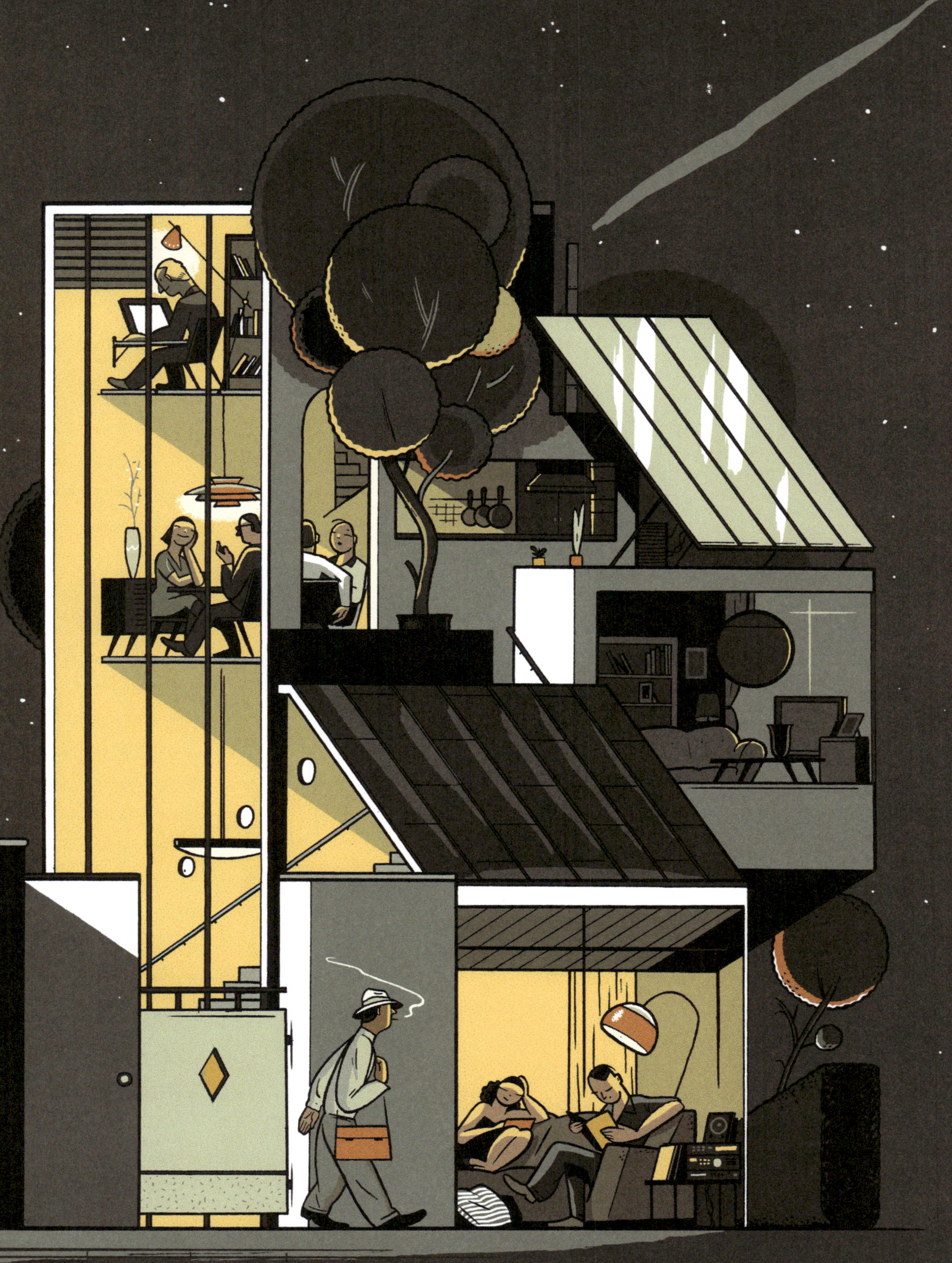

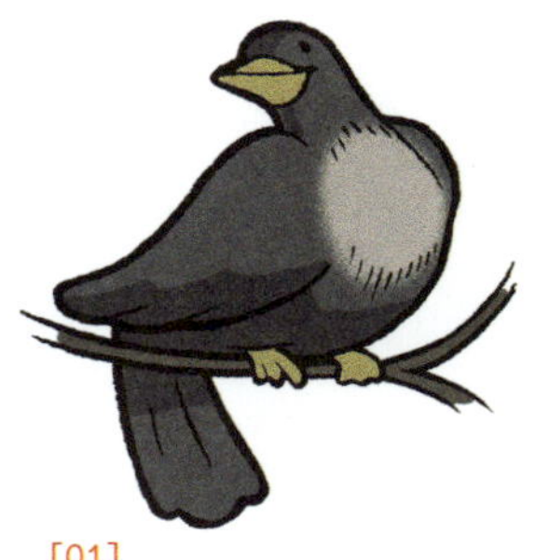

[01]

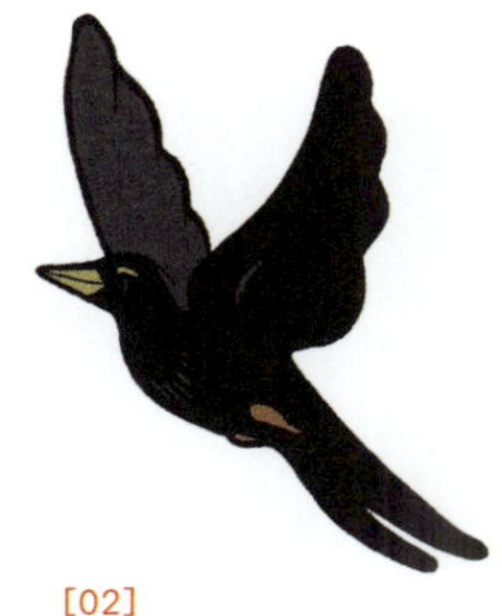

[02]

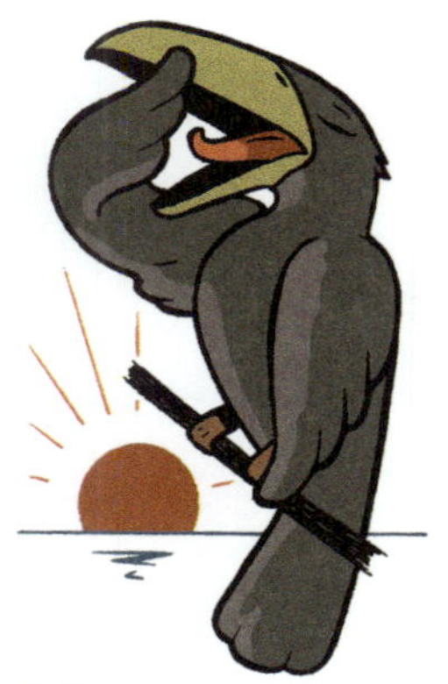

[03]

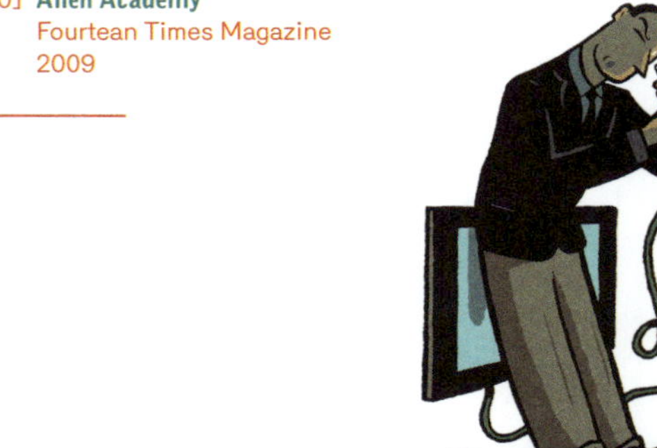

[04]

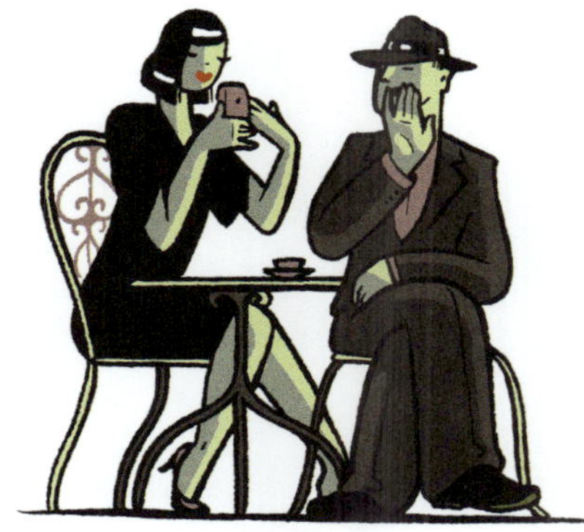

[05]

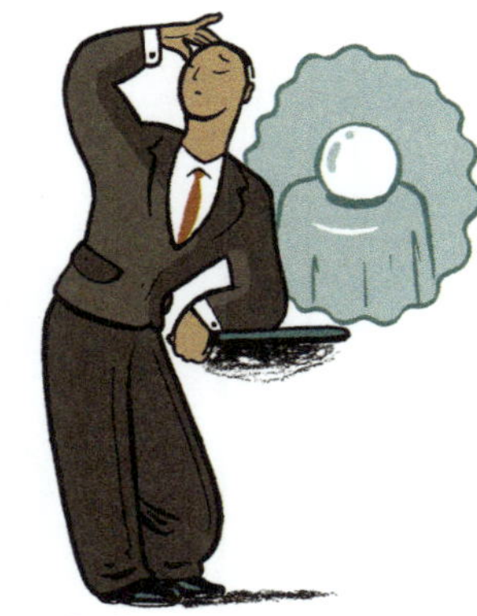

[06]

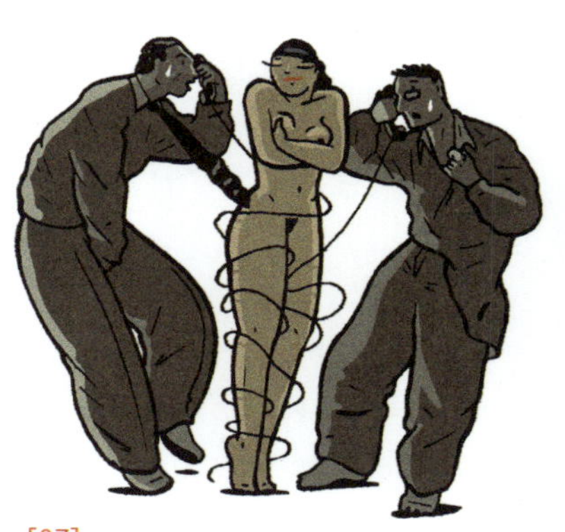

[07]

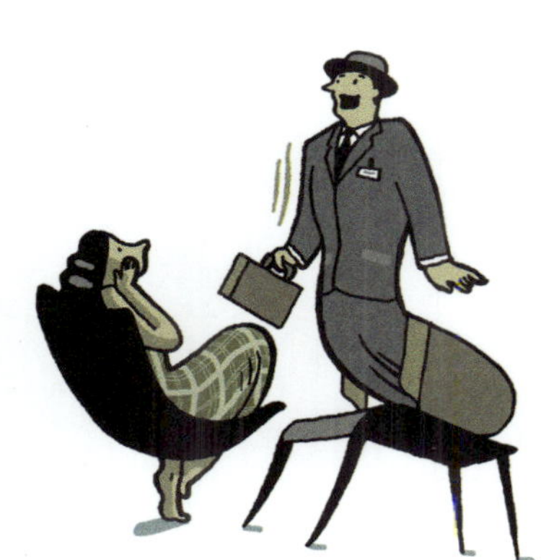

[08]

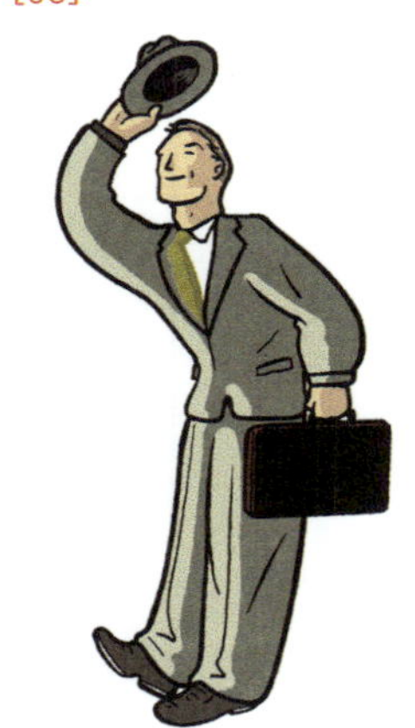

[09]

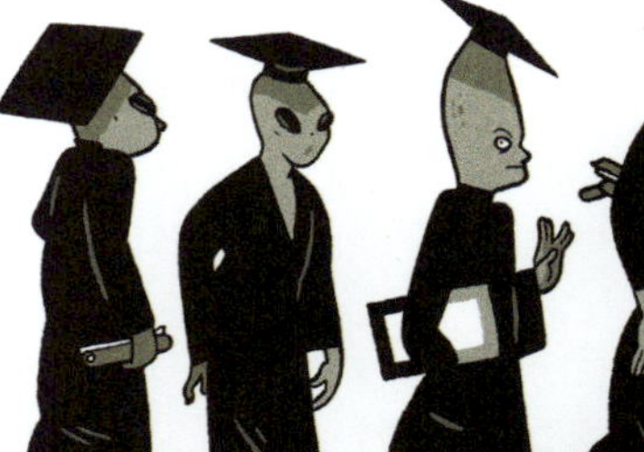
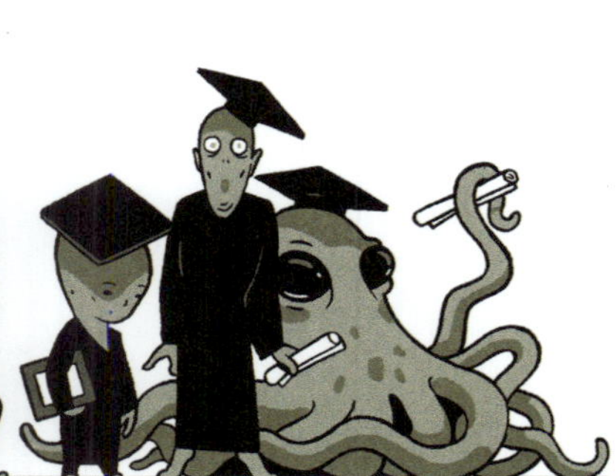

[10]

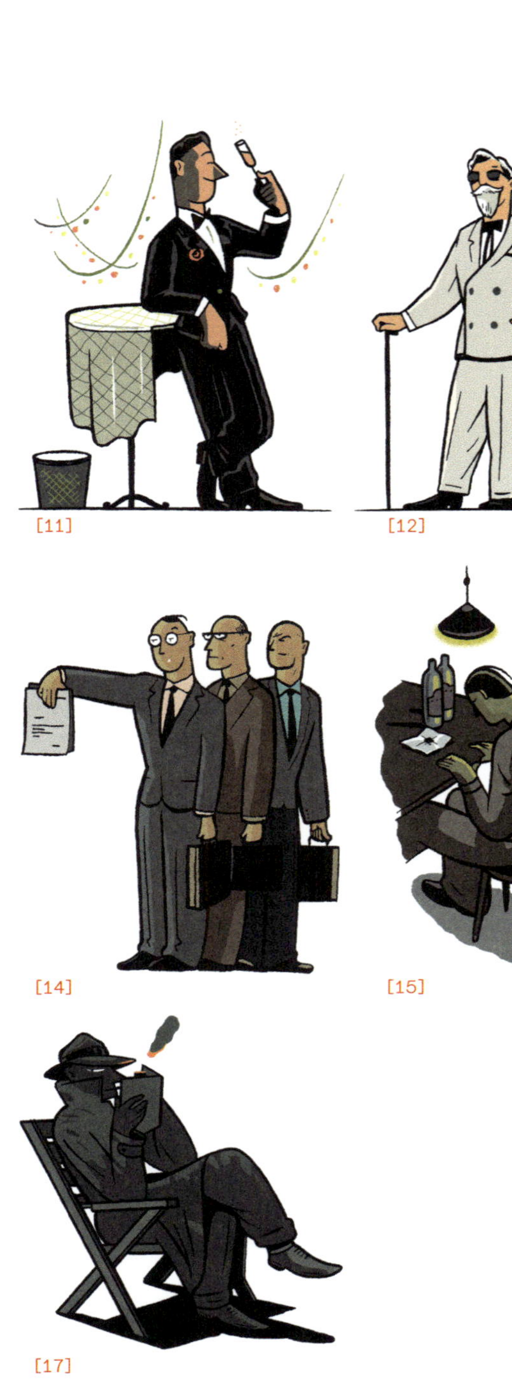
[11] [12]
[14] [15]
[17]

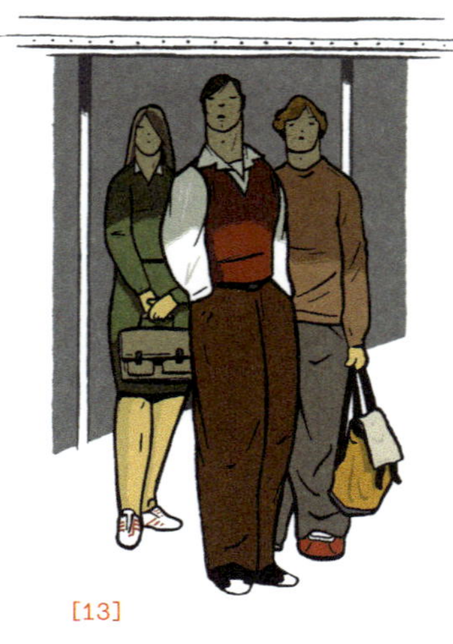
[13]

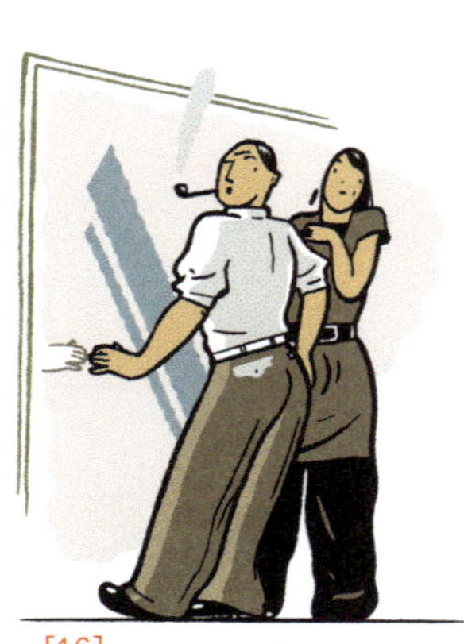
[16]

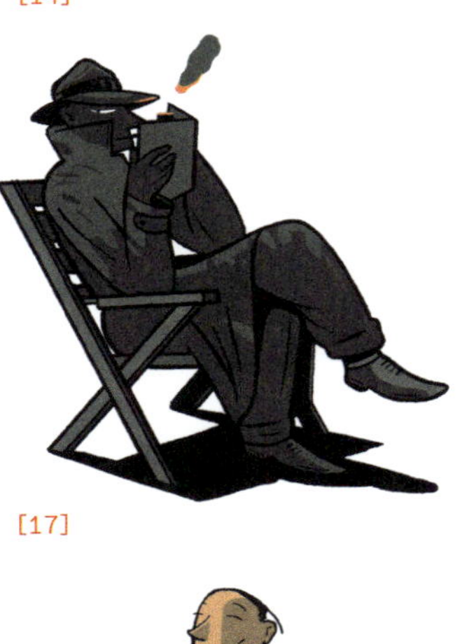

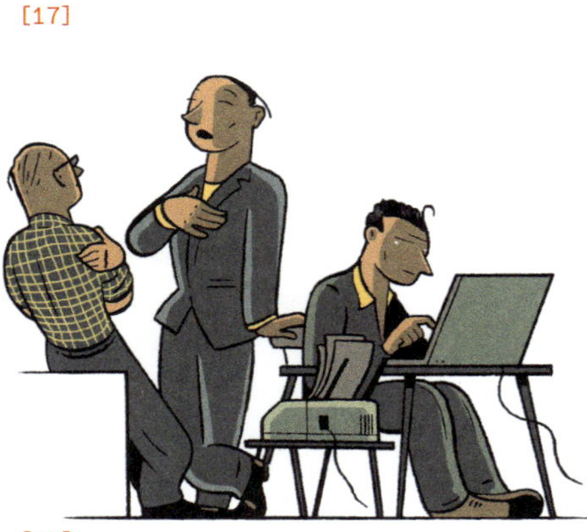
[18]

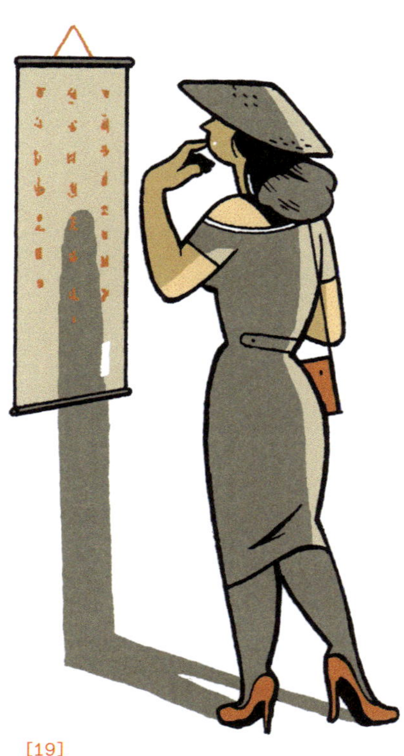
[19]

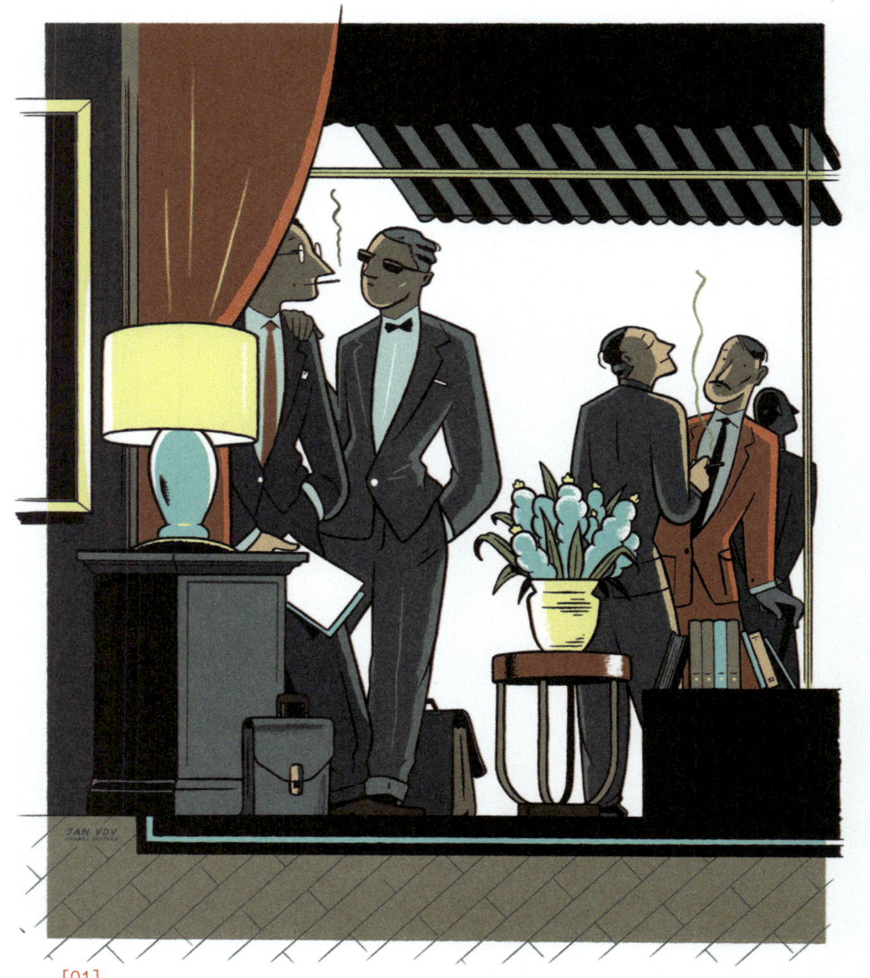

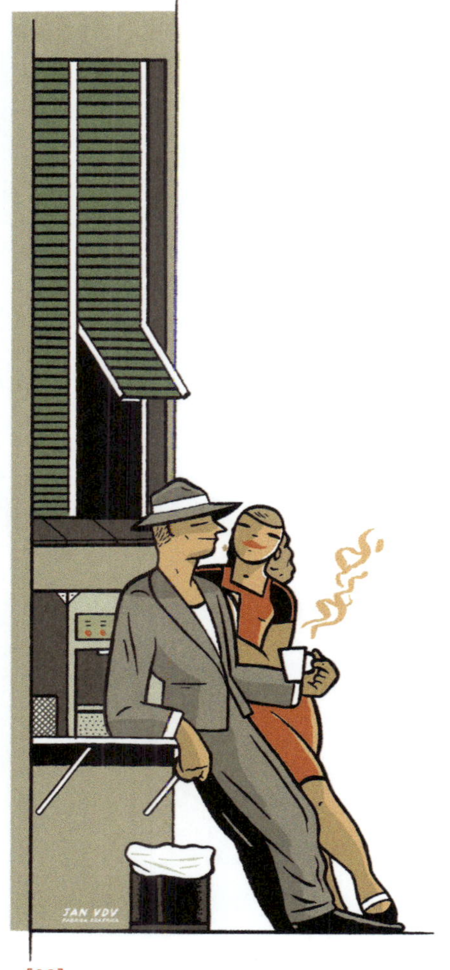

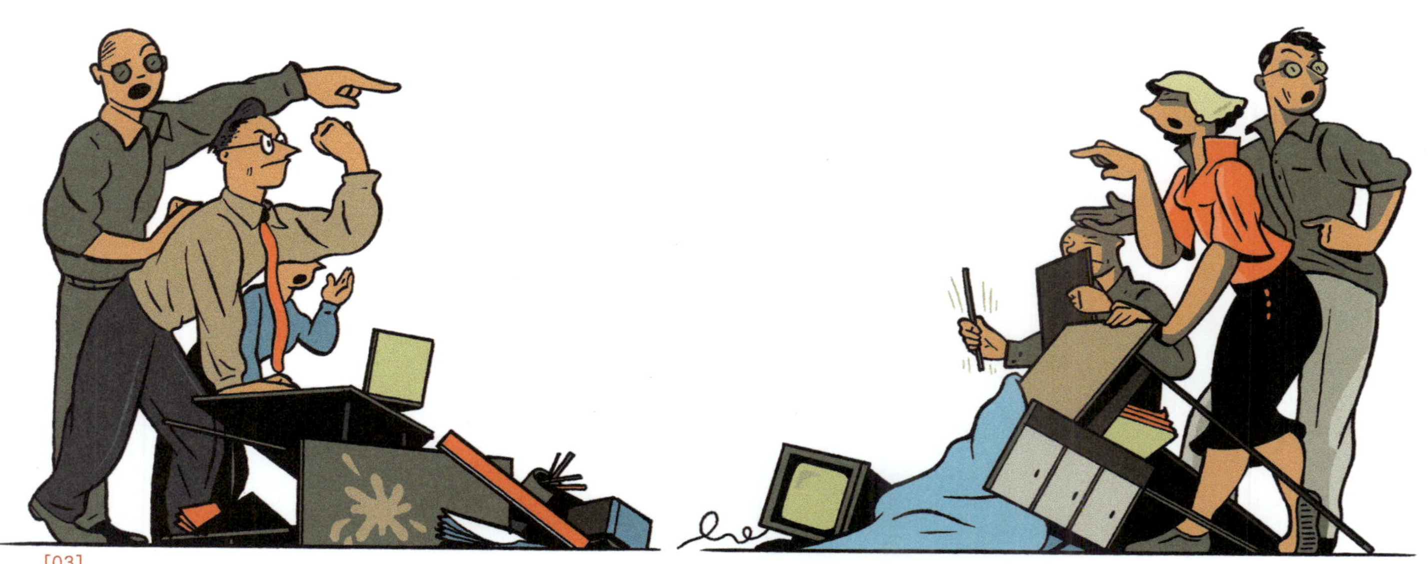

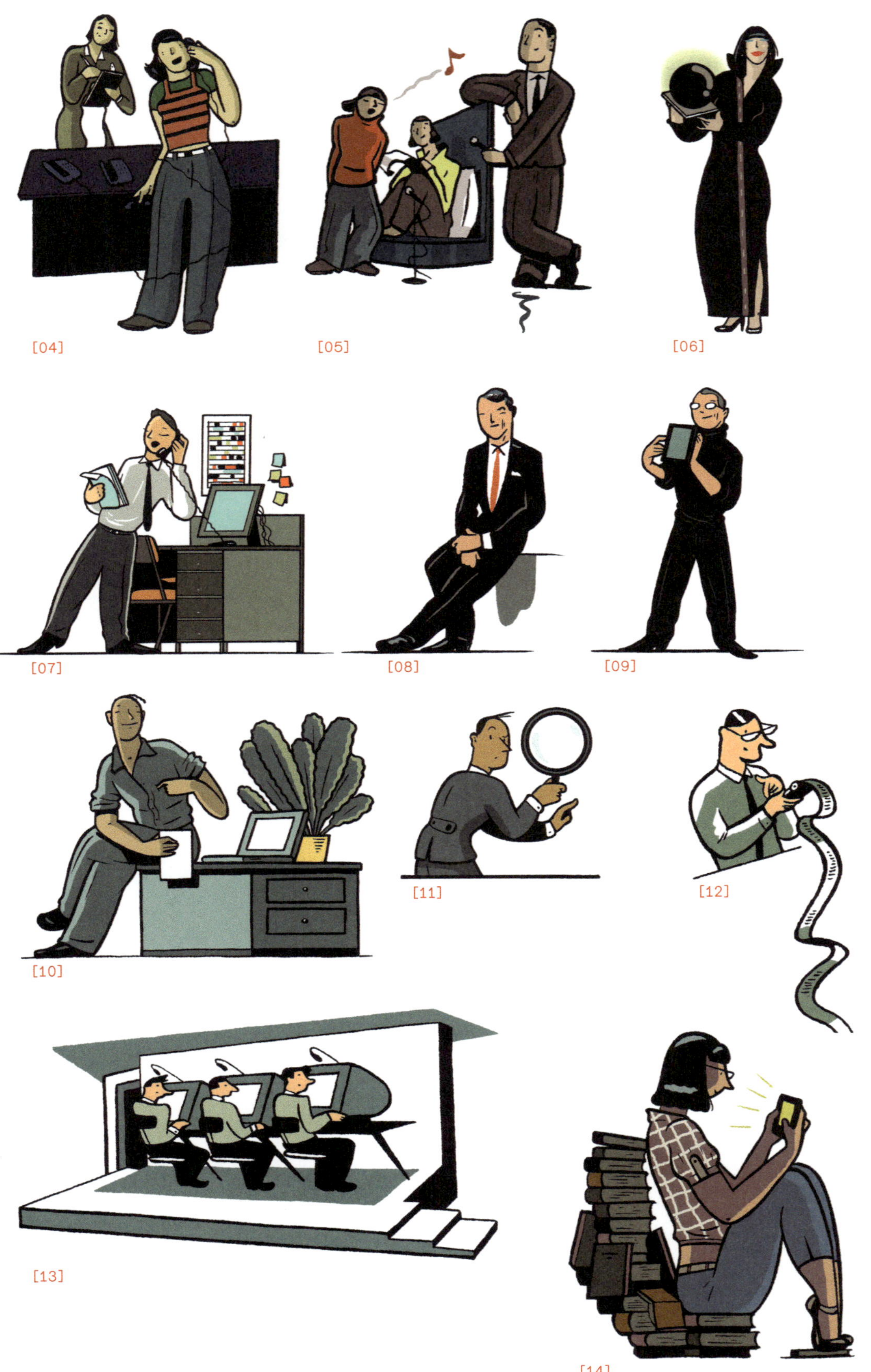

[04]
[05]
[06]
[07]
[08]
[09]
[10]
[11]
[12]
[13]
[14]

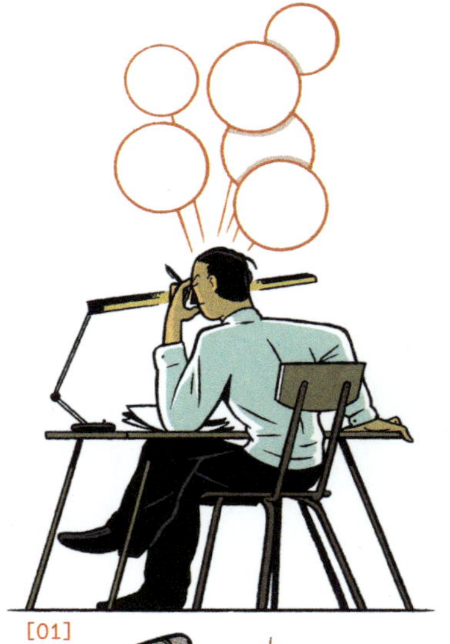

[01]

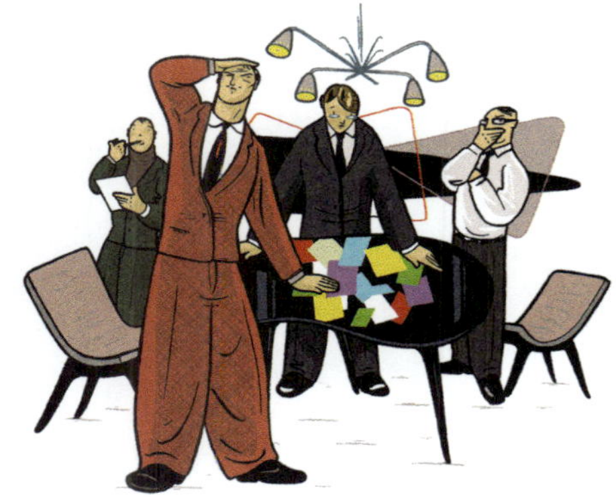

[02]

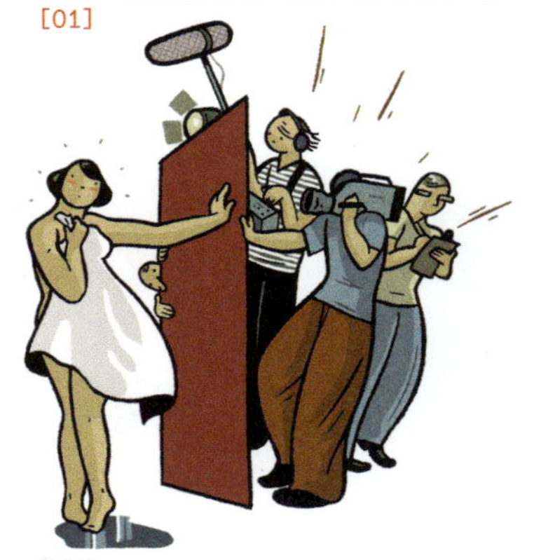

[03]

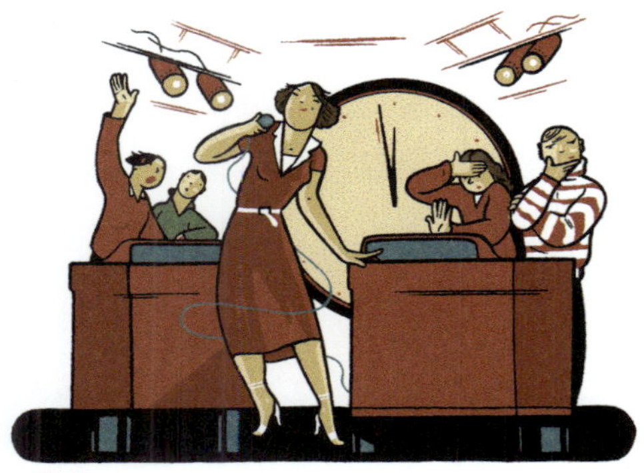

[04]

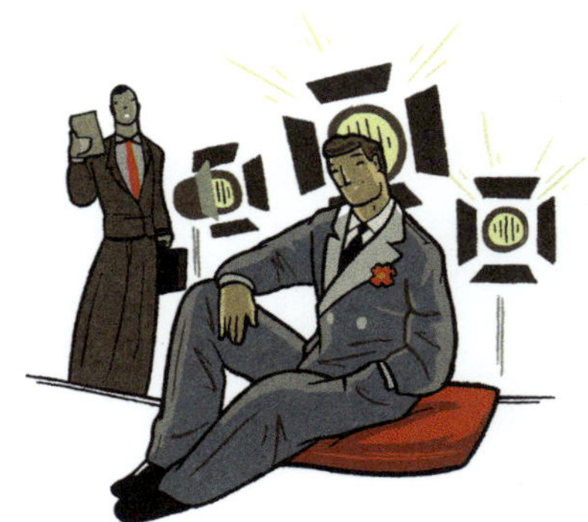

[05]

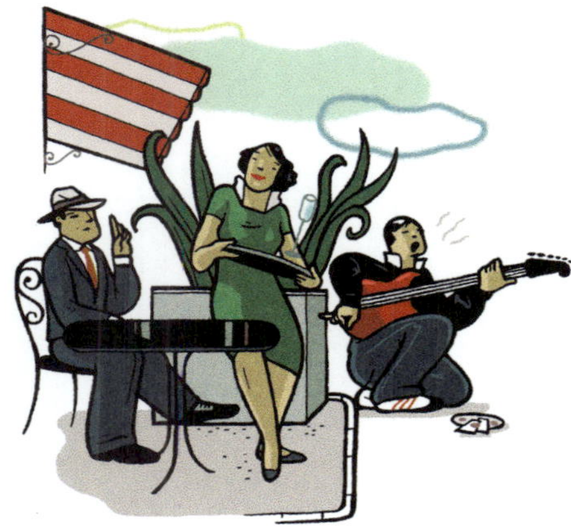

[06]

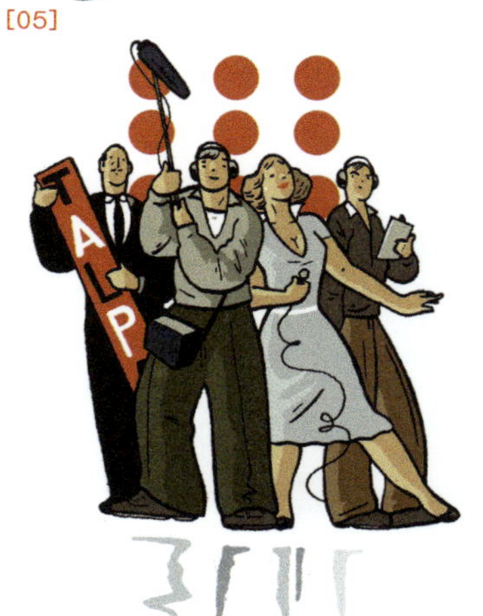

[07]

[08]

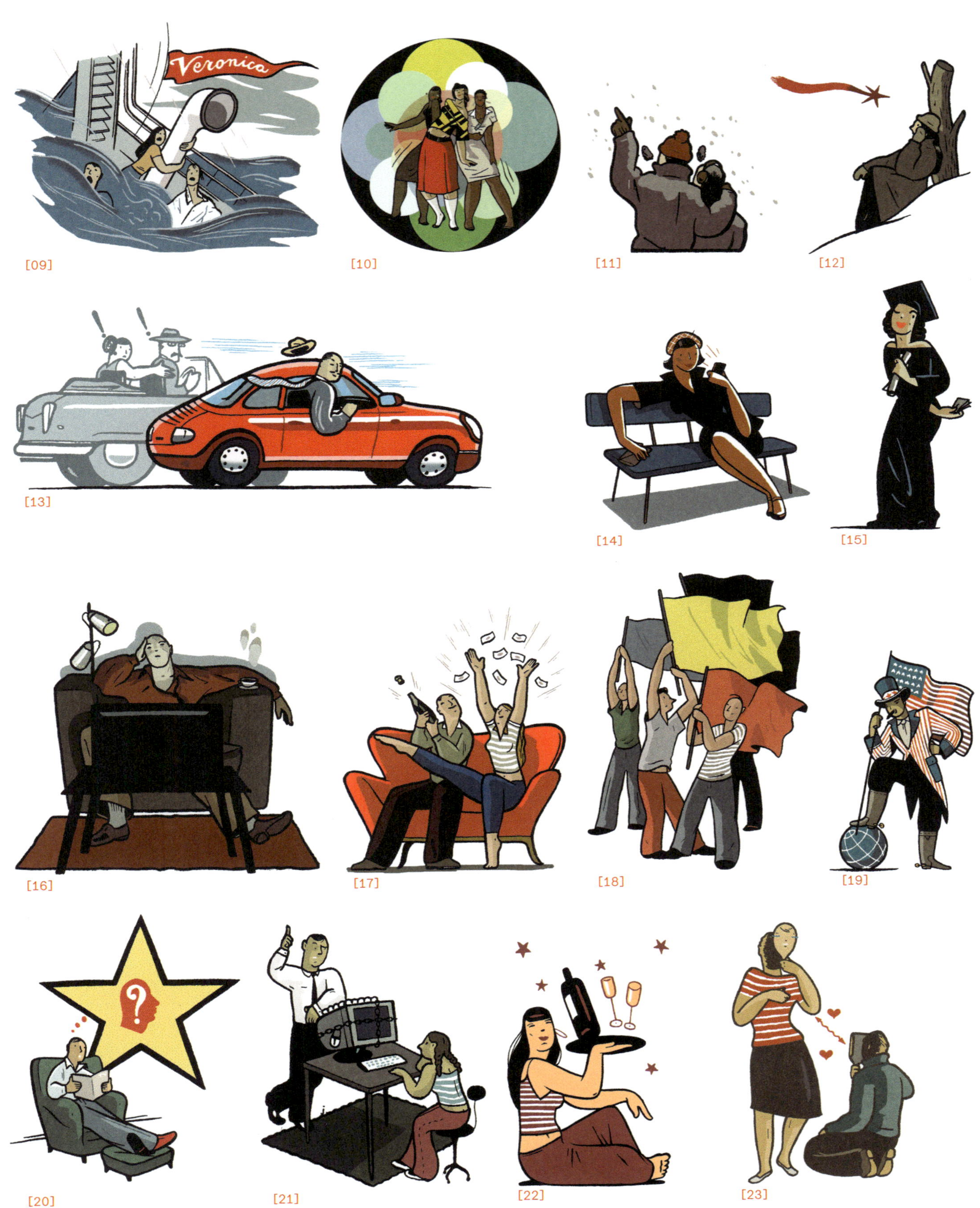

[09]

[10]

[11]

[12]

[13]

[14]

[15]

[16]

[17]

[18]

[19]

[20]

[21]

[22]

[23]

123

LA VILLA ARPEL / MON ONCLE.

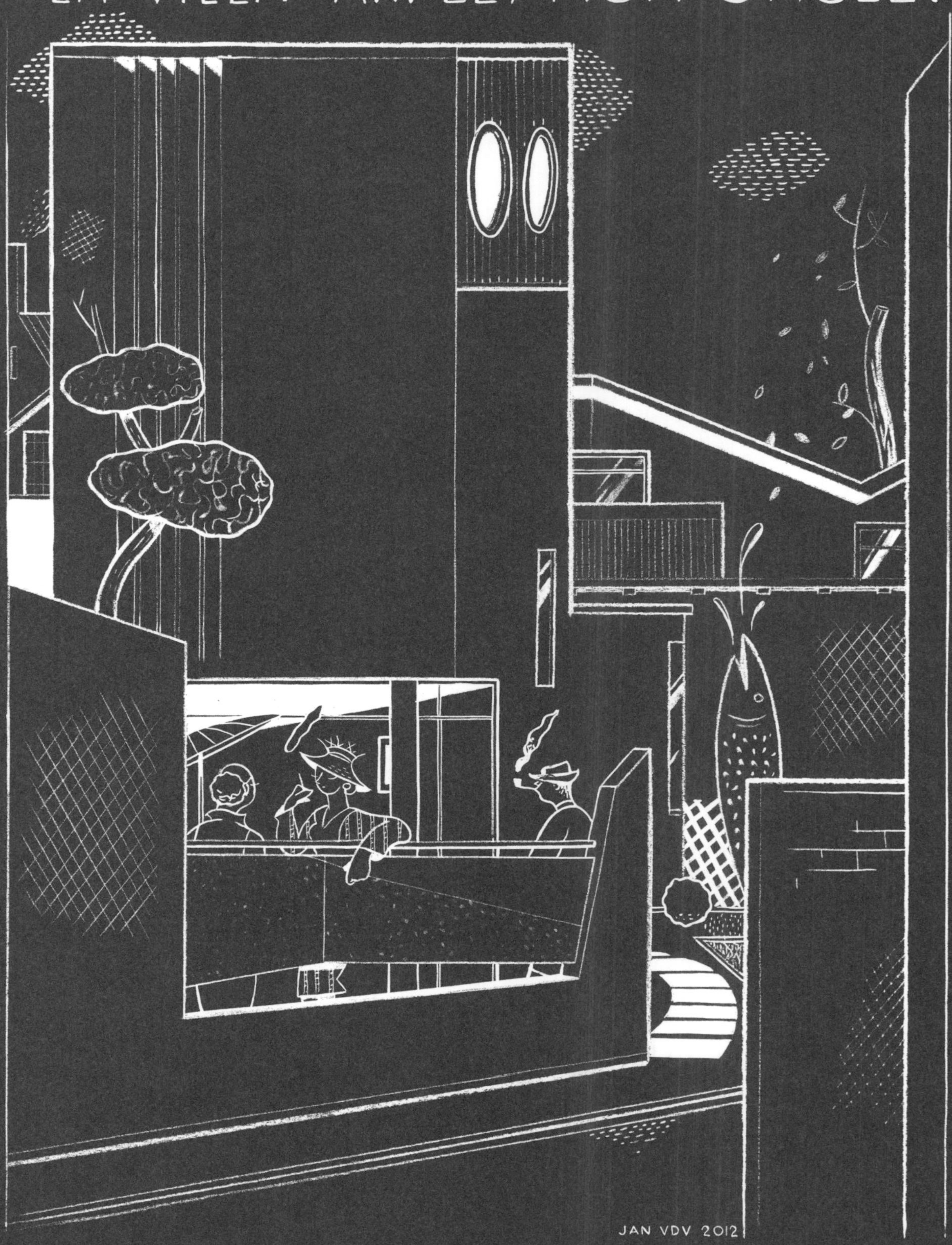

[01] **Villa Arpel-Mon Oncle**
Personal Work
✳ 2012

Thanks to :

My parents for their eternal support; Sylvie for being my tower of strength in rocky times; the honorable gentlemen Eddy Vermeulen and Joost Swarte, my two beacons of good taste; Kris Demey for the night-long conversations on graphic design, life, and the architect of this book; Nick Proot for being a friend and willing photographer; Bart Boel for the random selection tips; James Cartwright for being so out of the blue enthousiastic about my work; Luke Pearson for the coloring on the NoBrow poster; Jan Van Zeveren for the translation skills and Françoise Mouly for the kind words!

JAN VAN DER VEKEN, ILLUSTRIOUS ALL OVER THE WORLD AND ELSEWHERE

Paris artist and comic book illustrator François Avril is a great admirer of Jan's drawings. He heaps praise upon the graphic skills of this young Ghent artist in his amusing French; all rattling and high-pitched tones. But the tempo of his speedy sentences falters every time he tries to pronounce the name Jan Van Der Veken. He articulates the syllables with large intervals (Jan – Van – Der – Veken) and smiles apologetically for so much *couleur locale* and his inaccurate accent. Our French companion tends to have difficulty with most of the names of the Flemish Masters, but you can't say he doesn't know his classics. For him, Rogier Van Der Weyden is simply Roger de la Pasture. François tells me that Jan's name reminds him of an audacious cyclist in one of the historical Belgian teams. "A team with you as a coach," he adds jestingly. That's a good one, François. And I know it would make Jan smile, too.

I've known Jan since the nineties, when he first walked into my Illustration Workshop at the St. Lucas Art School. He never came alone. His buddies Peter Willems and Pieter de Poortere (both cobble stone-nibbling *Flandriens,* too, I guess) never left his side. As a teacher, the presence of this sacred trinity from Mariakerke – all graduates from the same printing school – was a true blessing and a great experience. The eagerness with which these guys transformed their technical knowledge into a fulfilling artistic practice was phenomenal to see – especially for Jan, whose quest for a professional existence as an illustrator was the most challenging. Almost twenty years later, he's succeeded with flying colors. Not a single assignment is too hard, too off-limits, too tight on time or not worth the effort. With his fast mind and lively spirit, Jan constantly delivers top-notch work under the strictest of deadlines. Because even the most touching illustration is worthless if the newspaper in which it should have been published is already printed.

Jan knows the ins and outs of his profession as a "serving creator". His work keeps impressing his clients and he knows how to charm a large audience. His insatiable desire to draw and his natural talent for stylization and color make every one of his drawings an improvement upon the last. He's also become an expert in drawing surprising perspectives, landscapes and contemporary architecture. Always with a cheerful and lighthearted nature, but brilliantly composed and skillfully executed.

Jan never avoids technical or educational subjects. He can always count on his craftsmanship, his immense reservoir of mental images, and his ability to find the right documentation. For instance, the air pilot in Jan knows the smallest details about aircrafts and aviation. He takes a lot of pleasure in rendering them in isometric projections. And, of course, an illustrator like Jan is also a *pur sang* calligrapher; meticulous as a goldsmith, he creates beautiful handwritten and self-designed typefaces.

Today, Jan Van Der Veken is a well-known and respected colleague, famous in Flanders and successful abroad – a silent celebrity (he likes it that way) in his well-equipped workshop. Somewhere in my extensive bookcase you can find *All Demons Day* by Herman Portocarero, illustrated by Jan. It's the most beautiful book I've ever seen, but now we also have this new volume by Die Gestalten to covet, with the handsome name of Jan Van Der Veken on the cover.

Keep on practicing in Paris, Jan – Van – Der – Veken!

Ever Meulen

A LETTER
TO JAN VAN DER VEKEN

Illustrators of Belgian descent should count themselves lucky. To be honest, I'm very jealous of my Belgian colleagues, though my mother is Flemish and therefore so is half of my family.
I often visited my Belgian family during my childhood. The fun began whenever I passed the Dutch border in the sidecar of my uncle Armand's Harley Davidson. Back then there was no highway between Breda and Antwerp. Our road trip went through villages and country roads lined with with sky-high billboards. Many people believed those ads spoiled the view, but I loved them. For a Dutch boy growing up in a straight-laced environment, those billboards were truly exotic. I saw unknown products advertised with appealing images. The ad for Spa mineral water in particular made a big impression on me – it depicted a huge clown leaping acrobatically over a water fountain. No matter where I stayed in Belgium the images were everywhere; from elaborate art books to huge piles of comics. That was how I came to know the comics of Madam Pheip, Jansen en Jansens and Sus Antigoon.

Later on, I discovered that the culture of imagery within Catholicism had a great influence on this Belgian comics tradition. Once, the Belgian bishops wrote a letter to their priests, advising them to publish comics in their free parish newspapers. That way, they hoped, they would expose more youngsters to Catholicism. The consequences were huge, and as a result all Belgian children grew up with comics. Of course church visits decreased progressively, but that early Catholic influence put comics on the map and boosted their popularity. The Belgian government also recognized the importance of comics and supported art academies in order to nurture young talent. Now there's not a country in the world that reads more comics and has as many brilliant illustrators as Belgium.

Jan Van Der Veken studied at the St. Lucas Art School in Ghent and learned the tricks of the trade from his teacher Ever Meulen. Jan was still a student when I met him for the first time and you could see the passion in his eyes even then; this man was determined to lavish the best of his abilities upon us – and he's not short on ability. Jan stylizes on different levels. First of all, the message, the story. He starts off with a subject and then reduces it to its very essence. Consequently, he often abandons realism and moves in the direction of infographics.

Jan's drawings sure as hell don't get boring. His colors are beautifully rendered, often utilizing a very limited color palette that really makes his work stand out. He's clear in his communication and his tight compositions are full of endearing characters; mostly girls who've thankfully escaped the skinny catwalk virus and dapper gentlemen. His protagonists don't act like the stars of a novel, but like extras, and by rendering them in this way Jan reminds us that really, we're just gawky extras, living in a world of our own construction.

Jan never repeats himself and he keeps on surprising is audience which is why I very much look forward to seeing what Jan Van Der Veken's pen still has to offer.

Joost Swarte

Imprint

JAN VAN DER VEKEN

fabrica grafica

This book was conceived, edited, and designed by Gestalten.

Edited by Hendrik Hellige and Robert Klanten
Preface by James Cartwright
Additional texts by Ever Meulen and Joost Swarte

Layout by Floyd Schulze
Layout assistance by Adeline Schöne
Typeface: Mercury by Radim Pešco
Portrait photo: Nick Proot / prootfolio.com

Proofreading by Transparent Language Solutions
Printed by Livonia Print, Riga
Made in Europe

Published by Gestalten, Berlin 2013
ISBN 978-3-89955-498-4

© Die Gestalten Verlag GmbH & Co. KG, Berlin 2013
All rights reserved. No part of this publication may be reproduced or transmitted in any form or by any means, electronic or mechanical, including photocopy or any storage and retrieval system, without permission in writing from the publisher.

Respect copyrights, encourage creativity!

For more information, please visit www.gestalten.com.

Bibliographic information published by the Deutsche Nationalbibliothek.
The Deutsche Nationalbibliothek lists this publication in the Deutsche Nationalbibliografie; detailed bibliographic data are available online at http://dnb.d-nb.de.

This book was printed on paper certified by the FSC®.

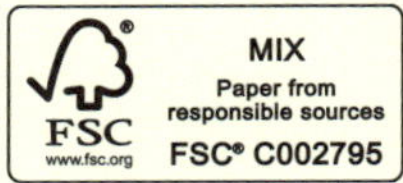

Gestalten is a climate-neutral company. We collaborate with the non-profit carbon offset provider myclimate (www.myclimate.org) to neutralize the company's carbon footprint produced through our worldwide business activities by investing in projects that reduce CO_2 emissions (www.gestalten.com/myclimate).

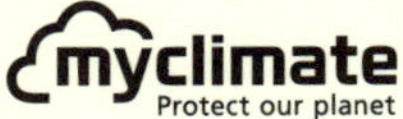

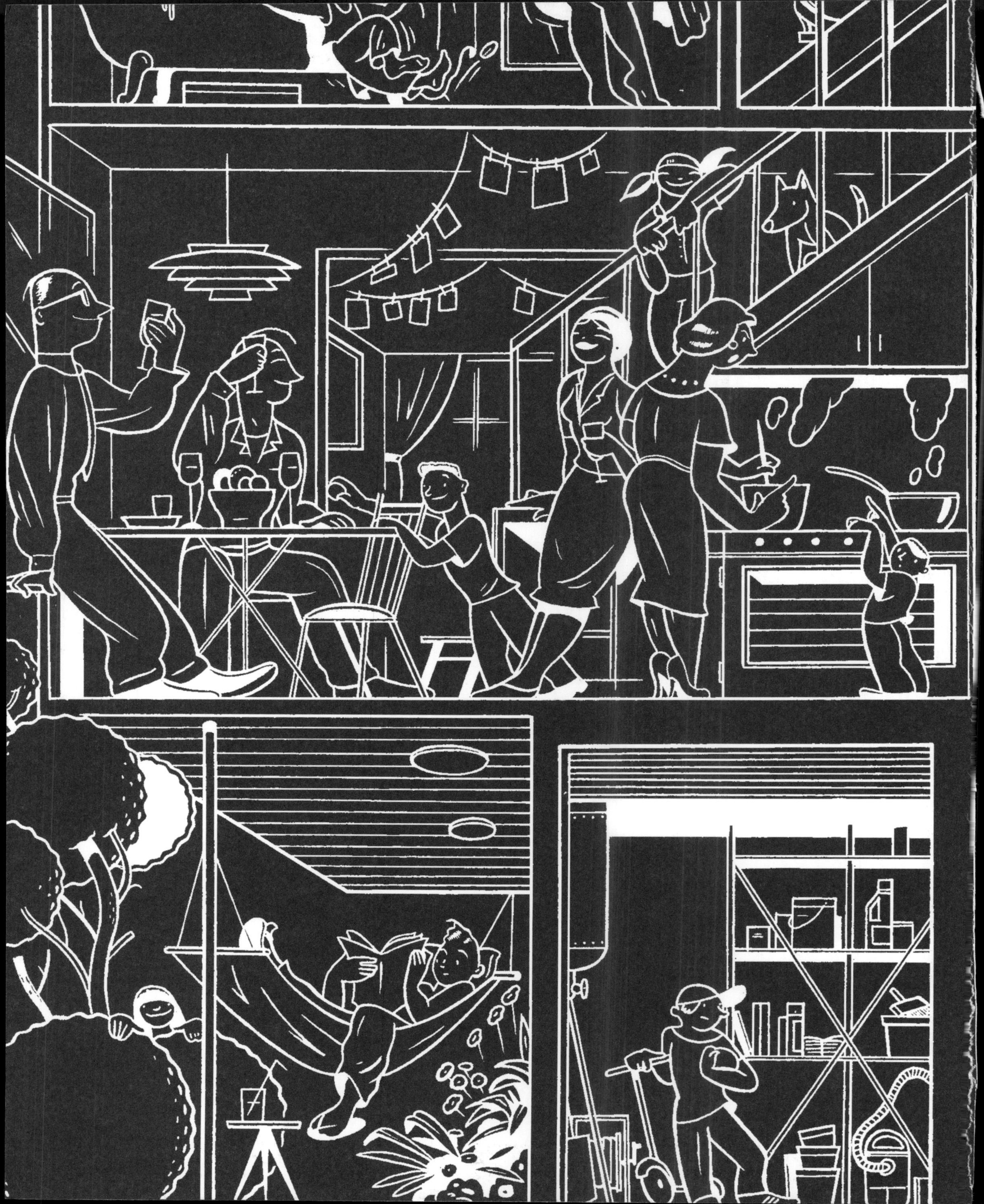